Politics of the Post - War: Assessing the Process of Disarmament Demobilisation and Reintegration in South Sudan (DDR)

PhD Marial Mach Aduot

BP

Bor Publishers

Bor Publishers - Australia

A catalogue record for this work is available from the National Library of Australia

First published in 2020

Copyright © 2020 PhD Marial Mach Aduot – Bor Publishers

Bor Publishers,

Perth, Western Australia

Phone: 08 9439 4704

Email: admin@borpublishers.com

Web: www.borpublishers.com

ABN: 45 867 024 044

ISBN: 978-0-6482848-4-0

Legal & Disclaimer

The information contained in this book and its contents is not designed to replace or take the place of any form of medical or professional advice; and is not meant to replace the need for independent medical, financial, legal or other professional advice or services, as may be required. The content and information in this book have been provided for educational and empowerment purposes only.

The content and information contained in this book has been compiled from sources deemed reliable, and it is accurate to the best of the Author's knowledge, information and belief. However, the Author cannot guarantee its accuracy and validity and cannot be held liable for any errors and/or omissions. Further, changes are periodically made to this book as and when needed. Where appropriate and/or necessary, you must consult a professional (including but not limited to your doctor, attorney, financial advisor or such other professional advisor) before using any of the suggested remedies, techniques, or information in this book.

Upon using the contents and information contained in this book, you agree to hold harmless the Author

from and against any damages, costs, and expenses, including any legal fees potentially resulting from the application of any of the information provided by this book. This disclaimer applies to any loss, damages or injury caused by the use and application, whether directly or indirectly, of any advice or information presented, whether for breach of contract, tort, negligence, personal injury, criminal intent, or under any other cause of action.

You agree to accept all risks of using the information presented inside this book.

DEDICATION

For my father, mother and siblings

Abstract

The Disarmament, Demobilisation and Reintegration (DDR) of ex-combatants is a critical aspect of conflict prevention in states emerging from civil war. It is often designed and implemented in post-war situations to contribute to broader national recovery efforts through Security Sector Reform (SSR), primarily to support the twin objectives of "sustainable peace" and "development". The justification for the DDR was based on the perception that "peace requires breaking the command and control structures operating over rebel fighters… thus making it more difficult for them to return to organised rebellion" (Spear, 2002, p. 141). Following the ending of the war between the Sudanese's Government and the Southern rebels - the Sudan People's Liberation Movement/Army (SPLM/A) in 2005 (Rolandsen, 2011), the Security Arrangements (SA) between the two violent actors mandated the implementation of a DDR. According to the peace accord, the main antagonists, the Sudan Armed Forces (SAF) and the SPLM/A should downsize their forces and disarmed and demobilised a substantial number of their forces.

The accord envisaged the DDR in South Sudan as a provisional security measure to facilitate the fundamental challenge of proportional downsizing of force, rationalisation, and standardisation of ex-guerrilla forces into a national army. During implementation, the DDR in South Sudan fell short of meeting its envisaged objectives. This failure formed the basis of this project's research question: What are the factors affecting the DDR in South Sudan? The main challenge cited by this project is that the civil war from 1955 to 72 and 1983-

2005 between military Islamists governments in the North and the radical secessionists in the South created a political situation characterised by conflicting security and political demands, which sought a military strategic balancing and manipulation. In the post-war South/ern Sudan, the effort to conduct the DDR was met with hostile socio-political conditions based on an attempt to maintain the status-quo of a united Sudan versus partitionist demands. This contradiction caused a tense post-war transition, a situation "best described as a no peace-no war environment" (Munive, 2013, p. 586).

Despite the importance attributed to DDR in the Comprehensive Peace Agreement, the unwillingness by the SPLM/A to downsize its force, and the perils of designing and applying such a complicated process, failed the initial CPA-DDR. The SPLM/A was extremely hesitant or unwilling to downsize its forces "due to a perception that the CPA was merely a ceasefire" with the North (Munive, 2013, p. 586). In South Sudan, however, the internal outlooks were not supportive of the DDR. The devastating civil war resulted in a humanitarian catastrophe that claimed the lives of millions and drove more away from their homes between 1983-2005. Since then, South Sudan has been undergoing a process of violence and security configurations between the different ethno-political groups. This condition makes it difficult for the Southern Sudanese to maintain the requirements for the DDR, especially the capacity to reintegrate the demobilised Ex-Combatants. Thus, this thesis identifies various socio-political and economic factors affecting the process of DDR in South Sudan. One of the main issues emphasised is that South Sudan emerged from war too fragile and fragmented along ethno-political lines.

In this challenging situation, the DDR confronts debilitating problems. This lack of capacity means the South Sudanese state cannot meet certain functions that require centralised use of force. The main emphasis is that South Sudan emerged from war to peace, from rebellion to government, and from contested territory to statehood, in quick transition. This region has been without government or supreme authority for a long time and hence developed alternative governments. This fragmentation of authorities allowed multiple armed structures to emerge, with intersecting influences on the use of force. After the secession, neither the incumbent nascent South Sudanese government nor its challengers, were in control of the use of force. The control over the use of violence became decentralised between armed factions, "with some areas under full control by either the government, the rebels or their auxiliaries, while other areas they control are contested" Kasfir *et al.*, 2017; citing Kalyvas, 2006, p. 210). This situation challenged the idea of DDR, which concentrates on re-establishing the state's monopoly on the means of force.

Acknowledgments

This academic journey involved the sacrifices and contribution of many people. I was born in war-torn South/ern Sudan during the civil war with the Sudanese Government, and learned to write on the ground with no writing materials in Kakuma Refugee Camp in Kenya. It was not an easy path to come this far, and that warrants a list of those worthy of acknowledgment. First thanks go to the humanitarian and the Australian community, which has given me security and a home. Second, there have been unimaginable contributions from family members, friends, and a group of academics. At this milestone, I expressed thanks to my chief supervisor, Dr Costas Laoutides, whose work is indispensable. On a personal note, I am indebted to the contributions rendered by my family. My sisters, Atong Mach Aduot, Yom Mawut Gai, and Aluel Majier Gai. Their unswerving supports would have been in vain without the guiding hands of a matriarch, Akon Achiek Wai.

The same can be said for those who have supported me in different ways. Those thanks go to General Mac Paul, Ayuel Martin Majier & Dr Mach Martin Majier, Mabior Maler Ajok, Ayuel Gai Ayuel, David Mabior Lual, Yuot Ayuen Yuot, Lual Andrew Makuei and Dr Clifton Evers, Dr Anne Bunde-birouste, and Alexander Balmer. With that being said, it does not withstand the support given by Anyang Gurech, Michael Thon Magok, Ayuel Mading Ayuel, Geu Ngong Athel, Peter Majak Kuol, and Agot Alier Leek, Jok Aguto Akuot, Panchol Mathiang Mach, Akoi Wut Lual, Guguei Gai Kuei and Garang Ateny Reng & Nicodemus Ajak Bior, to name a few. To my friends who have witnessed my journey to this stage: Achan Deng Kudum, Abul Manyoun Mayen, Deng-thie Mading Deng, Bishop; David Achiek Mach Luala, & Rev. Bol Amol, Angar Chating Abiel, David Ayuel Machar Thiong, Juach Garang Bul, to name a few. Your contribution pushed me this far. Last, I would like to convey my appreciation to content readers, Dr Kate Hall & Dr Leanne Kelly, and the entire team of academics of the Faculty, all the interviewees and institutions that provided access to first-hand information, I am grateful to you all. Without whom the preparation of this thesis would not have been possible. I am thrilled with all these contributions.

Definition of Abbreviations and Acronyms

AAA: Abyei Administrative Area

AAA: Addis Ababa Agreement

AU: African Union

BCSSAS: Bureau for Community Security and Small Arms Control

BFPS: Bergdorf Foundation for Peace Support

BICC: Bonn International Centre for Conversion

CCI: Compagnie des Constructions Internationales

CDR: Commander

CIDCM: Centre for International Development and Conflict Management

Col: Colonel

CPA: Comprehensive Peace Agreement

DDR: Disarmament, Demobilisation & Reintegration

DFID: Department for International Development

DOP: Declaration of Principles

ECOMOG: Economic Community of West African States Monitoring Group

ECOWAS: Economic Community of West African States

ELF: Eritrean Liberation Front

EPRDF: Ethiopian People's Revolutionary Democratic Front

EU: European Union

FDLR: Forces Démocratiques de Libération du Rwanda

Gen: General

GoS: Government of Sudan

GoSS: Government of South/ern Sudan

HRW: Human Rights Watch

ICC: International Criminal Court

ICG: International Crisis Group

ICISS: International Commission on Intervention and State Sovereignty

IDDRS: Integrated DDR-Standards

IDP: Internally Displaced People

IGAD: Intergovernmental Authority on Development

ILO: International Labour Organisation

INGOs: International Non-Governmental Organisations

IOM: International Organisation for Migration

IPA: International Peace Academy

IPF: International Partners Forum

IRIN: Integrated Regional Information Network

LRA: Lord's Resistance Army

MOU: Memorandum of Understanding

NANS: National Alliance for National Salvation

NCC: National Constitutional Conference

NCP: National Congress Party

NDA: National Democratic Alliance

NDDRC: National Disarmament, Demobilisation and Reintegration Council

NGOs: Non-Governmental Organisations

NIF: National Islamic Front

NRA: National Resistance Army

NSA: Non-State Actors

OAGs: Other Armed Groups

OECD: Organisation for Economic Co-operation and Development

OLS: Operation Lifeline Sudan

PKO: Peacekeeping Operation(s)

PMHC: Political-Military High Command

PRIO: Peace Research Institute of Oslo

PSO: Peace Support Operation(s)

RUF: Revolutionary United Front

SAF: Sudanese Armed Forces

SALW: Small arms and light weapons

SAS: Small Arms Survey

SIDDR: Stockholm Initiative on DDR

SPLA-IO: Sudan People's Liberation Army-In-Opposition

SPLM/A: Sudan People's Liberation Movement/Army

SRSG: Special Representative of the United Nations Secretary-General

SSDA/M: South Sudan Democratic Army/Movement

SSDDRC: South Sudan DDR Commission

SSDF: South Sudan Defence Forces

SSLM: South Sudan Liberation Movement

SSNLM: South Sudan National Liberation Movement

SSPS: South Sudan Police Service

SSR: Security Sector Reform

UCDP: Uppsala Conflict Data Program

U.N.: United Nations

UNDP: United Nations Development Programme

UNDPKO: United Nations Department of Peacekeeping Operations

UNITA: National Union for the Total Independence of Angola

UNMIS: United Nations Mission in Sudan

UNMISS: United Nations Mission in South Sudan

UNSC: UN Security Council

USA: United States of America

USAID: US Agency for International Development

WB: World Bank

TABLE OF CONTENTS

Introduction: Sudan's Comprehensive Peace Agreement and the Disarmament, Demobilisation and Reintegration (DDR) in South Sudan from 2005 - 2011

The most criticised process of intervention is a negotiated peace settlement and the liberal peace paradigm upon which the processes the negotiation is based. The disintegration of the Soviet Union and the wave of the 'new wars' that "followed ushered in a new era of international interventionism"; from humanitarian, to efforts to end civil wars and rebuild post-war states (Costantini, 2015, p. 1). Since the 1990s, the number of forcible and peaceful interventions in ongoing civil wars and their aftermath has increased (Richmond, 2013). The principles upon which these interventions, especially the armed intervention in Kosovo, Iraq, and recently in Libya were based, and the consequences, have caused a debate about their efficiencies (Paris, 2004; 2010), and motivations and the framework guiding those interventions (Chandler, 2010). In spite of its diversity, a reasonable body of literature has converged towards increasing criticism of the paradigm upon which international actors base such interventions (Richmond and Frank, 2009).

To end over forty years of civil war in Sudan, the Inter-governmental Authority for Development (IGAD), Eastern Africa region bloc, echoed an international framework guiding the interventions, hence choosing the negotiation settlement, drawing on the power-sharing model, which is a technical approach. Although Sudan's Comprehensive

Peace Agreement (CPA) ended Africa's longest and deadliest armed conflict (Haile and Bara, 2013), it did not bring about sustainable peace in South/ern Sudan during the transitional period and after the secession in 2011. This chapter introduces an argument that this negotiation settlement framework, associated with the effort to end the civil war and build peace, has given way to a bureaucratic focus on institutional approaches, without recognition of the effects that South Sudan's violent internal political dynamics can have on peace and stability. Following the end of the civil war between Southern Sudan and Government of Sudan on January 9th, 2005, the CPA granted Southern Sudan a semi-autonomous government and the right to self-determination after the six years' interim period.

The CPA also mandated the Disarmament, Demobilisation and Reintegration (DDR) of Ex-Combatants (Jabareen, 2013; Bell and Pospisil, 2017). Additionally, the CPA allowed "the Sudan People's Liberation Army (SPLA) to remain a separate army" (De Vries and Schomerus, 2017; citing; the CPA, 2005, p. 87). Among the most elaborate of these tasks was an attempt to disband informal armed structures in Southern Sudan and return ex-combatants to their communities. Moreover, this chapter will argue that the impact of separate armies; SPLA and SAF was ill-conceived or understated by mediators, and that led to the failure of the initial CPA-DDR in Southern Sudan. I base this argument on the history of perennial armed conflict in Sudan and the absence of "inclusive institutions", which are often prerequisites for centralising use of force (De Waal, 2018). The power and wealth-sharing between Sudan's Government and the SPLM/A enhanced conflict management between the CPA's partners, but that did not prevent conflict among South Sudanese. This project will argue that the government that emerges from the CPA was not inclusive, nor did it respect the interests of the political peripheries (Rubin, 1994).

Hence, the conceptualisation the CPA-DDR in South Sudan failed to reflect on Vallings and Magüi's argument that "if one ethnic group is dominant across the political spectrum and discriminates against the other, that state is at a high risk of fragility. Exclusionary politics motivates discriminated groups to resist" (2005, pp. 2-29). Unlike many civil wars in Africa, the war in Sudan was hinging on the Southern demand for secession. Since the origin of the war was not a mere dispute over power and resources, but rather a question of the groups demanding statehood, the logical construct of security perception between the North and Southern Sudanese was based on extreme political realism (Lacher, 2012). While various studies have been devoted to the detailed examination of the causes of civil war, dynamics of those wars and outcomes (Cabestan and Pavkovic, 2013; Pavkovic and Radan, 2011; 2007; Coppitiers, 2003), some academics have tried to define the factors that would explain the dissimilarity between different cases, for instance, between Ethiopia and old Sudan's approaches towards secession.

This is an essential omission in the post-war DDR because the state's attitude during, and after the war determines, to a large extent, the security strategy of separatist movements. This chapter will address the question: Why did Sudan frame the Southern demand for secession as an ultimate security threat? This chapter presents how such framing influenced Southerners' decision to frustrate the CPA-DDR, and thus, propelled post-war South Sudan into a militarisation. This chapter examines the essential strategic conditions between North and South, with a focus on how the lack of trust between the sovereign government and the secessionists in the South created a classic security dilemma based on the strategy of security balancing (Hartzell and Hoddie, 2007). This situation occurs because the entities (SAF and the SPLM/A) worry about the possibility that any single institution will dominate the use of force or state power, therefore, promoting their own interests, and threatening the security of others (Hartzell and Hoddie, 2019).

In this situation, the political and SA that distribute power in such a way as to preclude the armament were not there to support the DDR. The logic behind the above argument is twofold. First, insecurity in post-conflict of the South Sudanese can be experienced across multiple dimensions. Designing various means of addressing these forms of competing political and security interests can help to make actors feel secure, but these measures were not included in the CPA (Duursma, 2014). My thesis will argue that not all forms of power-sharing will be appreciated by everyone in post-war Sudan. However, by agreeing to multiple types of power-sharing, political, economic and security, Southern Sudan entered the CPA's contract prepared that, should the North dishonour one type of power-sharing, they would use their military might as a means to check the North. This strategic approach is in contravention of the principles of the DRR. The central part of this chapter emphasises how this kind of strategic dilemma allowed the GoS and the SPLM/A to increase their security capabilities at the expense of the DDR (Doyle, 2005). Second, while the CPA accord focused on ending this war, it did pay attention to Other Armed Groups (OAG's) impact on the DDR.

This project will emphasise that, while the literature is replete with lessons explaining factors of success or failure of a given DDR, the CPA was unfocused accord, and that provokes some questions: why, despite the best of intentions and investment of political and economic resources, did the CPA fail to lead to a consolidated peace in South Sudan? How do informal armed structures affect civil war related to public authority and their response to the DDR? When the CPA was signed, Southern Sudan was vacillating over its demands for secession and factionalism. This situation confirmed the uncomfortable truth that negotiated peace brings about a "false sense of peace that often comes at the cost of justice" (Herath, 2016, p. 106). This argument reflects Galtung's "negative peace", whereby the situation "may not see conflict out in the open, but the tension is boiling just beneath the surface because the conflict was never reconciled" (2016, p. 106). As Martin Luther King Jr. asserts: "Peace is not merely the absence of some negative force-war tension, confusion, but it is the presence of some positive force-justice, goodwill, the power of the kingdom of God" (Herath, 2016, p. 106; citing King, 1956, n.p).

This chapter explores the puzzles of post-war DDR and focuses on how mediators failed to consider the significant effects that entrenched situations of war would have on the DDR. Despite the design flaws,

21

the DDR was "envisaged as an interim security measure, to facilitate the core challenge of proportional force downsizing and to rationalise the creation of unitarian national Sudanese Army" (Munive, 2013a, p. 7). This thesis argues that, despite these intentions, it became a facade for the solicitation of international funds. One would ask why the SPLM/A needed such a large army; was it to seek "control over the military" (De Waal, 2018) as the main element of its political strategy inside South Sudan, or was it determined by the leaders' calculations based on their expectations of future armed conflicts with the North. This thesis argues that both assumptions played a part in such a strategic move. After taking over their respective regions, SAF and SPLM/A shelved the original objective to meet their competing political goals, the effort maintaining the status-quo of united Sudan and effort to secede from the union (Brethfeld, 2010).

It can be argued that the SAF and SPLM/A were having problems regarding the political will to pursue DDR. Thus, the failure of the CPA-DDR was not an accidental event, but a well-planned political and security strategy for two reasons. Despite entering into the peace agreement, the North-South relationship was termed as "a no peace-no war environment" (Jok, 2012, p. 6; citing Young, 2006) If the North and South regarding the CPA as a suspension of war, then it could not be a secret that they would approach DDR with self-security and survival in mind. So, what were the reasons that the South Sudanese regarded the CPA as a ceasefire? One reason is historically based on the North's behaviour towards the Addis Ababa Agreement (AAA), and another lies in the fact that Southern Sudanese has been mired in internal ethno-political violence throughout the war with the North (Wakoson, 1984; 1993). These conditions created the barriers that would later prevent the Ex-Combatants and armed actors in South Sudan from committing to the DDR. There was no political will to overcome stalemates in the DDR.

A senior South Sudanese political leader confirmed the above argument, saying that while disarmament programmes were essential for peace, security and confidence-building, the disarmament was unsuccessful in South Sudan because "no one trusted North commitment to the CPA" (P21/17/11/2017). For this participant, the DDR was agreed on paper, but its implementation was problematic, citing a lack of trust between the GoS and the SPLM/A. In her view, the CPA-DDR lacked credibility among the Southern Sudanese who have what she described as "good political and military reasons to be wary" of the regime in the North. In this case, one would argue that SAF and SPLA's readiness for DDR was not assessed nor taken into consideration by the CPA mediators. Bridging literature on post-war transitions and fragmented, and violent politics of Sudan, this research addresses the question of the relationship between the peacemaking process and failure of the DDR in South Sudan. Hence, my thesis suggests the CPA partners did not eliminate the option of violence to forward their political agenda of secession or to maintain the status of united Sudan.

Secondly, the CPA did not examine whether the SAF and SPLM/A were ready to engage in peacebuilding through a restructuring of political and organisational resources at their disposal. My project will argue that the old Sudan was a state whose socio-political systems, economic and security institutions were fragile, and the little that existed was contested (Jok, 2015). The IGAD noted that war between North-South, or among Southern Sudanese is the demonstration of state absence. However, violence may not be just the consequence of state fragility; violence can be a driving element of the state's fragility. Some argue that civil war is caused by "increased strain on political institutions, and the social tensions that often come to prominence because of violent conflict" (Vallings and Moreno-Torres, 2006, p. 15). This argument might be valid with the post-secession South Sudan, where political interactions and security based on the group's strategic dilemma. Instead of fighting its armed opponents who were the proxy of the North, the SPLM/A resorted to military integration, incorporating Other Armed Groups (OAGs) into a statutory security framework; but there was one problem with that military integration.

With the troubled politics of South Sudan, the term 'group' dissolved dissimilarities between criminals and resistance groups. As the interim period progressed, military integration became a lightning rod, causing war in South Sudan as it eventually disintegrated (De Waal, 2019). Moreover, the post-war setting in South Sudan has a culture of violence that has been cultivated by broken law enforcement and weak politico-military authoritarian institutions (Muggah, Colletta and de Tessières, 2009). While the DDR was due to start in 2006, it did not start until 2009. One year after South Sudan's secession, reports indicated that only 12,525 ex-soldiers out of a target figure of 90,000 had demobilised (Belitung *et al.*, 2016; Schirch, 2008). Yet, the reduction of the SPLA, even if successful, would not have prevented the war in South Sudan (Sudan HSBA, 2008a). To arrive at this observation, the project will present a succinct account of the Sudanese war and argue that, when an armed conflict erupts, it not only reverses decades of development efforts, but also creates costs and consequences—socio-political and economic—that continue for decades.

Even when the North and South ended the war, rents from natural resources and political suspicions weaken the post-war state, making the South Sudanese government ineffective and less accountable. Other political factions have good reason to suspect or fear the SPLM/A's ideas about re-establishing its dominance. These ideas of dominance do not form any positive programme but translate into s raw political and military power play centred on exacerbating the vulnerability of its opponents. After analysing all these factors, the chapter will then shift to the core objective of this study, which is to examine elements contributing to the shortcomings of the DDR in South Sudan, 2005-2011. One item of discussion is the collapse of military integration established by the SPLA. In addition to exploring the appalling consequences of civil war, the project examines the reasons that competing armed actors in South Sudan have been unable to reach a sustainable political consensus to avoid the costs of conflict. This problem requires analysis of the armies' motivation to participate in war, primarily, an understanding of the mobilisation process, and the discontent with policies on the DDR. It will be discussed in Chapter One that South Sudan was lacking institutional arrangements that focus more on addressing fear, insecurity, oppression, and inequality. Another issue which not emphasised in the CPA-DDR is an accumulation of small arms due to the decades of war. These arms are easily concealed by armed civilians and combatants alike in remote or ethnic territories across South Sudan. This situation makes it very hard for the government to trace and secure these small arms. When the cracks appeared between formerly parallel armies in 2013, each political order raced swiftly to their ethnic territories, and South Sudan descended into war and broke into various factions (Blanchard, 2016; Lyman and Knopf, 2016). To understand the conflict in South Sudan, historical accounts of conflicts will offer insight into the formation of armed factions, and the proliferation of arms, something that cannot be assessed without unpacking the country's history of violence.

Sudan's Violent History and Southern Sudan's Quest for Statehood

Post-colonial Sudan has become commonly depicted as a state plagued by war between the African-Christians in the South and Arabs-Muslims in the North, and the corollary of such animosities has afflicted the country with political woes (Ali and Albadawi, 2002). The first civil war broke out on the 18th of August 1955 when the Southern officers of the British-administered Sudan Defence Force mutinied against the post-Colonial transitional arrangements (Johnson, 2003a). Until 1956, the British governed Southern Sudan as a separate region, a gesture that honed the Southerners' appetite for statehood. Southern leaders were expecting to inherit sovereign South Sudan when the British left, but that dream turned into dismay as the British merged the North and South into a single administrative unit, Sudan in 1955 (Howell, 1978). In response, Southern Sudanese violently protested the merging. To put this rebellion in context, there was a growing number of charges against the incoming Sudanese government based on views that it usurped Southern Sudan's right to statehood to secure the territory and the resources therein.

What is apparent in the historical context of Sudan, is that there are links between civil war and state formation, and the same could be explored in South Sudan. When the state is fragile, the list of state functions diminishes (Ghani and Lockhart, 2008; Zürcher, 2007). Another observation is how the lack of democratic procedures increased the intensity of conflict among the groups (Gurr, 1993). One could argue that the armed conflicts in Sudan was a result of Britain disregarding its own Southern Policy. According to analysts, this policy allowed Southerners to "build up a series of self-contained racial or tribal units with structures and organisation based, to whatever extent the requirements of equity and good government permit, upon Indigenous customs" (Beshir, 1968, p. 115). In my view, Southern provinces were not autonomously governed, but because the North was mostly Muslim; the policy encouraged a divergence of customs and socio-cultural practices. Despite loopholes in Southern claims, the war was exacerbated as the formation of the Sudanese state proceeded with no strategy to create a cohesive state (Davidson, 1992).

"The Northern elites who inherit the state were the new colonisers", claimed a member of foreign mission interviewed for this thesis (P6/24/08/2017). This participant stressed the impact of post-colonial rulers; a notion reflected in Jean-Bayart's classic portrayal of African countries as buried deep in the messes of the past and the savagery of the present. Bayart emphasises "the persistence of entrenched patterns of African statecraft" and its impact on formal institutions of the modern state (1993, p. 221). He argues that "factionalism is not something that happens only at the periphery, but is a structural condition at the heart of African politics: the precariousness of national political equilibria is not a manifestation of the organic inadequacy of the state, nor even a supplementary proof of its extraneity" (Bayart 1993, p. 221). This argument is bold, with some truth in it given the savagery of old Sudan. However, Bayart's generalisation of Africa suggests that chaos in African states is entirely functional, a context which this study disagrees. Among the useful features of Bayart's hypothesis is the depiction of how formal political organisations are intermingled with "reciprocal assimilation of traditional and modern elites" (1993, p. 221).

Emboldened by their displeasure with this type of governance, Southern leaders denounced post-Colonial Sudan as a state built on "ethnically-defined administrative units allied to the local population by incorporation of pre-colonial patron-client relations" (Mamdani, 1996, p. 37). Despite their diversity, Southern Sudanese waged the war based on what some described as "political tribalism", or the composition of ethnicities by "competition for state power and largesse against others" (Lonsdale, 1994). For the decades of the civil war against the North, political tribalism that wove the southern groups together became their psychological depiction of the North.

Hence, the war of liberation was based on the way Southern Sudanese look at the North as outer groups from what they see in themselves. Such a perception exacerbates Southern Sudanese's views of Sudan as an oppressive, Arab-Islamic state (Lagu and Alier, 1985). In this situation, Southern Sudanese dismissed the legitimacy of the Sudanese state and attacked the essence of the state as an organised public authority (Beswick, 1991; 2004).

This conflictual interaction allowed the North and South to adopt an inward-looking socio-political process, which caused them to become inevitably adversarial (Khalid, 2003). If one defines the then Sudanese state in a Weberian view, as having the legitimate monopoly over the use of force, then one must regard the Sudanese state as being at an embryonic stage, as the Southern Sudanese were exerting substantial coercive power. This trend of violence continued until it triggered a coup in 1958, led by General Abboud (Deng, 2002a). Apart from appointing himself president, Abboud closed the British Mission Schools in Southern Sudan and introduced the Arabic language as a learning pattern; a move that Southerners perceive as a threat to their identity (ICG, 2002). In response, Southern Sudanese securitise their identity and territorial belonging. This project perceives belonging as the condition of being part of the shared identity group. Territorial belonging implies political group (s) belong to the part of a defined national territory.

The description of territory and belong, in Southern Sudan, has been a socio-political process connected with the group political stances towards the North that encourage the perceptiveness of boundaries

(Pollini, 2005). Southern leaders at the time identified some factors significant to the creation of Southern Sudanese socio-political systems, a cultural resemblance and shared destiny. These conditions are often described in politics as a "common fate" (Campbell 1958), to which the socio-political and economic traditions (Hawley, 1950, p. 258) add interrelationship among the groups, which is related to Campbell's (1958) idea of internal diffusion. This rising of Southern internal diffusion lead to social belonging, "the state in which an individual, by assuming some role, is characterised by his or her inclusion in the social collectivity, which is exclusive" (Weber, 1922, p. 136). Hence, social belonging is "relates to any form of social collectivity, whether this is primarily expressive or whether it is predominantly instrumental" (Pollini, 2007, p. 498). This study is not under any impression that the existence of political and cultural harmony in Southern Sudan during the war with the North entails the existence of a sustainable political organisation believed as a sense of shared belonging.

Nevertheless, the hostile environment in which Southern Sudanese were living stresses their sense of vulnerability and raised the strategic value of social belonging and the territory. This project argues that Southern Sudanese collective fears of the Sudanese government intensified the war and affecting their long-term security calculus and the acceptability of the state. Throughout years of impasse, the excruciating cost of war prompted another coup in 1969, led by General Nimeiry (Beshir, 1975). Nimeiry accused Abboud of "harming Sudan by dividing its peoples" (Deng, 2005a; 2005b). As a gesture of peace, he invited Southern rebels for peace talks (Khalid, 1990). The hypocrisy of Nimeiry is that it was premature for a military system without a codified constitution to call for peace without acknowledging that Sudan was in a crisis of military elitism. While Nimeiry was parading himself as an alternative to military elitism, he was disingenuous because he usurped power through military means, contradictory to the norm of the democratic governance or political franchise, to free Sudanese from the arbitrary exercise of power.

Despite his insincerity, Nimeiry's government signed the Addis Ababa Agreement (AAA) in 1972 with the South Sudan Liberation Movement (SSLM), led by General Lagu (Kasfir, 1977). Unlike the CPA, the Ethiopian Emperor, Haile Selassie, persuaded disputants to pursue peace negotiations (Wai, 1981). The question is, what were the inadequacies of the AAA, and how did those deficits contribute to the second armed conflict in Sudan and the proliferation of arms in South Sudan? First, the Emperor, Haile Selassie did not have the political power to enforce the terms of AAA, especially the Southern referendum. Despite these concerns, the AAA granted the Southern Region Semi-autonomous government and self-determination (Shinn, 2004). These processes appear to have allowed Southern Sudan to gain a permanent role in Sudanese politics, but the efficacy of that role was dubious due to the lack of ineluctable constitutionalism (Malwal, 1985). A war that warrants a call for secession is not an ordinary civil war. The passion with which the North and South fought the war greased the tracks leading to a destructive future. Hence, the lack of an external force to monitor implementation made the continuation of the AAA precarious.

Southern Sudanese's quest for statehood, democratic governance and social and economic equity, and the resistance by the elites in North created a competitive and distrustful political environment where supposed cooperative interests became conflictual with each other. According to Doki and Ahmad, 2014, n.p), "Sudan was awash with arms long before the country split in two. When South Sudan seceded in 2011, it was estimated that there were up to 3.2m small arms in circulation". Thus, the post-war transition from that kind of conflict is likely to be marked by an absence of positive peace, "a social condition in which exploitation is minimised or eliminated and in which there is neither overt violence nor the more subtle phenomenon of underlying structural violence. It denotes the continuing presence of an equitable and just social order as well as ecological harmony" (Barash and Webel, 2014, p. 7; also, 2009). This is because the government Nimeiry established did not recognise the effects of structural violence, and political institutions that have excluded the Southern Sudanese (Wakoson, 1984; Beswick, 1991).

This observation is vulnerable to criticism. Sylvester wrote that incidents occasionally mar harmony but proposed that those incidents cannot affect the essential achievement, which ensures "nothing on the horizon that could seriously upset the present arrangement" (1976, p. 184). He was wrong. While Sylvester recognised Nimeiry's opposition to secession, he did not emphasise the effect of Sudan as an Islamic-military state on the Southerners (Kasfir, 1976). In the security context, Nimeiry was acting without fear of consequences from the

South for two reasons. First, the AAA's Security Arrangements mandated the merging of the SSLM forces into the SAF. While the merging of SSLM's forces did not go smoothly, the South was no longer in any position to deter the North. After years of an unsteady implementation, the worst that the Southerners feared came to fruition, as the AAA came under pressure from Islamists who pressured Nimeiry to function like previous leaders, a demand he succumbed to, abrogating the AAA in 1983. This is because there was no mechanism for deterrence to allow the North to evaluate cost-benefit calculus of abrogation of the AAA (Collins, 2007).

Annoyed by this move, Southern army officers in the SAF staged another mutiny, launching a second civil war (Lesch, 1998). John Garang (1987), a leader of the new rebellion, described the war as "a reaction of the oppressed". Garang derided the system as the euphemism of theft. To him, the SPLM/A was going to waged war to reinstitute a legitimate political organisation to function as a "machines designed for the efficient transformation of material inputs into material outputs" (Scott, 1987, p. 31). Given the political stances, the Sudanese war became partisan until it involved more coups and reached a stalemate in the 2000s where neither SAF nor SPLA stood a chance of winning the war militarily, and the costs of continued escalation were becoming unbearable. Capitalising on this impasse, the IGAD started a peace process to end the war. After five years of negotiations, the CPA was signed on January 9th, 2005. Chapter Six of this thesis will provide critical reflections and present how the CPA replicated the AAA, except for the separate armies and peacekeeping mission (De Waal and Pendle, 2018).

Nevertheless, this project argues that the CPA was not sufficient to address Southern Sudan's fears of the North. As observed by Biel and Ojok (2018, p. 2), "although IGAD was successful in brokering an agreement among the parties", the mediation process suffered from zero-sum thinking. Rather than dealing with the actual situation, IGAD took a political high road; ultimately, the CPA became too political, focusing on how to end the war in Sudan. This study argues that the CPA provided no strategy to address historical mistrust between North and South, and among Southern protagonists. Thus, it "contains loopholes coupled with a lack of political will in the implementation process by one or both parties to the agreement, and that paved the way for the chain of actions and reactions that produced a series of violent conflicts" (Rottenburg and Komey, 2011, p. 22). Second, Southern Sudan was not a country, nor a functional central authority when the CPA was signed. Hence, despite ample literature on lessons learned from earlier DDR programmes, this project argues that there was little to no evidence that the CPA-DDR would produce the desired outcomes.

This is not only because of critical loopholes in the design, but also the lack of mechanisms to ensure socio-political and economic reintegration of Ex-Combatants. Young alluded to these deficiencies, arguing that the SPLM/A "had never succeeded in overcoming the tribal identities of its soldiers and developing a national ethos. As a result, the army often operated as a collection of militias and warring factions whose members were more loyal to their tribe or individual leaders than to the SPLA hierarchy" (2012, p. 323). The deficiency of a central mechanism to ensure collective security was among many problems not considered in the CPA. Given these situations, the DDR ran into trouble by default as various armed groups defined the violent political landscape (SAS, 2012). Hence, assessing the challenges of the DDR in South Sudan required emphasis of contradictory North-South relationship and disintegration of South Sudan after the secession.

The Politics of the CPA-DDR and its Challenges

The United Nations Secretary-General's report on peacebuilding after the civil war notes that "the ability of the U.N. to design and implement effective DDR programmes will be limited unless basic political and security conditions are in place" (The UNDPO, 2010, p. 11). As stated above, emerging states strived to conduct the DDR even in situations where these conditions do not exist. The quest to engage in the DDR derived from the early 2000s when the Secretary-General concluded that DDR is "has repeatedly proved to be vital to stability in a post-conflict situation" (U.N., 2000, p. 1). Efforts to assess the factors affecting the DDR in South Sudan "require a source of variation in the use of DDR programmes" (United Nations, 2008, p. 2). This project argues that possible challenges in South Sudan lie at the national and local level. By assessing the motives of individuals and groups that resisted the DDR, this research asks: Does DDR work for individuals in a country due to the nature of war and armed actors? What explains whether Ex-Combatants and groups can demobilise and reintegrate into society after the war? After the signing of the CPA, the DDR was initiated to guarantee coordination and synergy as well as to be responsive "to the dynamic and often volatile post-conflict environment" (IDDRS, 2006, p.1).

This approach was based on an attempt "to prevent a return to violent conflict" (IDDRS, 2006, p.1). Practically, this objective is carried out through providing ex-fighters with other means of livelihood and military support systems "that they may have relied upon during the war, but which are no longer relevant in the post-war situation" (Jooma, 2005). In contrast, Southern Sudan was lacking these pre-conditions. The North and South were fighting with various armed groups (Jacoby and Özerdem, 2008). Thus, "sensitivity to such ontological security dynamics can help explain the apparent alluring attraction of more traditional geopolitical scripts" between North and South (Browning, 2018, p.5). This fear was based on historical mistrust between North and South, based on an abrogation of the AAA. While it is hard to test the role of trust in the outcomes of the DDR, it is the main precondition for successful DDR (Lamb, 2018). Instead of focusing on transparent disarmament, South Sudan maximise force and arms as mentioned by a participant. "We were integrating forces from the ranks of militants for a political purpose. We were waiting to go back to war with the North if they interfered with referendum" (P23/21/09/2017).

The North, in contrast, was not exempt from uncertainties facing the South, as a member of foreign mission confirmed: "our main concern was not only to be overrun by the SPLA. We were also fighting in Darfur" (P3/08/07/2017). These arguments hinted at Sudan's Armed Forces and SPLA's intention to hold on to their armies due to lack of political will and commitment (The UNDPO, 2010, p. 13; also, Hartzell *et al.*, 2001). Hence, although the North-South war has ended, the existing of the regional wars and ethno-political competitions remained a substantial threat to the CPA-DDR. The concern arose when armed groups-maintained vetoes on contentious political and security issues. The absence of the focus on these conflicts saw a flurry of wars in both North and South, in part because although the North-South war end, the incidence of local violence did not evaporate. This thesis uses political will to link the challenges of the DDR to the competing centres of power in the post-war situation. The CPA-DDR was built upon the premise of the international prism, rather than the promise of armed actors, representing groups' interests.

Lack of Political Will and Commitment: North and South Sudan Perspectives

An interpretation of the above arguments leads to the conclusion that there was an absolute lack of political will. First, the success of the DDR needed commitment and the political will of ex-adversaries (IDDRS, 2011). Besides, such commitment indicates "trust in the peace process and willingness of the parties to the conflict to engage in DDR" (IDDRS, 2011, p. 20). However, what happens when warring parties engage in the anti-DDR process? As an example, in Sierra Leone, despite reaching the 1999 *Lomé Peace Agreement,* (RUF) snubbed the DDR and resorted to violence (Call, 2009). Following violent political predicament that threatened to destroy the peace, a robust regional military intervention and international pressure were launched, leading to the forcible removal of the RUF's obstinate leader, Foday Sankoh (Call, 2010). So, RUF finally accepted the terms of peace and entered the DDR process in late 2000 (Colletta and Muggah, 2009). The context of a much-revamped pressure in the outcome of the DDR is discussed in Chapter One.

Unlike the situation in Sierra Leone, the Sudanese factions signed the CPA without a minimum guarantee of security. "The UN forces in Juba here and many other towns are just there to escort their bosses and water tankers. I am not sure those soldiers ever saw any battle, let alone protecting our people" (P26/23/09/2017). This participant stresses the lack of security climate in South Sudan. Thus, the mindset of security has the potential to hinder the DDR. Despite the existing of the *United Nations Mission in South Sudan* (UNMISS), the security situation remains unstable in South Sudan (Childress, 2011). Instead of focusing on how these armed conflicts can affect the DDR, the SAF and SPLA proceeded with the programme from a tunnel view of the CPA of SA which entitled them "to deal with any OAGs in whatever manner they so wished" (De Waal, 2017, p. 180). In February 2006, Bashir formed the *National DDR Commission* (NDDRC) tasked with "policy formulation, oversight, review, coordination and evaluation of both North and South DDR Commissions" (NDDRC, 2006, p. 3). There are several effects of this order in terms of practical procedures of the DDR. First, the order goes against the primary purpose of DDR. Such exclusive nature of the DDR lacks policy orientation but is derived from the process of the CPA negotiation itself, which was to CPA and not to ensure reform in governance. The IGAD approach was less about internal disquiet in the North and South, but to end the war between North and South. When Bashir issued an order, he was following the talking point of the CPA disregarding an accumulation of arms and the ongoing-armed tribal conflicts. The problem with that approach, however, is how it affects the integrity of the NDDRC. When the DDR is used for political expediency, it contradicts the notion that DDR must facilitate sustainable, community-driven efforts aimed to alter the mentality of communities and individuals from war discourse towards notions of DDR. Failing to meet these pre-conditions means failing to urge those affected by the war to accept their new post-war environment and to engage with the national reconciliation. Both commitments to the DDR and reconciliation sought local knowledge about security and causes of conflict, noting that this information can be an indispensable tool, not only for preventing future armed conflict, but also for general socio-political cohesion.

What is essential in the DDR is not just the collection of arms, but a "fundamental question about the degree to which intended beneficiaries are consulted about the DDR" (2014, p. 277). This approach cherished "sophisticated understanding of reintegration and the way it can relate to post-war reconstruction" (Kilroy, 2014, p. 277). Instead of this question, Bashir tasked NDDRC to report to the 'Presidency', himself and his two deputies, one of which was the president of Southern Sudan. Lamb and Stainer (2018, p. 6) argue that "decision-making and the management of the DDR process were highly centralised and based in Khartoum". Therefore, the "overall management provided very little autonomy to key local stakeholders in

South Sudan, and there was a general lack of transparency, inadequate consultation and the absence of regular meetings" (2018, p. 6). This assertion was confirmed by those who involved in South Sudan DDR. "I have not done anything relating to the DDR since my appointment to the role. The SPLA controls the decisions about the DDR and its policies" (P19/17/11/2017).

This participant emphasises that South Sudan DDR Commission was existing in name but was "relegated to a bystander role in terms of leadership, oversight and coordination" (Lamb and Stainer, 2018, p. 6). What followed was a dishonest and politically charged DDR process. In early 2006, the SPLA started what observers described as "a mock DDR" focusing on non-essential combatants (The CPA Monitor, 2006). This conundrum confirmed existing of "acute political tension and a lack of trust between Khartoum and those in Juba" (Lamb and Stainer, 2018; citing Breitung *et al.*, 2016, p. 7). What SPLA achieved in this crisis is the incorporation of 50,000 soldiers from OAGs, though observers described these numbers as doctored or understated (Mazurana *et al.*, 2002). The SPLA maximisation of force comes with enormous impacts on the disarmament in South Sudan. Sustainable peace and security "require breaking the command and control structures operating over rebel fighters… thus making it more difficult for them to return to organised rebellion" (Spear, 2002, p. 141). Southerners maximises their force because it was idyllic for the relationships with the North built upon a mutual distrust and competition.

Armed and Insecure: An Impact of SPLA Maximisation of Force

on DDR

After the signing of the CPA, the SAF and the SPLA were still fighting on multiple fronts. Hence, the primary factor that hinders the disarmament programmes in South Sudan was the fear of the North, and perhaps also various competing security preferences: "we disregarded the DDR because we must protect ourselves" (P4/08/11/2017). What this interviewee failed to mention is the impact of the historical accumulations of arms, and how both North and South held autonomous socio-political and economic interests. That mindset is dangerous for the DDR when armed actors could not figure out how to reduce the size of their forces and still feel secure. The competitive relationships between different armed groups and political rivals created political and security system where arms and armies became factors of crucial importance. Therefore, the proliferation of arms can be a result of problematic cooperation among the groups. Because of this stance, SPLA institutionalises its purpose and responsibilities vis-à-vis a rigid militarisation.

The lack of cooperation and maximisation of force can be modelled with various theoretical approaches, including those beyond the scope of this project. However, what was apparent in Southern Sudan in relation to the North was that each group approached the DDR for strategic reasons. While Southern Sudan was not a country when the CPA was signed, the SPLM/A was operating under "the basic assumptions of the realist approach that nation-states are motivated only by their own interests" (Evans and Newnham, 1998, p. 645). In the intra-state war, this school of thought stresses that each group considers the needs and interests only when the other group can enforce their demands by threatening or performing damaging actions. This situation reflected an inter-group prisoner's dilemma (Kareva, 2011). In Sudan, secession is one threat that GoS feared because it has been the primary source of war. However, the main issue relates to the location of natural resources: "natural resources are usually geographically concentrated in a particular part of a country, so countries that are heavily dependent upon natural resources are likely to be prone to secessionist movements" (Collier and Hoeffler, 2006, p. 41).

It was apparent that control over Sudan's oil played a decisive role in escalating competing interests. In contrast, the CPA established an even division of revenue, shrinking the North's ability to finance the war, most notably in Darfur and other emerging fronts (Suleiman, 2011). With Southern Sudan gearing towards secession, there was ambivalence in the North to prevent this event (Jenne, 2006; Scroggins, 2002). There is an essential context in these preferences. First, the Southern Sudanese see security as self-reliance, and this creates suspicion and uncertainty (Smith, 1996; Yiftachel, 1992). Given the nature of historical problems between North and South, this emphasis shifted the ontological focus away from civil war management to prevention, but not according to ordinary terms of stopping the war. Southern Sudan's approach was the projection of power, though military. Aside from the traditional relevance of balance of power concepts in intra-state conflict, it can be more intricate where multiple actors seek a balance of power. In this case, resistance to the DDR is not equivalent to combatants' economic uncertainty.

This observation is not emphasised in the old theory of the DDR. Marshall and Gurr (2005) saw uncertainty in ex-combatants' economic needs, contrary to fear. As mentioned earlier, both parties were harbouring aggressive intentions (Winkler, 2010). Thus, my thesis argues that CPA-DDR failed not just because of the flaws of the design, but also due to an acute security dilemma that made defensive mechanisms unavoidable (Jervis, 1976). The solution to this uncertainty is the balance of power, as mentioned above (Eriksen, 2004; Chazan *et al.*, 1988). A balance of power in a place where a chunk of the territory is seeking to secede and minor groups fear domination, places domestic cooperation under "a paradoxical and unfortunate dilemma" (Walter, 1997, p. 339). In context, Butterfield emphasised how security dilemma can influence actors' security thinking (Butterfield, 1951). This context increases a crisis of distrust between North and South, as well as SPLM/A and local opposition in the South.

Although the CPA allowed GoS and the SPLA to dismantle' OAGs, this approach was counter-productive. It failed to appreciate that not all OAGs will be lured into submission or crushed without maintaining a cache of arms. This research considers this factor to be a contributor to the failure of DDR. These puzzles reject the state's monopoly on violence, as well as warlordism. The panic among different armed factions showed that success or the failure of the DDR might not depend on economic incentives (Ahmed, 2009; McEvoy and Lebrun,

2010). The success of the DDR, in this situation, may require reapproaching strategic interaction of groups eager to avoid disaster (Muggah, 2010. SPLA as a movement started as a revolutionary armed struggle, and as a result, attracted thousands from the North, mostly in the Blue Nile and Nuba Mountain (Woodward, 1990). These regions also protested North oppression, but because CPA was approached in the context of North-South conflict, these Northerners were excluded.

Unfinished Business: Contested Territories and Proxy Armies

CPA was incomplete, but its critics focused on its lack of broader participation in negotiations and implementation (Rolandsen, 2005; 2011). In reality, the CPA was exclusive; hence, several issues that could help or hinder the DDR were pushed aside (Munive, 2013). This criticism is explored deeply in Chapter Six. While some analysts described the CPA as a mere 'ceasefire', violence and security uncertainty in South-South relations was severe (Rogier, 2005). Other scholars argue that the resumption of armed conflict between North and South was unlikely because of war fatigue and the win-win peace dividends (Grawert, 2010). These arguments are valid in part, but the resumption of North-South war was not obsolete. OAG groups were not Civil Society, but hard-to-reach armed constituencies of various warlords with real grievances against GoS and SPLA (O'Brien, 2009). Because CPA design was exclusive, OAGs considered its DDR as a reinforcement of the traditionally exclusive politics in both North and South Sudan.

Branch and Mampilly (2005) argue that the CPA did not address the 'how' of cooperation through the tangible 'what' of solutions. It is apparent that the CPA ended the North and South civil war, but that conceptualisation ignores the fact that the whole of Sudan was an enduring site of multi-layered violence (Guelke, 2012). In the absence of an inclusive peace agreement, it is challenging to frame the DDR programmes as acceptable to those who feared massacre (Nichols, 2011). The proposal on how to resolve disputed borderland of the Abyei region states that the Ngok Dinka inhabiting Abyei region will take part in different poll after the plebiscite of Southern Sudan to decide whether to remain in North or join South (The CPA, 2005, p. 65). This protocol was a mischaracterisation of the people of Abyei and the political decision that transferred them administratively to the North. Abyei is the "area of the Nine Ngok Dinka Chiefdoms transferred [administratively] to the North in 1905" under British colonisation (The CPA, 2005, p. 65). This transfer of the Dinka sub-clan was an administrative procedure instead of a transfer of the people and their territory to the North. In the CPA, Abyei remained contested territory.

Despite these challenges, the CPA set up the Abyei Administrative Area (AAA) where the North and South rotated an appointment of the head administrator of the area. This administrative covenant did not cease South Sudan's claim on Abyei: "we have, up to now, over two divisions of SPLA in the disguise of police in Abyei. They are not the police but our special commandos" (P37/10/01/2018). In this argument, one critical idea emerges. The purported SPLA divisions in Abyei were not the police per se, but special units ready to counter the SAF right on the border if the war resumed (Rands and LeRiche, 2012).

This means South Sudanese intentionally disregarded the DDR in anticipation of war. Second, the CPA granted Southern Kordofan and the Blue Nile, politically unspecified "popular consultations, a democratic right and a mechanism to ascertain the views of the people of two regions on the CPA reached by the GoS and SPLM" (The CPA, 2005, p. 74). The problem with that consultation is that ethnic groups in those regions are non-Arabs, although some are Muslims (Young, 2012).

According to a political figure from the region, widespread consultation was insignificant: "we suffered from the same government as Southern Sudanese, and we have fought the same regime" (P2/07/07/2017). In an analysis, this situation provoked a "paradoxical political and security dilemma" (Booth and Wheeler, 2008). Before secession in 2011, these concerns forced the SPLA divisions in two regions to start a pre-emptive war (Breitung *et al.*, 2016). This war did not affect the referendum. On July 9th, 2011, South Sudan declared its independence, but this achievement was not a panacea to chronic violence and fragmentation among the Southern ethno-political groups. This project argues that the CPA and the secession were not a panacea because they allowed politically unprepared insurgents to ascend to power. After Garang's demise on July 30th, 2005, the SPLM/A did not just lose its direction, but its vision. The residue that remained was a group of ill-equipped ex-rebel combatants who undermined the state's procedural system and appointed themselves the rulers of the law. Thus, the supposed liberators turned into rulers without social graces but vested in the nepotistic system and violent power struggle.

Post-Secession DDR in South Sudan and its Challenges

South Sudanese independence was a euphoric moment, defined as the triumph of a liberation (LeRiche, 2013). Like many rebel groups who came to power, South Sudan's claim was based on overcoming some types of political hegemony (Mamdani, 2014). Nothing was unusual about South Sudan; in fact, it emerged in worse shape. South Sudanese state formation follows "a version of Tilly's (1985) idea of how to create a state through internal violence between competing groups, which often ends with the production of a criminal or predatory state" (Tilly cited in Richmond, 2011a, p. 419). Whether South Sudan is a criminal or predatory state will be assessed later. However, it was evident that the war was applied to shape Sudan according to South Sudanese's socio-political customs. With common challenges baffling post-war states, South Sudanese delight was deemed pretentious. This is because transitions from war to peace, rebel to government, and contested territory to sovereignty required building a state from scratch.

South Sudan emerged as an interim state, without central institutions (LeRiche and Arnold, 2012). Chapter Four confirms that South Sudan is, indeed, an interim state where the centralised use of force has collapsed in infancy. South Sudan emerged too fragile, unable to meet the duties of the sovereign state; a contradiction of the perception of the state as "a compulsory political association who upholds a claim to the monopoly use of force within a given territorial unit" (Weber's (1995, p. 3). This normative principle is vested in the state's autonomy and freedom from any invasion from other states or institutions. The autonomy of states is integrated into world politics, and it provided arrangements that uphold the state monopoly of force within its territory. This projection of the state as omnipotent within its boundaries, a dominant form of political authority that eclipses other authorities has never existed in South Sudan. Given this deficiency, the shortfalls of the disarmament may lie in the state's lack of exclusive control over a violent informal military organisation, as well as its inability to ensure collection protection. The collapse of the state monopoly of force is a significant indicator for the decentralisation of violence.

Thus, the Republic of South Sudan is characterised by the decay in law and order, a demise in state centrality, and the fracturing of state security systems. The nascent state has lost its legitimate monopoly of and over organised use of violence and found itself increasingly incapable of monopolising the use of force emanating from different armed actors sponsored by competing elites. Based on the challenges posed by the decentralisation of violence, this project will weigh the concept of South Sudan's sovereignty against the effects of the informal armies. The argument to be made, in this case, is that South Sudan has lost the absolute power over armed non-state actors that supposed to be disarmed. Thus, South Sudan's sovereignty is morally expressed in the political and legal definition of state supremacy, but not in the empirical projection of the state's supremacy. This study provides empirical understandings of the link between civil war, faulty state formation and weakness following South Sudan's declaration of statehood in 2011. It has identified numerous influencing conditions leading to this situation.

The empirical data hinted that the war in South Sudan lies in the "state failure and a broader process of state formation" (Pella, 2015, p. 211). Every aspect of statehood was crafted from the ruins of the civil war and ill-trained SPLM/A's guerrilla leadership (Lacher, 2012). This analysis illustrates that the country is struck by the deficiency of central authority to control the use of force. Faced with the multifaceted challenges, South Sudan emerged lacking the necessary capability to cope with the difficult transition from the civil war to peace and the statehood. These debacles of fragility and violence widened the meaning of security and those providing security. The contraction of the state as a sole legitimate actor has opened the enquiry into the relationship between the failure of the DDR and the mindsets of those providing security (Lacher, 2012). The above issues prompted the need to understand the governance as: "the structures and processes which enable a set of public and private actors to coordinate their independent needs and interests through the making and implementation of binding policy decisions in the absence of a central political authority" (Krahmann, 2003, p. 11).

In contrast, security governance relates to the instruments and structures through which security is provided. In a post-war state, security governance is "the organisation and management of the security sector, understood here to comprise all the bodies ranging from armed forces, police and intelligence agencies to those institutions that formulate, implement, and oversee security policy whose main responsibilities are the protection of the state and its constituents" (Bryden *et al.*, 2003, p. 3). As discussed earlier, South Sudan is a state without dimensions of "stateness" (Fukuyama, 2004). Without a capable state to supervise armed actors, South Sudan struggled to control the use of force. As Wilson explains, "the most important thing to know is how that coordination is accomplished" (1989, p. 24). This research argues that South Sudan confronts a multifaceted array of socio-political and security predicaments, many of which derived from the SPLM/A as a violent liberation movement, as well as the South Sudanese state's loss of control over the means of force. While re-establishing this monopoly signifies one of the critical challenges of any peace-and-state-building process, in the meantime, a wide range of various security operators marks post-war contexts and not all of whom share comparable political goals.

The actors may range from international military elements, state-level military, ethnic armies and their informal structures loyal to local warlords. In this situation, all socio-political levels of engagement are involved in public authority and security governance. Arms control may not be achieved in this situation because all actors militarised the interactions and resisted this DDR effort. Despite these concerns, President Kiir, issued an Executive Decree in August 2011, upgrading the SSDDRC into a national body and appointing the board, which he chaired (UNDP, 2013; Gebreselassie, 2018). Per this order, South Sudan aimed to reduce its armed forces by 150,000 and facilitate the reintegration of ex-fighters into civilian life (GoSS, 2011). It was clear that President Kiir had not learned from the flaws of the CPA-DDR.

First, the institutionalisation of the DDR body was too political, rushed, and ambitious, as it was for the CPA approach to the DDR (Sudan SHBA, 2012).

If the aim was the downsizing of the SPLA, one must also talk about how to rise livelihood prospects for ex-fighters in terms of economic reintegration. The DDR also must redress security instability and ensure the ex-guerrillas are transformed into responsive representatives (UNPSO, 2012; Ball and Hendrickson, 2009). This emphasis was captured in one participant's argument:

It is one thing to know how to organise an attack against the government garrison town during the North-South war, but it is another to function as a legislature, a judge or minister. The current leaders treated South Sudan like any other town they seized from SAF where they (senior generals) must take first from what had been captured, and the rest goes to subordinates (P26/23/10/2017).

In this view, the GoSS aspiration to reduce the excessive army failed from the beginning because no one wanted a transformation of the security system, or the inevitable transformation of lucrative roles with that system. As per the Presidential Order, this DDR followed the exclusive trend of the CPA-DDR. The Presidential Order, at the time, and the mandate for the commission did not explain the causes and manifestations of violent conflict and political instability in the country. It seemed, in that case, President Kiir understates South Sudan's political situation, activities of OAGs or pattern of violent behaviour in his army. That approach to conducting the DDR without consent or meaningful consultation is insignificant in a situation where contesting authorities dictate control strategies for armies (Baaz and Verweijen, 2013). Warner argues that "despite the benefits that military integration can provide during the war to peace transitions, the process is a quick fix that runs the risk of creating a demonstration effect, showing that violence and disobedience can be translated into benefits" (2016, p. 10). In contrast to Warner's analysis, the open-ended rebellion-reintegration cycle echoed what De Waal (2014, p. 347) described as "rent-seeking rebellion". These behaviours are dangerous for the DDR because they created a perverse incentive for rebellion, as groups seek to advance their political and security advantage. Decreeing the formation of the DDR board has adverse effects on the management of armed structures. Some researchers argue that this DDR encountered substantial delays in allotting resources and had to contend with violence (Brethfeld, 2010; Gebreselassie, 2018).

Third, there was "the stigma attached to SPLA fighters" because they were hated for their wartime actions (Stone, 2011, n.p). According to De Waal (2017, p. 182), "the SPLM was a guerrilla dictatorship". Thus, those who rejected the DDR based it on historical fears. Much of this context is discussed in Chapter Five. While fear may have temporarily glued different factions together, factionalism and groups' fears of Dinka dominance continue (Rolandsen, 2014). This power struggling became prudent after the death of South Sudanese leader, Garang, in 2005 (Malwal, 2014). After the period of ambiguity, a military hardliner, Kiir, a Dinka, assumed power in 2005. This installation of the militaristic system was popular in the net values of North-South relations, but not so much in South-South relations where each group have established competing armed structures. As South Sudan inflates its army, it brings about political and economic militarisation. It is vital to stress the effects of this militarisation on the DDR and the dire state of security. Two decades before the CPA, "the SPLA started as a mob and swelled in time bec[a]me a large semi-conventional infantry, only to collapse and fragment" (De Waal, 2017, p.187; also, Snowden, 2012).

After the secession "the SPLA had 745 officers of general rank, 40 more than the four U.S. armed services and second only in the world to Russia" (De Waal, 2017, p.187). While De Waal is right in his assertion, he fails to mention that these Generals did not just emerge from the original crop of the SPLA. Most of them came from a blotted rank of ex-proxies of the North incorporated into the SPLA, as well as from violent and self-decorated ethno-political warlords. In 2006, "the Southern Sudan legislative assembly voted to pay private soldiers U.S.$150 per month and increase this amount to the U.S.$220 in 2011 (De Waal, 2017, p.187; citing The Sudd Institute, 2014). After this pay rise, the SPLA budget "was overspent by 363%', meaning almost the entire defence spending went on salaries" (De Waal, 2017 p. 187). This deficit makes it difficult to concentrate on elements crucial for addressing the political dimension of DDR (Bior, 2014). Analysts believed the military integration might have averted a potential civil war in South Sudan before secession, but there is also a curse of military integration.

Fragmentation of Post-War Military Integration in South/ern

Sudan

The "factionalism of Southern politics had continued during the 1980s, but an internal split of the SPLM/A in 1991 proved militarily and politically disastrous" (Rolandsen and Daly, 2016, p. 120). Thus, the current proliferation of arms and war are not different from the various cases of factionalism before the CPA. In July 2013, President Kiir issued Republican Decrees dismissing the Cabinet, including his Nuer deputy, Machar (HSBA, 2014b). Given the history of power struggle, the dismissal of Machar surfaced tension between the Dinka and Nuer. This argument was based on the speed of mobilisation with which the tribal sections of SPLA fragmented and confronted each other. After five years of violent factionalism, "South Sudan has ceased to perform even the minimal functions and responsibilities of a sovereign state" (Knopf, 2016, p. 15). While South Sudan wielded "juridical sovereignty, its domestic sovereignty is contested, and nearly all the warning signs of impending" collapse was present, with extreme ethno-political polarisation fuelling a cycle of war (Knopf, 2016, p. 3). This situation appeared in total contrast to an economic theory of mobilisation. The logic is that if ethno-political mobilisation for civil war is founded on economic pull factors, then military integration should have provided a much-needed alternative (Hoddie and Hartzell, 2003). This argument is hard to dismiss, but this thesis states that military integration needs to be implemented together with other peacebuilding measures (Krebs, 2015). It is harder to isolate military integration's specific effects to determine how its success prevented the failure of the DDR. However, experts argue that 'the structure of military integration' holds the key to a successful DDR (Warner, 2016, p. 3; citing Glassmyer and Sambanis, 2008). Some integration falls short because of poor design (Burgess, 2008; Hall, 2009). Thus, potential disintegration of the world's newest state poses a challenge to western models of DDR (Musso, 2011). While the South Sudanese need a stable state, that quest is not synonymous with adapting the technical DDR.

Academics have proved this point, arguing that today a proliferation of armed groups in "the territories is intimately related to a full spectrum of sources of contestation. Although diverse in scope and form, they all seem to revolve around the issues of who has the right to rule where, over whom and what" (Vlassenroot et al., 2016, p. 7). Post-war/secession DDR in South Sudan was based on strengthening the governing system. This failed, leaving the rebel-led transitional state mired in a capacity gap. To highlight this shortfall, Fukuyama, and Levy (2010) proposed an integrated approach for institutional governance, suggesting that development plans must consider the complex interplay of political and economic dynamics of local contexts. Fukuyama postulated four "development sequences", each defined by its entry point: State capacity-building; transformational governance; "just enough' governance; and bottom-up development through Civil Society" (Andrews et al., 2012, p. 9; citing Fukuyama, 2010).

Many elements of fragmentation are unusual in South Sudan. Thus, the DDR provision created flexibility, which resulted in loose and distrustful military integration. This approach requires an understanding of whether ethno-political violence continues because armed factions have not forsaken a military solution. This analysis attempts to situate the challenges of the DDR within a broader portfolio of overlapping insurgencies in South Sudan. Some people might see a lack of centralised state in public sector performance, but in terms of fractious societies, it can be seen as the lack of sustainable legitimacy (Pritchett *et al.*, 2012). If a state cannot exist without an apparatus of government, one could argue that it is even worse in South Sudan, as a country where the notion of the state government is not "deeply rooted among the population" (Buzan, 1991, p. 64). These dispersed systems of governance lie in how North ruled Southern Sudan through militarised interactions. To understand why it is challenging to promote the demilitarisation of public space, it is essential to recognise the networks of armies and the reasons for their existence. It is then equally crucial for any DDR to deal with structural causes of local militarisation, including reforming the conduct and behaviours of the national army or security forces.

The SPLM/A governed as a military with a country, intransigent to the civility of power. An analysis of guerrilla groups in power offers a vested emphasis on how the group's behaviours and motivation formed hostile structures that led to war. This project will show that these dynamics of conflict led to a disintegration of the armed forces landscape. Hence, the proliferation of arms is built on what I describe as disputed assumptions and fragmented political idealism. With that, the transition period did not put an end to the arms race, leaving South Sudanese state in the grips of competing powers (Morrisey, 2010).

Organski's *World Politics* (1958) stresses how a system with two or more comparable powers is "unstable because the rising powers will be dissatisfied with the systems upheld by the dominant power" (Gilpin, 1981). While Organski was referring to the international system, civil war states are a smaller scale of the international system. Without denying the vital role of the state in security governance, this project asserts there was an under-estimation of OAGs' power during the formulation of South Sudan (Adekanye, 1995).

Thus, the SPLM/A brought into government a system "coupled with an overlay of conflicts and personal ambitions" (Arnold, 2007a; 2007b, p. 489), where the powerful seized the state and its means of production (Kimenyi and Mbaku, 2011; Kimenyi, 2011). This project seeks to emphasise the effect of substantial dual limitations identified in the post-war DDR literature. First, the propensity to present state fragility as the main goals of analysis have excluded a rigorous exploration of the informal structures and effect of their interaction with the DDR. Second, an over-reliance on institutional analysis as a descriptive variable of success and failure of the DDR obscures the main aspects of the challenges of state formation in South Sudan and absence of formal control over informal armed actors. The basic tenet here is to introduce this project by arguing that the armed conflicts in South Sudan embed the continued perception among armed actors/partisans that they are waging war against existential threats.

Aims of the Research

This research explores the critical factors that lead to the shortcomings of the DDR in South Sudan. The basis of this inquiry lies in the context of instability taken to represent various problems that prevent the creation of a functioning South Sudan. In this context, the DDR in South Sudan appeared to be the strategy to redress security instability and transform the former guerrilla army into a national army capable of reducing the risk of violence. This understanding will be the primary starting point for the examination of the challenges hindering the DDR in South Sudan. Accordingly, this thesis will explore how the armed factions are involved in a conflict that destabilises a sensible DDR. In other words, this thesis examines how the groups' reliance on the use of violence has influenced DDR shortcomings in South Sudan.

Research Questions

This research poses two important thematic questions regarding the complex ways in which post-war disarmament programmes interact with factionalism in a violent, fragmented state:

- **What are the significant factors affecting the operationalisation of the DDR in South Sudan (2005-11?**

  - **What realistically was expected from new efforts of DDR after the secession of South Sudan from Sudan in 2011 given security constraints on the ground?**

Thesis Structure and Outline

The history of Sudan is stained with civil war. Since 1956, Sudan has been without a functional central authority. When the CPA was signed in 2005, SA between the North and South did not explain how to entice armed groups to relinquish their political and security objectives. The introduction started with contextualising the bitter disputes between the North and South as competing protagonists. These contradictions allowed both North and South to engage in armaments as a means of maintaining the status-quo.

Hence, the chapter presented how the North's and South's fear of each other, and the exclusion of OAGs, influenced the outcome of the DDR in South Sudan. The factors affecting the DDR in South Sudan may revolve around an accumulation of arms, flaws in the designs, and designers' inability to understand the history and dynamics of the conflict. South Sudan's DDR suffered from 'complex motivations' among armed groups, but that concern did not receive significant attention in the DDR literature. Thus, this research will advance the DDR literature through a discursive approach to, and analysis of the socio-political networks of belligerents in South Sudan, and their effect on the disarmament of ex-combatants. In Chapter One, the project presents a literature review beginning with an examination of the DDR as a process aimed to prevent post-war states from relapsing back into war. That emphasis requires a conceptual underpinning of DDR and its execution as a process. Such understanding requires a brief discussion on uses and practices associated with DDR, as well as an assessment of operational challenges. This briefing is essential when assessing the failure of disarmament and demobilisation of Ex-Combatants because it grants specific attention to how groups relate in violent situations.

In South Sudan's situation, the disarmament could not be described in terms of tentative results, as it was an absolute debacle as the state broke apart. Thus, operational definitions of DDR as "the transition of being a member of an armed group to being a civilian" cannot be operationalised successfully due to political and economic factors that may explain why groups resort to violence in South Sudan (Humphreys and Weinstein, 2008). In this case, a question of who controls the use of force remains open. This situation allows criticism of the traditional convention of DDR, as I will argue that disarmament in South Sudan suffers from the absence of centralised public authority. Thus, Chapter Two applies hybrid peacebuilding modelling as a theoretical framework to provide comprehensive insight into South Sudan's violence, and the factors contributing to the decision of armed groups to engage in violence. Hybrid modelling is included through a "composite of exogenous and Indigenous forces" (Mac Ginty 2014, p. 392).

Mac Ginty and Sanghera (2012, p. 4) define hybridity as "a condition that emerges from top-down and bottom-up interactions". This study draws upon re-conceptualisation of ex-combatant reintegration and rethinks DDR from the conventional standpoint, to evaluate the impact of the complex and persistent armed conflicts in South Sudan. To contextualise the factors affecting the DDR in South Sudan, Chapter Two discusses the proliferation of arms as condition fuelled by a network of competing structures which do not lend themselves to prevailing institutional approaches because of the hybridity of security systems. The hybrid theory considers the limitation of the state, which created local structures of governance that resisted the DDR. This approach brings the analysis beyond institutionalist limitations and focuses on the contesting authorities. Chapter Three will present the research methodology based on a qualitative approach. The rationale for a qualitative approach is explained as this study is not trying to establish generalised relationships between variables but seeks to understand phenomena as complex units. The focus is to assess the factors affecting the DDR within peace support operations.

To identify these factors, this project applied a qualitative approach because it is "discursive in method and concerned with a comprehensive account of some events or unit" (King *et al.*, 1994, p. 4). The qualitative approach acknowledges that all actors are relevant in peacebuilding, although some quantitative researchers regard such data as unreliable (Denzin and Lincoln, 2003; 2005). This project is aware of the state's turbulent politics, but the extant information is insufficient at explaining why groups resorted to war. Thus, interviewing stakeholders allowed this project to apply a curious lens to examine the nuances of the situation. This interaction creates a systematic effort to hear people's perspectives and lived experiences about war. The interviews provide a valuable way to learn about others and their world. It would be an ambitious undertaking for this study to provide a comprehensive analysis of the DDR in South Sudan from functionalist views because the CPA's functional approach still has ramifications for the DDR because it did not include all political parties (Haas, 2014; Klabbers, 2008).

As such, the chosen approach aims for depth rather than comprehensive coverage. Even with such cooperation, the success of finding credible information is still conditional on additional factors. This concern forms the basis of Chapter Four. Chapter Four suggests that the post-war government of South Sudan lacked control over a monopoly of force, even though some researchers have attempted to exaggerate the capability of the South Sudanese state. South Sudan was not a state requiring rebuilding after the war. In 2011, South Sudan emerged with nothing more than a declarative qualification of statehood. These arguments advance the notions that state-society synergy is violently fragmented, and that has reduced "a routine submission to the state" (Grafstein, 1981, p. 456). In this situation, South Sudan cannot shepherd its citizens without a competent governmental authority. As a result, one can expect violent ethno-political discourse, which is the core argument in Chapter Five. Like many African states, South Sudan is built on a precarious national foundation of repealing socio-political identities.

These groups have waged fierce civil wars both against the North and between each other. While the bond of political regionalism was useful against the North, analysts believed the tribal fault-lines informed how the groups conducted their politics in post-secession epoch (Brown, 2014). This project argues that identity silencing could be a strategy in conventional fields of interaction, subject to political determinism. The group attempt to escape poverty, and exclusion does not show that they make a free choice to escape (Le Billon, 2012). It shows, instead, that their situation influences them to strive for a better alternative. Finding what is influencing South Sudanese groups' behaviour requires analysis of how the seeds of violent were sown long before the CPA. Chapter Six is dedicated to the role of the international community in peacemaking, and efforts to prevent the relapse to war. It argues that despite ending the war, the CPA was not inclusive enough to address divisions in South Sudan. Lamb and Stainer (2018) cited the lack of interplay between the incentives of the CPA and OAGs. They emphasise how the CPA-DDR were predicated on the effort to consolidate the power of those perceived to be in charge.

Thus, the CPA negotiators did not consider how an exclusive CPA could incite an illiberal regime, given the fact that there was no proportional allocation of positions and protection of some ethnic factions that rebelled "against the political order imposed by other identity groups" in Southern Sudan (Lamb and Stainer, 2018). Such a situation hinted at the intricacies of security concerns. Thus, this study builds on the work of critics who decry that the 2005 CPA was incomplete. Hence, the CPA offered a ceasefire, especially in South Sudan (Young, 2007). Finally, in conclusion, the researcher presents a summary of the research's main points and asks a provocative question about the future of South Sudan: so, what have we learned about the challenges facing the disarmament? The response to resistance may be seen, not as a residual product of politics, but rather as a critical component of the socio-political and economic process. With that condition, DDR needs to include the effect of violent division among elites and groups.

Chapter One: Literature Review: Disarmament, Demobilisation, and Reintegration of Ex-Combatants (DDR): The Case of South Sudan

Ex-combatants can become the primary cause of instability and disruption in post-war states and escalates the possibility of armed conflicts being resumed if these armed actors reneged or rejected peace and the DDR process. This challenge is magnified in war-ravaged countries, which are characterised by weak political and economic institutions, insecurity, and the proliferation of arms. These conditions are conspicuous in South Sudan, and they have a substantial influence on the outcome of the DDR and other peacebuilding initiatives (Haywood, 2014). After ending the war, North and South embarked on an effort to prevent relapse to war, by initiating the DDR. As presented in introduction chapter, the CPA mandated that the SAF and SPLM/A disarm a combined 180,000 soldiers by the end of the six-year interim period (The CPA, 2005, p. 87). This was ambitious for several reasons, as the following paragraph explains. The track record of the previous peace accord between North and South has earned the Sudanese government the dubious distinction of intransigence when it comes to Southern Sudanese secession claims.

South Sudan fear the North might renege as it did on a past agreement, and this is considered a significant impediment towards their commitment to the DDR. Second, the CPA did not bring about peace (Goodhand, 2006). This outcome led to the research question guiding this thesis: What factors and circumstances affect or contribute to the failure of DDR in South Sudan? The introductory chapter offered a multi-dimensional view on the CPA-DDR and the factors contributing to its failure. Thus, by examining the process of the CPA, this chapter will demonstrate that the violent political situation has emanated from that process. From 1955 to 2005, Southern Sudan has been without a compelling state system and government, making it the perpetual situation of the absolute absence of stateness in post-Colonial history. In this institutional vacuum, South Sudan continued to function in governance without government mode, and that experience is of a broader interest in the failure of the DDR for two purposes.

First, South Sudan's case helps refine academics' conceptualisation of the complexity and nature of armed actors in protracted violent predicaments. Most assessments of the spoiler problem, like Stedman's research, concentrate on armed groups seeking to destabilise peace or procedures sought to prevent the resumption of war, like the DDR (Stedman, 1997). The notion of spoilers is entirely appropriate to this situation, as spoilers dedicate their time and resources to blocking DDR and perpetuating conditions of conflict and violence. In contrast, DDR needs to be understood and approached within the framework of armed actors (De Vries and Schomerus, 2017). The context of the violent split of the SPLM/A and various ethnic conflicts were not included in the CPA-DDR. In short, this was designed for short-term stabilisation missions, to prevent war between North-South. Such an exclusionary approach fortified armed structures, who continued to marshal the scenes of horror, forcing a collapse of the state envisioned by the IGAD (Tschirgi, 2004). This research argues that the CPA-DDR did not have sufficient understanding of the dynamics of the discord, and thus lacked an understanding of whether the DDR was susceptible to co-optation by powerful domestic elites in pursuit of military supremacy.

Although the CPA had ended the North-South war, these respective regions were chaotic, making it difficult to predict the line where the hostilities ended. Significant challenges were coming from below [informal security and political systems] that did not accept the authority and legitimacy of any dominant groups. This limitation in statehood creates opportunities for informal armies to resist the disarmament, hence, rendering the post-war states incapable of monopolising the use of force (Jackson, 1990). Understanding the interplay between groups' grievances or fears could explain their resistance to the DDR. Such an approach rejects the institutional approach to the DDR, in favour of a context-based approach. This project will argue that South Sudan state has not attained the Weberian shape in function. Establishing this observation is vital for supporting the argument that the challenges of the DDR lie in OAGs' security.

1.1 Civil War in Africa: Conceptual Explication with Reference to South Sudan

The history of post-Cold War Africa includes many civil wars (Anderson, 1983; Lake and Rothchild, 1998). Although "states have always grown out of competition for control of territory", the violent factionalism in Africa represents unsystematic causes (Tilly, 1990, p. 4). An analysis of why South Sudan continues to face a prevalence of war often mischaracterises the causes of war as products of acrimonious ethno-political competition over oil wealth (El-Batahani *et al.*, 2005). More nuanced evaluations by regional experts, like De Waal, (2017), have concentrated almost entirely "on infighting among elite politicians and military officers based in Juba and other major cities who use patronage networks to ethnicise conflicts", and that have created "autonomous groups mobilised to defend their interests" (Stringham and Forney, 2017, p.178). This chapter argues that a focus on violent political competition or local politics of ethno-political warlords has led some scholars to misinterpret the interests of informal armies, parochial armed actors and the role they played in the failure of the DDR. Scholars of African politics often portrayed local armies as loyal ethnic militias, although the literature of civil wars on other continents consists of similar techniques of analytical thinking (Van Evera, 1994).

Some researchers focus on economic elements, while others use social divisions and negative interactions to show that a handful of factors, such as repealing socio-political characters, are causal determinants of war (Horowitz, 1985; Muller, 1985). These scholars invoked Gurr's (1970; cited in Spears, 2002, p. 123) social discontent; a "discrepancy between the conditions in life that people inherently expect and the social conditions that limit what they are capable of achieving". In his book, *The Clash of Civilisation (1993)*, Huntington asserted that differences, like sociocultural dissimilarities, would be a reasonable cause of identity conflicts. His thesis has significantly impacted the understanding of conflict, but it came under a barrage of criticism from those who perceived his conclusion as far too early for a definitive historical verdict (Murshed, 2002; Senghaas, 2002). Critics saw civilisations as one of many causes of conflict. In a rebuke, Berger (2010) argued that if the thesis has plausibility at all, it is with reference to the Muslim world.

Berger reacted to Huntington's claims of the culture conflict nexus, in which he wrote, "Islam has bloody borders" (Huntington, 1993). While this assertion does always not describe Islam, it does fit various conditions in which Islam confronts other religions, and the civil war that led to the division of old Sudan is an example (Otterbein, 2004). Like most scholars, Huntington's thesis made him a creature of his time. As the Soviet collapsed, he spent much of his work dissecting the war in the Balkans, focusing on what he described as the "fault line" between Islamic and Christian civilisations (Bradley, 2016; Russett, O'Neal and Cox, 2000; citing Huntington, 1993, p. 3). This study concurs that the clash of civilisation conflicts existed, but it is timely in light of current wars to revisit Huntington's prescient essay and the debate it engendered. There is not enough statistical evidence of civilisation as the cause of conflict in South Sudan. What might be causing the war in South Sudan is "elite predation or ethnic entrepreneurs" – political leaders who articulate beliefs in kinship bonds or common destiny, and who mobilise and organise groups to press group claims" (Sisk, 2009, p. 19). Huntington also ventured toward a Confucian culture and emphasised how it would fit China against the West in ways that do not now seem probable.

These flaws are magnified by Huntington's failure to foresee the deep cracks within the Islamic culture, between the Sunni and Shiite. The second group draw a link between civil war and the availability of natural resources. Collier found natural resources to be a significant factor in causing civil war (Collier, 1998; 2009). In Collier's explanation, conflict stems from the presence of economic inequality. Thus, ethnic wars are based on the interaction of preferences, opportunities, and perceptions. These findings were based on statistical modelling with large sample sizes. Despite this size of the sample, the cause of civil war in South Sudan, based on Collier's findings, can be seen as the result of excluding some groups from access to resources. This argument ignited a consistent debate among academics. However, no ostensible answers on the connection have emerged. Some scholars argue that only oil fuelled the civil war (Ross, 2004; 2007), while others argue that what is essential is how dependent a state is on those resources (Basedau and Lay, 2009; Le Billion, 2008; 2009). There is an even more significant difference in the mechanisms associating natural resources to the cause of civil war.

Some scholars claim that natural resources lead to the armed conflict based on their effects on the politics of the state (Humphreys, 2005; 2004b; Lujala, 2010). My thesis argues that an analysis of the connection between onsets of armed conflict and the natural resources is problematic because some civil wars are fought for political emancipation. This situation is apparent in South Sudan, where "the state only exists judicially, not as social facts" (Booth, 1991, p.313). As argued in the introduction, South Sudan "resembles a mafia neighbourhood", rather than a coherent and functional national society (Booth, 1991, p. 313). This breakdown of a centralised system of government and security requires understanding civilisation, security and war economies, as the factors causing the war. Collier's view may lead to the characterisation of civil war as an ethnic conflict because of subjective use or mobilisation of the ethnic group to differentiate one group from another (Kustov, 2017). This distinction leads to armed conflict when ethnicity is used as a tool for a power struggle.

While the primary data collected for this project has found some link between civil war in South Sudan and natural resources, that link does not explain the causal mechanisms behind the correlation without a variety of other mechanisms. When there is no fair governance in a divided state, such as in old Sudan and now in South Sudan, the outcome is an ensuing breakdown in trust between those who felt excluded. Hence, citizens resort to accessing public utilities via violent ethno-political elites. When that is the case, the cause of war may involve national politico-military leaders who invoke ethnic enmity and dupe civilian militias into war via tribal pandering. As Lynch has emphasised "ethnic discourses are deployed, manipulated and understood in a myriad of sophisticated ways by parochial fighters as well as by warlords" (Stringham and Forney, 2017, p.180; citing Lynch, 2011). In this case, patronage and clientelism fuelled violent politics vested with a "politics of symbolism" (Chua, 2003, pp. 74-75; also, Htun, 2004). Again, this assertion sees ethnicity as the cause rather than the interest each group is trying to achieve.

That interest might not be economical. Aside from the impact of ethnic tension, the armed conflict and factional wars in South Sudan can still be considered preventive violence against genocidal acts of the dominant group(s). Despite the politics of symbolism and ethnic subjectivity, the outbreak of violent conflict in South Sudan is not defined only by emotional appeal or motivations (Green, 2006; 2012), but is "a prime example of how governance arrangements can either achieve and maintain peace, or become the trigger for civil war" (Radon and Logan, 2014, p. 149). The gap in the above literature thus far is a failure to emphasise complex motivations for war. The debate paid less attention to local issues in divided states, especially how relationships between groups could lead to a war that fuelled corrupted flows of arms. This research argues that there is a connection between locals' grievances and disarmament failure. That situation sought consideration of how national-and local leaders' ambitions intersect with the politics of DDR. Based on these arguments, the project will ask how DDR has attempted to address civil war in Africa when it still experiences armed conflicts.

1.2 How DDR has Attempted to Address the motives of the Civil War in Africa

While the prevalence of civil war has decreased since the 1990s, the threat of surplus arms remains the main challenge to peace. In the last decade, "there were approximately 500,000 individuals, a variety of non-state militias, national armies, and paramilitary groups slated to undergo DDR programmes across Africa" (Zena, 2013, p. 1). Given this estimation, one may ask why DDR is essential, and why the DDR and Security Sector Reform (SSR) are linked. DDR was established as part of efforts to control arms and actors (Bryden, 2007). The aim of the DDR in South Sudan, for instance, derived from an attempt "to contribute to security and stability in post-conflict environments so that recovery and development can begin" (Knight, 2008, p. 29). Based on this argument, most post-war states have engaged in the DDR. For decades, states such as Ethiopia, Uganda, and Liberia, to name a few have engaged in the DDR (Afolabi, 2009). Additionally, since the genocide in Darfur, the U.N. has deployed multiple multidimensional peace support and conflict prevention missions across Africa, with no substantial results.

According to Knight, "by 2005, 75 per cent of U.N. peacekeeping resources were devoted to dealing with African conflicts" (Knight, 2008, p. 34). Despite these interventions, the peacekeeping and the DDR result in several African countries are far from the objective envisioned by the U.N. Some, such as in South Sudan, is an absolute failure. Most observers of the DDR in Africa blamed the failure of programmes on a security environment that "continues to be precarious and unstable", as well as insignificance of the reintegration packages (Afisi, 2009, p. 59). Harsch's research from *Africa Renewal* "shows that reintegration is a complex and long-term process. It is fraught with difficulties and depends on the success of wider efforts at economic recovery and political reconciliation" (Harsch, 2005, n.p). Harsch's observation emphasises the persistence of conflict in African countries where peacebuilding and the DDR have been tried. A core argument regarding the failure of DDR in Africa surrounds "the overwhelming need for and significant difficulties in establishing

72

conditions for sustainable peace" (Knight, 2008, p. 34).

The discussions in the literature showed broad differences in DDR programmes in Africa. The nature of war influenced the outcomes of the DDR, along with the peace settlement approach, the "political will" of the signatories, and the capabilities of the post-war governments (Fithen, 1999; Vinck *et al.*, 2011). In some states where only conventional armies have been involved, DDR processes have been direct. In Eritrea, over 100,000 ex-fighters were disarmed after a peace accord with neighbouring Ethiopia in 2000, annulling a reference to Eritrea as "a mobilised nation" (Healy and Plaut, 2007, p. 6). The explanation for this success lies in the dynamics of war. Eritrea's dynamics were different from South Sudan, where armed factions faced off within the country and each other. The Eritrean government's challenge was to orient its soldiers away from a war mentality with another state. In contrast, DDR in South Sudan was contending with the dynamics of conflict. Munive identifies two significant challenges facing DDR situations in South Sudan. First, he noted that "there is no peace to keep due to on-going hostilities" (Munive, 2014, p. 13).

When this situation unfolded in South Sudan, the challenge became the "lack of a political agreement and political buy-in from warring parties" (Munive, 2016, p.10). Armed combatants doubted whether DDR would work in such violent settings (Lamb, 2018). The second issue identified by Munive is that continuing armed conflict-affected the "stability required to facilitate the economic reconstruction needed to provide ex-combatants jobs" (Munive, 2016, pp.10-11). It became challenging in this situation to carry out DDR programmes that prevent relapse to war. Thus, the DDR process in non-compliant situations must address, not only the fear of the groups of an institution conducting the DDR, but also the public perception of armed groups as security providers. The DDR in South Sudan would need to recognise and legitimise armed actors who had the authority to persuade militias. Arnold and Alden argue that "the DDR of the so-called White Army militias" [Nuer civilian armed group in South Sudan] highlights the complications innate in management of the DDR aimed at local militia (2007, p. 5). Instead, they explain the prospects for successful DDR inherent in dealing with regular force (2007, p. 5). South Sudanese signed the CPA when they had no comprehensible national armed force. Hence, experts have either understood the prevalence of war as "a contest among elite patrons who command hordes of tribal clients, loyal proxies for whom tribalism masks class privilege, or as the financial collapse of a state held together by ethnic patronage alone"(Pinaud, 2014, p. 211). Moreover, De Waal's (2014; 2017) analysis presents a perspective of what he described as "the elite agency" in the civil war in South Sudan. That view neglects the locally influential ethno-political leaders who recruit and lead militias. This situation was encountered in Mozambique when its war ended in 1992 as well as in Sierra Leone (UNSC Report, 2011). In Sierra Leone, however, the insurgent Revolutionary United Front (RUF) initially failed to adhere to the peace accord. After suffering severe military reversal from U.N. forces, RUF disarmed. A survey conducted in 2003-4 by the U.N. found that the RUF did not resume the war, not because of DDR incentives, but due to the lack of support for resuming armed action (Solomon and Ginifer, 2008).

Although some researchers articulated their discontent with the situation in Sierra Leone, a majority saw their arms groups as organisations from the past because the war has not resumed (Rufer, 2005; Ball and Hendrickson, 2005). This is because many of Ex-Combatants had already left the army to become civilian and "were working as cocoa farmers", carpenters, and "small-scale traders" (Rosen, 2005; Sanford, 2006). This transition does not mean that Sierra Leone is perfect. Unemployment in the country remains very high (UNSC Report, 2011; 2013). Some Ex-Combatants were stuck in limbo, but this is still preferable to the resumption of war. When there is no defined front line, combatants and war become predatory rather than strategic, and the conventional procedure for security reform becomes obsolete. The fall of the conventional security reform occurred in South Sudan because violence frequently revolves around the political interest of groups (Jok, 2012). Some have argued that DDR must constitute "a comprehensive, integrated, and coordinated approach from the planning to the implementation stages" (Knight, 2008, p. 30); a procedure they believe has not been followed in Africa (Zena, 2013; Pugel, 2009).

Lamb et al., (2012) emphasise the lack of combatants' views in conventional DDR. As Harsch (2005) suggested before, there is a need for peace agreement mediators to address the specific needs of combatants. Since Africa does not have its own medium of the DDR independent from the global context, the African Union's (AU) and the IGAD procedure remained within the ordinary discourse (Bryden and Scherrer, 2012). AU's DDR-Capacity Programme 2013 has raised awareness about the kind of help required by countries engaging in the DDR. Yet, that push fails to contextualise the emerging context of violence, and how to utilise lessons learned from previous cases within Africa. Since the CPA, South Sudan has been confronted with numerous local rebellions emanating from historical political rivalry within the SPLM/A, and disputes arising from the 2010 elections. The GoSS and its army, the SPLA, depict external threats, mostly from the North, as considerable. However, the GoSS and its army have not secured ultimate control over means of legitimate force, with many political factions and ethnic armed youth (Munive, 2013).

This situation requires a grasp of motivations and interests that mobilise violent actors, and the concerns that encourage resistance to the DDR. The success of DDR may result in improvements in security's performance based on who is demobilised or retained. At the same time, SSR produces professional security forces that can control spoilers by setting "the terrain for future reform efforts by establishing the numbers and nature of the security sector" (Hänggi, 2005, p. 95). These aspirations failed in South Sudan. In the words of one participant: "the biggest problem we had is that integration was not done properly" (P17/14/12/2017). This participant argues that the DDR was designed outside the parameters of the SSR. This argument discounts ethnic divisions but emphasises that the army was not professionalised, labelling the SPLA as "a collection of militia, organised based on personal loyalty to its commander, in effect, ethnically-based armed units" (Stringham and Forney, 2017, p. 186). The gap in the above literature focusing on the state-centred DDR model in South Sudan, and emphasise the failure to conceptualise hybrid/multi-layered security providers in areas of limited statehood.

1.3 A Security Governance Concept to Post-War Peacebuilding

The notion of security governance encompasses two perceptions that have evolved since Sudan's CPA; security stretched to include "socio-political, economic, societal and environmental as well as military threats of armed factions" (IDDRS, 2006, p. 29). The idea of governance in security has appeared in peacemaking to echo the disintegration of state system or power among "public and private actors on multiple levels and the emergence of formal and informal cooperative problem-solving arrangements" (Scheye and Peake, 2005, p. 240). In this case, the "governance discourse attempts to understand the multiplicity of actors beyond the state. Security governance thus considers complex governing mechanisms in the broad security field" (Bryden and Hänggi, 2005, p. 34). Hence, security governance is a useful analytical perception in fragmented states where armed groups are embedded in local communities (Kupchan, 1998; UNRPPO, 2000).

It is essential to recognise how various armed actors involved in national power struggles and the use of that power, including in the provision of public security. In an analysis of DDR in Burundi, an estimate of over 75 per cent of Ex-Combatants said the training and reinsertion packages of DDR had prepared/equipped them for the transition into civilian life and employment (Hanson, 2007). A similar argument resonated with the outcome in Angola, but with little emphasis on how to connect community security and DDR (ICG, 2003). The main intention is Multi-purpose training of Ex-Combatants, based not just on how to be economically viable, but also on how to be a good citizen. There is a critical need for facilitated dialogue between Ex-Combatants and their communities (Willems *et al.*, 2009; 2010; Touray, 2005). What became apparent during the fieldwork for this project is an inconsistency between the expectations placed on the DDR and the experiences of war-affected states. To some extent, the expectations of the DDR did not encompass every armed actor and their security needs.

1.4 DDR: Theoretical Understanding

DDR is a reasonably well-researched area of the international community's war prevention efforts. Those researches were advanced by the work of Lamb and Berdal, (1996), who are vulnerable to criticism from the new groups of thinkers who want to surpass the old ways. This group includes Pugel, (2003), who seeks to explore how fluid networking among distrustful factions hinders the DDR. Thus, as in other avenues of technical expertise, critics argue that, the DDR policy reaches practitioner in an imprecise manner. Despite engrained instability and new areas of insecurity, the U.N. agencies continued to follow their norms, beyond the reach of field practitioners. The academic gap in DDR is existent, but it is shrinking as ideas drift towards a critical analysis of how insecurity discourages participation in DDR. Most DDR practitioners work for the U.N. So, they tend to drive a specific agenda, as post-war operations rely on global bureaucracy as they seek international political necessities to pursue the desired action (Porto and Parsons, 2003).

This liberal practice originates in the official discussion in former U.N. Secretary-General Boutros-Ghali's utilisation of the term, *An Agenda for Peace* (1992, p. 11). The U.N. linked DDR with all peace efforts; a perception explained by Kofi Annan, who emphasised peacebuilding vested in SSR (Annan, 2000; 1999; Tschirgi, 2004). In fractured states, however, capacity development may be relevant, but it does not often surpass entrenched perceptions of self-security (Schelling, 2012). The ethno-political minority groups' fear induces ontological insecurity, which sets a hostile socio-political dynamic in motion, leading to the re-securitisation of the post-war socio-political disputes. What is needed in this situation is a context-driven process of DDR coupled with a reconfiguration of incentives in a way that maintains ontological security. DDR in South Sudan, in contrast, offers an entry point to argue that transition from armed conflict to peace, rebels to government, and territory to the sovereign state encompasses intricate political procedures shaped by simmering tensions and violence (Sorbo and Ahmed, 2013). The question thus must be how context-based approaches to DDR could navigate multilayered conflicts.

This questioning seeks to go beyond conventional state-centric concepts of security. To explore the depth of post-war security hurdles, it is helpful to recognise that liberal interventions are inherently paradoxical, where the OAGs approached political and security issues in term of the threats to their survival (Chesterman,

2004). This securitised worldview merits emergency and exceptional security measures (Waever, 1995). As this is the case in South Sudan, DDR "thus belongs to the same crop as the strategic concepts of effects-based and comprehensive approaches to operations" (Andersen 2012; citing Egnell and Haldén, 2009, p. 30). This view necessitates the analysis of different researchers' arguments and their failure to recognise the critical challenges posed by subnational armed groups that do not accept the state monopoly of violence.

1.5 Concept and Definition of DDR

States emerging from war are confronted with one prime security concern; what to do with the massive armies and arms acquired during the war? The response by the post-war state and the international community is DDR (Doyle and Sambanis, 2000). Most scholars argue that "for the peace to fail, a dissident organisation must have the capacity to mount an armed challenge to the post-conflict regime" (Mason *et al.*, 2011, p. 172). Hence, DDR is meant to disrupt the capacity of armed groups for hindering peace. Despite consideration devoted to DDR, implementing it requires more than symbolic or ideal driven initiatives to collect arms and disband armed structures. DDR is most effective when its coordination includes national and subnational umbrella policies designed to root out covert armed groups (Scheye and Peake, 2005). Since its emergence, DDR has been held as essential, but it is not a panacea for post-war troubles (Hamer, 2011; Lewis *et al.*, 1999). In South Sudan, the capacity of armed groups to mount new wars thwarted DDR because of widespread violence, which does not end with peace agreements. Hence, the resistance to

DDR may lie with factionalism and groups' impetus to rebel. A groups' impetus to rebel created multiple sovereignty (Tilly, 1978). Multiple sovereignty exists when informal armies organise resistance and command significant legitimacy.

In Tilly's argument "multiple sovereignty is the structural condition that makes civil war possible" (Mason *et al.*, 2011, p. 172; citing Tilly, 1978). Such groups do not adhere to the aim of disarmament: to re-institute legitimate state domination over the means of violence (Humphreys and Weinstein, 2004, p. 2). This foundation of a DDR does not focus on the political inclination of the group to commit to disarmament and sustainable people. This factor of armed actors can be modelled as the armed group's leaders' choice between war versus the peace, an option that is anchored in leaders' approximation of the costs and benefits analysis. Besides, as Banholzer points out, problems of reintegrating ex-fighters into "civilian life can be powerful triggers for combatants to take up their weapons again and resort to war" (2014, p. 3). This understanding was not in place during the CPA-DDR. The focus on downsizing the SPLM/A ignored the fact that "combatants who have been members of an armed group for many years are less likely to participate in the DDR process" (Baholzer, 2014, p. 2; also, Schauer and Elbert (2010, p. 312).

Before Baholzer's emphasis, Schauer and Elbert (2010, p. 312) stressed that "the risk of re-recruitment is high when Ex-Combatants fail to reintegrate economically and socially into their civil host communities, which may cause substantial economic development issues, and a new turn in the cycle of violence becomes inevitable". When the above situations unfold, DDR became difficult because of conflict and complex militaries (Glaser, 1990). This situation allowed actors to adhere to pursuing an inter-group and intra-group deterrence model, with the former derived from the South Sudanese fear of the North and the latter based on minor groups' fear of the new dominant group in post-secession South (Schomerus and Allen, 2010). It is evident in South Sudan that the minorities, and other ethno-political groups' fear the dominance. Hence, the informal armies and armed political factions who choose to fight or resisted the DDR draw on various ethno-political grievances as an organising principle (Sorbo and Ahmed, 2013). To contextualise this argument, the next section will define and discuss DDR and the literature on how the DDR attempted to improve the situation for ex-fighters and prevent relapse to war.

This analysis demonstrates what can occur when there are no "functioning government institutions to help to ensure that emerging countries fulfil their economic promises and provide the security needed for combatants to disarm" (Schauer and Elbert, 2010, p. 312). This situation requires a much better understanding of DDR and the counter-logics that encourage combatants to resist the DDR. The fundamental precept of the DDR process lies in efforts to prevent countries emerging from war from relapsing back into civil war. This procedure of transforming soldiers into non-combatants citizens is presented in the definition below.

(a): Disarmament is the collection of small arms and light and heavy weapons within a conflict zone. It frequently entails the assembly and cantonment of combatants; it should also comprise the development of arms management programmes, including their safe storage and their final destination, which may entail their destruction. De-mining may also be part of this process.

(b): Demobilisation refers to the process by which parties to a conflict begin to disband their military structures and combatants begin the transformation into civilian life. It generally entails registration of Ex-Combatants; some kind of assistance to enable them to meet their immediate basic needs; discharge, and transportation to their home communities. It may be followed by recruitment into a new military force.

(c): Reintegration refers to the process which allows Ex-Combatants and their families to adapt, economically and socially, to productive civilian life. It generally entails the provision of a package of cash or in-kind compensation, training, and job- and income-generating projects. These measures frequently depend for their effectiveness upon other, broader undertakings, such as assistance to returning refugees and internally displaced persons; economic development at the community and national level; infrastructure rehabilitation; truth and reconciliation efforts; and institutional reform (UNPKO, 2005; Secretary-General Note to the General Assembly, May 2005 (A/C.5/59/31)).

In context, DDR cannot succeed only through "collection, documentation, control and disposal of small arms, ammunition, explosives and light and heavy weapons" (UNPSO, 2012, p. 13). DDR must involve the needs of child and female soldiers and the wider community affected by war (Alexander, 2006). A child soldier is "any person under 18 years of age who forms part of an armed force in any capacity, and those accompanying such groups, other than purely as family members, and girls recruited for sexual purposes and forced marriage" (The UNSGR, 2000, p. 3).

Yet, it is worth arguing that we must not ignore the context in which these children armed themselves or were armed by others (Swarbrick, 2007). This project stresses the importance of the power dimension when the primacy of the state is weak or absent. As it is the situation in South Sudan, the absence of the state leads to the emergence of the multitude of security providers. What is lacking in DDR literature is a consideration of the complexity of violent actors, and how they can negate the success of DDR. Given that this condition defines South Sudan, DDR operators work blindfolded because they cannot tell who governs the use of force (Risse, 2011). Thus, the demobilisation, instead, should turn rogue soldiers into peaceful civilians, which has not occurred in South Sudan. This stage of demilitarisation does not end with the dismantling of armed structures when the state is absent or weak (Specht, 2006). Thus, the demobilisation phase involves setting up cantonment centres to assess and determine who should be assigned to the next stage before undertaking skills training and providing Reinsertion packages (UN-DDR, 2009).

Reintegration is the process by which Ex-Combatants acquire civilian status and gain sustainable employment and income. Reintegration is essentially a social and economic process with an open timeframe, primarily taking place in communities at the local level. It is part of the general development of a country and a national responsibility, and often necessitates long-term external assistance (Secretary-General Note to the General Assembly, May 2005 (A/C.5/59/31).

These packages often contain financial assistance, as well as some household materials, but how long these packages can compensate for what ex-combatants lost? The success of DDR in Sierra Leone, for instance, was not based on how DDR would bring about greater security, or address political grievances that underlie or trigger armed conflict (Lamb, 2011). What is needed here is DDR capable of offering a means for the state to reach out to the war-affected society, and to rebuild its legitimacy (Stone, 2011). In contrast, post-war DDR in South Sudan hardly had any functioning security to entice the ex-fighters. Periods of protracted civil war "meant that virtually every male has been involved in the fighting in one way or another, and a large number of women have also participated in the war, either in a combat role or a support role" (SAS, 2011, p. 2).

But, Stone (2011) argues that, since its launch, the South Sudanese disarmament and demobilisation commission approach to the new security issues had just been to replicate the CPA-DDR text. In the Small Arms Survey (SAS) report, Stone wondered whether the South Sudanese disarmament and demobilisation commission board "grasped the issues of DDR" after some senior officials at SSDDRC argued that "the purpose of DDR is to replenish the army, taking out the old so that the new can enter" (SAS, 2011, p. 8). Thus, a question worth answering is: what is post-secession disarmament aimed at achieving? Is it to enhance physical security, as defined in the CPA? If so, the SSDDRC has not established any gain from what they have been doing. "I risked life to surrender my gun", said ex-fighters. "I am unemployed for over four years now, and I am unable to feed my family; that is why I re-joined the rebellion" (P21/21/07/2017). This example emphasises lack of the state's absorptive capacity in South Sudan.

Instead, Warner (2013; 2016) focused on the lack of economic capacity and what she described as "vertical dimension of power" to ensure the provision of public security. Warner argues that the success of reintegration depended on a political settlement and political will from the warring parties, and perceived reintegration from technical, economic perspectives emphasised earlier. The gap in Warner's analysis is her failure to provide answers identifying who the combatants are in South Sudan. Warner mischaracterise what is occurring as products of divisive ethnic rivalries, failing to emphasise how the legacy of political division within the SPLM/A, lead to the proliferation of political militias and vacuuming all the sense of a collective system of government and security. Even if that is the case, achieving successful DDR is not hinged on the state's absorptive capacity alone. Warner did not emphasise that such capacity should also take place in communities where ex-fighters lived before the conflict. While deficient reintegration packages were provided to the few disabled SPLA officers, lack of pension support, and employment fuelled remobilisation (Rands, 2006; 2010). Sudan provided reintegration packages worth USD 1,750 per–ex-fighter (MYDDRP, 2008).

This approach was not available in South Sudan. Nichols blamed this issue on the South Sudanese disarmament and demobilisation commission's inability to "build its capacity to the point where it is fully functional" (2011, p. 32). However, this thesis argues that Nichols has read too much into the economic designs of the DDR. While he is partly right, he failed to mention the incorporation of the DDR within larger peacemaking to address state-society/group-group relationship requires sustainable employment and social connection.

1.6 The Rationale for Successful Reintegration

The rationale for reintegration is simple. Ex-fighters without a sustainable way of making a living outside the army are likely to hold on to war (Lemasle, 2009; Rozema, *et al.*, 2008). Analysts saw disarmament and demobilisation as a core component of a broader strategy aimed at creating the situations conducive for sustainable peace (Nezam *et al.*, 2009). Thus, the main aim of "reintegration is to enhance national and community security and recovery by supporting Ex-Combatants in their efforts to find a new role in society and the economy, through sustainable, peaceful livelihoods for them and their families" (Lamb *et al.*, 2012, p. 58). Despite the merit of this argument, violence characterises South Sudan's fledgling capacities (McNeish and Nicholls, 2014). Even if the disarmament programmes considered the reintegration as a chance to enable ex-soldiers' transition to normal civilian life, nothing would have supported such a transition.

In part, the focus on wider armed combatants is justified to redress an imbalance in the conceptualisation of the DDR. A large body of literature is narrowly focused, and liberal policy-driven in character, dealing with the bureaucratic activities of the DDR. This argument stems from concern surrounding the tendency to focus on the nuts and bolts of operations. This treats the challenges of DDR as problems of effective delivery, an absence of the state, abstracted from any "specific historical and political frame of reference" in South Sudan (Berdal and Ucko, 2013, p. 9). This deficiency is no trivial matter. The mediators in Sudan's CPA have not departed from a managerial approach to DDR, divorced from a deeper engagement with the dynamics of conflicts.

The focus on ex-fighters represents a misunderstanding of war-affected states because the success of integration must address both physical and human security. Given the fact that DDR takes place in South Sudan as one of the fragile states, it, thus, makes sense to ask whether the reintegration, even when successful, could arrest physical and human insecurity through the related process. Or, accordingly, create a responsive political condition in which peace and development can thrive. Without such factors, DDR may not engender "the restoration to individuals of a sense of their value, strength and capacity to handle life's problems" (Bush and Folger, 2005, p. 2). Instead of this context-based approach, DDR was based on a numeric definition of success, and that falls short in South Sudan. Further, the reintegration is political because of the difficulty of disarming wartime forces (Solomon and Ginifer, 2008). When the security situation remains a disincentive for participation, DDR needs strategies that do more than just aiming to stop the war; it must involve multi-dimensional spheres of actions to build peace (Castaneda, 2009).

Achieving positive peace requires political relations capable of fostering reconciliation (Rasmussen, 2007). Such a situation can occur when a vital core of human security is protected. In that case, the emerging states need to have the political, economic and security institutions capable of protecting human security; a notion not mentioned in either the CPA-DDR or post-secession programmes in South Sudan. This lack of measures for safeguarding lives implicates not only DDR, but also envisioned political and economic institutions intended to promote physical and human security overtly (Solomon and Ginifer, 2008). The above arguments led to a call for DDR to be 'an interplay' between the dynamics of conflicts (Kimberly, 1996; Carbonnier, 1998). This criticism lies in the fact that most post-war states hinge on armed systems with convoluted authorities (Di John and Putzel, 2009). However, the estimates and debates of different scholars suggest various arguments on how to address ex-fighters' experience and to prevent them from remobilisation and resuming the war. Among these scholars is Nat Colletta, and his study of the DDR in Uganda in the 1990s.

1.7 Nat J. Colletta

Coletta's study of DDR in Uganda emphasised that "the political commitment, realism, and pragmatism of the national government and the international community towards implementation" determined the success and failure of the DDR process (Molloy, 2013, p. 54; citing Colletta *et al.*, 1996). In Coletta's view, a simplified DDR cannot thrive without considering the context of the violence. He believed that DDR must contribute to the building of a cohesive society (Colletta and

Muggah, 2009). That was not the case in South Sudan. There is no scientific description or meaning of social cohesion, but it is based on the willingness of groups to band together in socio-political, cultural and security fronts, to survive and prosper (Green *et al.*, 2009). The perceived intention of cohesive society lies in an attempt to build a wide variety of socio-political outcomes such as political inclusion and economic prosperity. This project will argue in Chapter Five that the South Sudanese, even though they fought the North as the collective, they never had a sense of belonging that gives a semblance of shared identity and inclusiveness.

When the governing system seeking to monopolise the legitimate use of force lack tolerance and capacity to protect and respect groups and communities' opinions, mutual distrust and uncertainty encourage inter-group and factional violence. Having socio-political and security co-operation, provision of good governance may increase active participation in disarmament. Since DDR seeks to restore the state's authority, it must navigate these volatile settings to find ways of moving warring parties toward reliance on "soft power" (Nye, 2008). Colletta *et al.*, (2008) agreed with Nye's principle of "soft power", arguing that DDR must meet these demands, beyond the mere projection of the state's ability to monopolise violence. This shift in Uganda's government expenditure entailed not just the SSR, but also the phased DDR of ex-combatant into productive noncombat socio-economic and political life. What the Ugandan government did well, in Colletta's view, is a segmentation of DDR through *Uganda Veterans' Assistance Programme* (UVAP). There were three main aims of the

UVAP identified in Colletta's thesis.

These aims were "(a) demobilisation and resettlement of veterans, (b) facilitation of their socio-economic reintegration into a peaceful, productive, and sustainable civilian life, and (c) restructuring of public expenditure to increase the funds available for priority programmes, especially those allocated for economic development and social infrastructure and services" (Colletta *et al.*, 1996, p. 2). The problem with DDR in Uganda, as Colletta pointed out, it was inspired by the donors' model (Wolfram, 2012). Like Nye's (2008) analysis of the impact of soft power, Colletta's view on DDR in Uganda does not reflect upon sites of production in fragmented states. What Colletta failed to mention is the outright military victory achieved by the *National Resistance Army* (NRA), and the role it plays in the success of DDR. Uganda was not faced with the question of who governed the use of force. Thus, the frequent economic implication of an unproportioned army was the main issue when Colletta studied the post-war DDR in Uganda. From the onset, Colletta stress that demobilisation and reintegration focused on the rationalising of wartime armies and economic revitalisation (Hoeffler and R-Querol, 2003).

Despite the years of war and coups in Uganda, Colletta's studies of the DDR did not cover the impact of war and who governed the use of force (Knopf, 2016). While Uganda had suffered from violence and war, it did not suffer from the spread of ethno-political militias like South Sudan. This was Cleaver's (1992) criticism, that Colletta did not consider insubstantial situations in Africa. Although protracted civil wars could end, a breakdown in the rule of law gave rise to 'warlord rule', and this has been the case in South Sudan where multi-layered systems of violence characterise political realities. The gap in Colletta's argument is the failure to recognise that different states need varying political, security and economic institutions to establish cohesive society. In the case of Uganda, the monopoly over violence at the time was held by the NRA, which established institutions for the protection of the vulnerable in society. Although the NRA did not institutionalise the practice of democracy, it was able to control the use of force. This argument echoed Berdal's analysis that focused on belligerents, discussed in the following section.

1.8 Mats R. Berdal

Berdal's *Disarmament and Demobilisation after Civil Wars* (1996) is another influential survey of the post-Cold War DDR period, focusing on both state and guerrilla forces. Berdal emphasises the importance of better management of DDR and how international assistance can be used for the SSR. While DDR is essential for security, Berdal argues that it should be a confidence-building strategy. This argument reflected Colletta's assessment of DDR's capability to influence the political will of the warring parties when "peace agreements are lacking or non-inclusive" (UNDP, 2010, p. 2). Berdal considers the impact of belligerents where a peace deal is achieved without an outright military victory, emphasising the dependency of DDR "on its linkages with parallel efforts of socio-political reconstruction aimed at addressing the root causes of the conflict" (Molloy, 2013, p. 18; citing Berdal, 1996). This argument focused on "combatant", including their associates often excluded from the programme because they were not fighting. This position is the blueprint of the second-generation of DDR (Chambers, 1997; 1998). The UNDP's *Practice Note* (2005) recommended many objectives since fiscal deficits could lead to unfinished DDR.

Instead of focusing on active military personnel, the UNDP called for an inclusive approach (Smith *et al.*, 1996). This concept categorised DDR in four distinct but overlapping goals: preventing the civil war from recurring; "crime and violence; stimulating civic and political participation; and healing trauma caused by war" (Berdal, 2006, p. 14). One may ask why Berdal deserved different treatment from Colletta. This research argues that Colletta laboured under an illusion of idealism; of fixing a perfect state's security, but Berdal emphasise participatory DDR. This approach recognises the inadequacy of states in question to meet the requirement of fixing such security as well as the effect of security sector fragmentation (Waner, 2013a; 2013b). This research argues that the option to integrate OAGs into the SPLM/A may have enhanced the appeal of and participation in DDR-SSR. When war broke out in 2013, the SPLM/A violently disintegrated, launching a hyper-militarisation of ethno-political identities (Keriga and Bujra, 2009).

1.9 Participatory Approach

Most countries affected by war suffer overwhelming destruction of both economic and political institutions. These conditions make it difficult to sustain the peace, as well as to address the factors that often influence the relapse into renewed armed conflict. Based on these situations, it is necessary to ask, "why does a participatory approach matter?" (Kilroy, 2015, p. 203). One of the most challenging aspects facing DDR is the fact that causes of armed conflicts, and the actors involved, stipulate a set of socio-political, economic and security issues that render an emerging state more susceptible to civil war and armament (Reynol-Querol, 2002). This study explains these issues conditioned both the resistance to DDR and the war in South Sudan. Thus, the participatory approach is applied in this study to expose the intricate context of the causal elements of conflicting relations in post-conflict South Sudan. An understanding of the factors affecting DDR in post-war South Sudan needs to be based on the fact that interaction between the actors and post-war factors are substantial in influencing the outcome of war recovery efforts.

Both armed conflicts and resistance to DDR are linked with locals' complaints and fear. Thus, these problems necessitate a need not just to reconsider how South Sudanese elites' ambitions intersect with informal armies, but also to contribute a thorough bottom-up analysis of how these militias have organised themselves. What could be deemed a successful DDR is open to debate in the complexity inherent in South Sudan. Thus, a participatory approach offers a lens for analysing DDR more holistically because it involves diverse stakeholders (Kilroy, 2015). Kilroy deemed this approach essential because it engenders a systematic understanding of post-war situations. Kilroy explained that those who fought the war or have been affected have a right to determine the process of DDR. In his view, DDR requires a different level of interaction, where the beneficiaries "make an input to its planning and implementation" (2008, p. 5). What is essential about the participatory approach lies in design and execution. It means that the timing of the DDR is of the essence to its success, and programmes need to meet the target groups' interests.

Adhering to this approach creates an inclusive DDR process which encompasses the Ex-Combatants and the community, particularly those affected by directly or indirectly by war. Proponents of the participatory approach argue that DDR necessary at the local levels to re-educate the communities that peace and security also depended on their commitment to resettle ex-fighters. With Sierra Leone, for instance, Ball (1997, p. 103) emphasises the importance of "community sensitisation", argue that it can "enhance local understandings of challenges facing veterans and their families". The basis of this argument lies in attempts to engender socio-political healings and reconciliations at the community level. Hence, a participatory approach is applied to build consensus whereby armed structures can reshape their concerns of how DDR may positively influence their daily life. This matching of DDR with the target groups was lacking in South Sudan. This argument means that South Sudan suffered from systemic flaws, as mentioned earlier, and from excessive accumulations of small arms. It also indicates that the plan and coordination of the DDR-CPA were not situated within the framework of broader security concerns.

Introductory Chapter contends that the procedure of the CPA-DDR was "overly formal, hierarchical" and vested with "opaque control mechanisms that are pursued in the absence of social controls that promote regular interaction, mutual respect, and the development of shared values at all levels" (Lamb and Stainer, 2018, p. 5). That approach may undermine trust between DDR operators and those designated for DDR (Wilkof *et al.*, 1995). This process was deemed as an essential factor in Sierra Leone, other successful cases, like Burundi. Schulhofer-Wohl and Sambanis (2010, p. 19) argue that the capacity of the disarmament programmes to prevent war lies in improving "the psychological health of beneficiaries". This approach was not implemented in South Sudan because the DDR programme was highly centralised. The report by the UN argues that "the overall management structure provided very little autonomy to the key local stakeholders in South Sudan and there was a general lack of transparency, inadequate consultation and the absence of regular coordination" (Lamb and Stainer, 2018, p. 6; citing UNDP 2013, p. 8). The effect of centralised and rigid DDR programmes reduced communities and other beneficiaries to what we described in an introductory chapter as "a bystanders". In this context, the South Sudanese disarmament process was lacking the potential benefits of involving all actors. South Sudanese DDR lacked local ownership, therefore, unable to build enduring capacity for resettlement of Ex-Combatants (Kilroy 2008, p. 5). Some blamed such centralisation of the DDR on acute political tension between the CPA's partners and insecurity in South/ern Sudan as cited in the introductory chapter (Munive, 2013a). However, some observers believed there was no consensus between the CPA-DDR partners, and that makes it challenging to utilise DDR as a mean of moving Ex-Combatants "beyond peacekeeping and mediation" (Vangen and Huxham, 2003). Despite these insights, some scholars criticise the participatory approach and exhibit how the translation of these ideas into policy/practice is not consistent with the desired impacts (Cleaver, 1998a; 1998b). Lamb does not blame a group for wanting to maintain its arms, but he cited a necessity to focus on the structural conditions and causes of militarisation (Lamb, 2013).

This analysis does not refute the importance of dialogue-oriented peace and DDR of Ex-Combatants. Lamb and Stainer, 2018, p. 9) argue that such desired impact may not be achieved in fragmented states "strained with low levels of goodwill and trust between parties". This argument accused proponents of participatory approaches of conflating efficiency and empowerment. Lamb, (2013, p. 5) citied how numerous Ex-Combatants in Mozambique remain in abject poverty, a situation he blamed on the country's economic outlook rather than a failure of the DDR. An analysis finds that full integration was not achieved yet the county did not relapse to war (Ngoma, 2006). In South Sudan, DDR was taking place in a country without any capacity to integrate ex-fighters. Thus, while studies of the DDR in Liberia, Mozambique, Burundi, and Angola offer some refined analysis, and understandings into the aspects of conflict, they are not integrated into the spectrum of what causes war, nor the fundamentals and casual agencies hindering the success of disarmament, and this is the gap the case of South/ern Sudan is filling (Ansorg, 2017).

The project argues in the introductory chapter that while the CPA-DDR was designed as an overall strategy for peace in whole Sudan, and most importantly, South/ern Sudan the programme "did not stipulate the specific implementation details, other than a small project for elderly and disabled combatants, and child soldiers" (Lamb and Stainer, 2018, p. 9). Given the scope of what was occurring before secession in 2011 and the 2013 civil war, academics doubted the effectiveness of the DDR in South Sudan (Lamb, 2013). Brewer argues that, although the CPA ostensibly ended the decades of war, "one form of conflict has been replaced by another" (2010, p. 1). Brewer recognised how the CPA established a progression of events, but the DDR alienate other security providers and clashes in South Sudan. Re-ignition of war between the two regions was still on the cards due to disputed resources and territories (Breitung *et al.*, 2016). What academics blamed for the violence in South Sudan was the pressuring of the bitter factions towards an election in a winner takes all approach (Stedman, 1991; Lamb, 2013).

These scholars questioned the importance of democratisation and unfocused DDR. They argued that it was not the generic factors of post-war states that led to the resumption of war. Yet, it is rather the "numerous and complex interactions" among political leaders that may explain the different outcomes (Höglund *et al.*, 2009). While the UN was hoping for South Sudan to fall into the tide of democratic revolution, its interior was mainly resisting that tide. In this case, democracy and DDR were faced with ethno-political armies and the impact of protracted war. In 1997, Lamb conducted a review of the interconnection between democratisation and peace to "contribute to the general dynamic of demilitarisation" (Lamb, 2013, p. 2). To make his case, he deliberates on both democracy and DDR. Lamb considers early attempts as myopic, to both political and security interests of armed groups. Lamb want DDR to be not just the "placing of surplus and offending weapons beyond use", but an improved political system, economic empowerment of the post-war states and community security (Lamb, 2013, p. 2). This position is not without its critics, who argue that violent actors must be included in the DDR (Sahlin, 2004; Ball and Goor, 2005).

1.10 Measuring and Evaluation of Successes of DDR

DDR of ex-fighters aims to create a conducive socio-political situation "by dealing with security problems that arise when ex-fighters are trying to adjust to normalcy during 'the critical transition period from conflict to peace" (Williams, 2014, p. 2; citing Miliken and Krause, 2002). The task of DDR is to remove surplus arms from circulation (Faltas *et al.*, 2001). Based on these emphases, a measurable indicator of a successful DDR is security. Utilising the concept of security as a critical indicator of success raises questions: whose security, from what, by whom and by what means? These questions are essential for explaining the failure of DDR in South Sudan. De Waal (2017, p. 4) described South Sudan as a violent kleptocracy, and its nascent "institutions are subsidiary to the transactional politics pursued by a narrow group of elites". Security remained contested in this situation and can be a hindering factor to the DDR (Cox, 1981). Security and securitisation, and how those in need of the security struggle to achieve it, is discussed in the next chapter.

One may ask why security is a crucial factor prominent to the failure of DDR in South Sudan. In post-war DDR, stability is seen as an objective of security, but that perception does not consider the protection of individuals and groups from violence induced by their own state as the primary indicator of DDR success. As Alkiri (2004, p. 360) argues, successful DDR requires "protection of the vital core of all human lives in ways that advance human freedoms and fulfilment". With South Sudan, the security envisioned in the CPA was about a reversal of North-South war conditions. It did not bring about what Humphreys and Weinstein, (2005, p. 2) described as "peaceful conditions and improvement of security through transforming the role and posture of armed combatants and making war no longer attractive to them as a means to an end". Thus, the success of the CPA-DDR would have been defined by its capacity to downsize the SAF and SPLM/A, preventing the war between North and South, and to disband OAGs. These aims are limited, and that has allowed this research to criticise the ineffectiveness of such policies.

The current proliferation of arms in South Sudan requires moving beyond honing the ruling elites to focus on what militarised civilians say about their motivations for such armaments (Basedau and Köllner, 2007). This means DDR programmes are essential, but not adequate for normalising societies in which violent players disagree on the political, security and economical offers of DDR. This criticism is necessary because it urges a question: what factors enable the practitioner to determine whether DDR was successful? This question seeks to interrogate the mixed record of DDR programmes in South Sudan, which were not designed to solve critical political instabilities

(Ginifer, 2003). The aim here is to argue that DDR literature did not take into account the "ulterior elite's motives for disarming enemies of the state" (Karazsia, 2015). The success of DDR in Mozambique presented quantifiable indicators and refocused DDR's attention away from the security dilemma (Meek and Malan, 2004). DDR in Mozambique continues to be judged as one of the most effective and comprehensive DRR processes to date. Despite this optimism, high unemployment among ex-fighters marked the years that followed (Shikhani, 2012).

Further, DDR in Sierra Leone is seen as a success, but it did not stop the continuing rate of unemployment among ex-fighters, nor the incidence of violence. This context was the basis of the World Bank's report on Southern African states, which focused on the vitality of economic reintegration (Kalyvas, 2001; 2006). Thus, those DDR activities did not overlap with developmental activities. This highlights the lack of consensus regarding the definition of success. Questions on measuring success provoked the call for specific success criteria. Further, "counting weapons is not enough" (Tatjana, 2014, p. 4). This thesis argues that DDR without adequate control of firearms cannot be considered successful. Two decades after the war ended, the Mozambican government was still struggling to resolve a lack of economic opportunities. While Oryema, (2013, p. 10) believed "proper targeting of low, mid and high-level combatants in DDR might prove effective". Alden indicates that "the bulk of the leadership of criminal gangs operating in Mozambique today is drawn from the upper echelons of the former military" (2002, p. 350).

Alden showed that ex-soldiers were accused of running organised criminal activities, including trafficking firearms. Critics argue that employment-oriented training is inadequate in fragile economies when the country cannot absorb ex-fighters (Dos Santos, 2000). This limited capacity afforded inadequate opportunities. Hence, ex-fighters join already unemployed society (McMullin, 2013). Despite its importance, reintegration cannot address ethno-political factors interfering with DDR. If individual social outcomes decide DDR success, the Mozambican case would have been declared a failure (Dryzek, 2005). In South Sudan, however, the reintegration process needs to do more than that. The process needs to understand how rival groups have preserved informal armies. In South Sudan, the extent to which these groups are preserved is determined to some extent by the impact of previous conflicts and how they ended. Those who have studied such systems linked the failure of the CPA-DDR with a lack of true reflection on these situations. Even when the conflict ends, sustainable peace requires a holistic approach to understand the ontological implications of security on DDR (Carment, 2005).

This thesis discusses how the CPA-DDR proceeded mainly in an ad-hoc manner without answers regarding the security of resisting groups. Here, effective DDR is defined "as policy change or as a movement away from the status-quo that is the presence of fully armed and mobilised warring parties" (Ansorg and Julia, 2019, p. 114). However, the notion of informal armed structures in South Sudan provides a useful context to explore this puzzle of resistance to DDR by analysing the impact of different "veto players", or a specific configuration of armed actors and their interests that makes the relinquishing arms less likely. We can base this challenge on the group's strategic reasoning (Menkhaus, 2007; Rabassa *et al.*, 2007). These conditions hinder management of DDR between the various organisations. The rise of politically competitive and centrally inclined armed groups makes it difficult to determine the number and identity of the groups concerned, their precise locations, and other information vital to the DDR process.

1.11 Organisational Dynamics, Informal War and Security as a Hindrance to DDR

The basis of success or collapse of DDR depended on the reintegration of ex-fighters and dismantling of the militias. This argument derived from academics preoccupied with fragile states. Basing the entire process of DDR according to the fragile states' context is myopic about the complexities of conflicts and their causes that fuel an internal arms race. This fragile states' literature missed more nuanced analyses by not focusing on infighting among South Sudanese who use patronage networks to ethnicise conflicts. Because of these intricacies, one could argue that some post-war states cannot mobilise resources and manage DDR according to liberal intentions because of violent interactions that reinforce an escalation of the conflict. Thus, the gap in the literature is the lack of contextual understanding about why groups resisted DDR and the strategy to induce fence-sitters who need viable security. As briefly discussed in the introduction, it takes a mere ethno-political disagreement for the faction or village to raise an army in South Sudan.

Hence, local politics are interlaced with the proliferation of arms, and that provides a rationale for why South Sudan still experiences endemic armed conflicts. The CPA-driven literature focuses on peaceful spells between the SAF AND SPLM/A, not on the termination of civil war in the two regions. These armed factions "mobilise to defend their interests and then compete for the loyalties of fighters" (Stringham and Forney, 2017, p. 179). The analysis supports Reno's (2011) argument on the rise of "a new class of parochial fighting groups", a context absents in DDR literature. Reno emphasises that such groups "operate as a parallel, local alternative to both the rebel and pro-government forces led by national-level "warlords" whose appeals may have contradicted more local agendas" (Stringham and Forney, 2017, p. 179; citing Reno, 2011). The resistance to DDR in South Sudan hinted that the armed groups have both the motivation, and the capability, to rebel (Mason *et al.*, 2011). This view builds the link between factionalism and the failure of DDR on Richards's (1996) idea of "New Barbarism", which derived from those who peddled stereotypical account about irrational wars and massacres in the 1990s (Kaplan, 1994).

This argument treats armed groups in South Sudan as "loose molecules". As Richard, (1996, p. 16) established that (RUF) in Sierra Leone had a "clear political vision", South Sudanese's factions oscillate between parochial political and ethno-political objectives. The motive and actions of South Sudanese factions also intersect with the research that seeks to explicate why African armed conflict has become ever more diverse (Willems, 2010). In referent to the case of Burundi, Willems applauded the prioritisation of "working through the national government and the extent to which the programme was embedded at the sub-national level" (Willems, 2010, p. 1). The vital aspect he emphasised is that Burundians were not harbouring deeper ties and stakes in warlordism (Berdal and Ucko, 2009). With South Sudan, the dominance/supremacy of one identity/political group has contributed to violent opposition of the government, and that has created a vast distance between armed actors and the incentive for DDR. Stedman argues "the biggest source of risk comes from spoilers who believe DDR threatens their power" (1996, p. 371).

Often these groups profit through the trafficking of plundered natural resources. Stedman's emphasis included other essential aspects that fuel spoilers' resistance to DDR. Some spoilers may be prosecuted for civil war-related crimes. The combination of the fear of losing access to power and resources, and the potential for prosecution, has led to relapse to war from Liberia to the Balkans (Suhrke, 2011). The accounts of some scholars claimed most groups resisted DDR because it put them out of the bargaining business (Leuprecht, 2010). This observation might be accurate to some extent, but it lacks an understanding of societal security (Kaufman, 1996; Theiler, 2003). Waever (1998, p. 23) "defined societal security as the ability of a society to persist in its essential character under changing conditions and possible or actual threats". While there are differences in opinion about the proper procedure for DDR, scholars saw a correlation between a chaotic arms race and the failure of DDR in South Sudan (Hazen, 2010). This situation needs a hybrid theoretical approach to provide an examination of the correlation between the dynamics of civil war, including local ethnic violence and the failure of DDR (Mutengesa, 1990).

This analysis renders the "opportunists-economic hypothesis" problematic and calls for a shift from battles over the supremacy of either economic or grievance theories to a rigorous exploration of the conditions under which the two concepts can overlap (Mueller, 2000). This thesis argues in Chapter Two that an understanding of the factors affecting DDR in South Sudan should not be based exclusively on either model, because the situation was impacted by warlords whose political appeals contradicted the DDR. Such an idea attributes the challenges to the history of war, born of the state's inability to restrain the strategic interaction of rivalling groups.

1.13 Conclusion

The accepted reality is that civil wars have impacts that exacerbate insecurity and conflict. Thus, DDR becomes integral and part of broader efforts to reform the post-war government's structures, including security (Hoddie and Hartzell, 2003). Apart from the fact that DDR seeks to control illegitimate use of force, it also involves institutional redesigning, as well as provision of the channels through which the warring factions can commit to a permanent peace. In particular, DDR is designed to prevent war by encouraging parties to take part in new political process and institutions with a potentially high cost to themselves, thereby helping them overcome mistrust. However, this dream of ensuring it is difficult to achieve in a post-war system struggling to maintain law and order and gain legitimacy to govern (Berdal and Malone, 2000; Chacha, 2004).

This chapter reflected on scholarly critique and analysis of DDR and argued that the programme's collapse in South Sudan not only due to the fragility of the state's political and economic institutions. DDR failed due to the macro and micro-levels of armed conflicts and the proliferation of arms. These factors were not considered explicitly in the CPA. This chapter have emphasised how less attention has been paid to socio-political fragmentation of South Sudan and their political and security systems. Despite these factors, the designers of the CPA-DDR failed to consider whether DDR, with related programming, would be in tune with fragmented political, economic and security demands of the different armed groups.

Conceptualising the challenges to the success of DDR in South Sudan requires a qualitative research methodology to integrate the approaches and procedures of observing, recording, examination, and understanding characteristics of the research phenomena, which in this case, are South Sudanese political actors and other stakeholders (Gillis and Jackson, 2002; Leininger, 1985). This case study aims to observe, understand, and interpret how the behaviours and actions of armed actors contributed to the failure of DDR in South Sudan.

Chapter Two: Beyond the Liberal Peace Approach Debate: Rethinking the Limits of Liberal Peacebuilding through the DDR Process in South Sudan

The collapse of the Berlin Wall in the 1990s assure some liberal scholars of the triumph of western democratic ideology, and the duty of the democracies to intervene in global crisis (Chandler, 1999; 2006; 2010). The negotiated peace in Sudan and the recent forcible intervention in Libya derived from the doctrines of liberal democratic peace (Owen, 1994; Kuperman, 2013). Immanuel Kant's *essay Perpetual Peace: A Philosophical Sketch* explored the essence of political liberalism as the criterion for peace (Pugh, 2005; citing Kant, 1795). The idea in this argument is that "the interaction among republican states leads to peace, since states with a republican form of government are more transparent and accountable to their citizens, and hence their commitment to the consent of the voters reduces the chances of engaging in war" (Bindi and Tufekci, 2018, p. 2).

This argument reproached dictatorial states as "more likely to be motivated to wage war, putting the states in a constant state of aggression towards their citizens, as they do not require their approval" (Bindi and Tufekci, 2018, p. 2). Kant's thesis focuses on politics as the cause of war. Thus, citing Kant, Bindi and Tufekci (2018, p. 2) appeal for the adoption of the universalisation of "liberal republicanism to prevent non-republican states from oppressing their citizens". In this context, the sustainability of peace is perceived to rest upon the commitment of each country to embrace the norms of liberal governance (Doyle, 2005; Paris, 2004). This view has fuelled Western-led interventions in war-affected states in the post-Cold War era.

On January 9th, 2005, the CPA, mediated by IGAD, ended half a century of armed conflict in Sudan. The CPA provided a roadmap for ending the war; however, my thesis argues that it was hastily crafted, and driven exclusively by the norms of power-sharing between GoS and the SPLM/A even though they were not the only armed groups involved in the conflict (Grawert, 2010). Despite this concern, the implementation of the CPA saw great international support in South Sudan, focusing on sustainable peace through statebuilding processes (Dobbins *et al.*, 2003; Berger, 2010). The focus was based on DDR of ex-fighters. Contrary to this intention, South Sudan topped the 2015 "Fragile States Index for the second consecutive year" (Barreau, 2016, p. 2), and has been lurking at the top of this list since that time. The emerging state has joined the ranks of long-lasting failing and failed states. Hence, the South Sudanese state is, to this date, one of the rare places in which humanitarian aid delivery are nearly impossible. The civil war among various factions has killed thousands and displaced millions of inhabitants (Richard, 2015).

The proliferation of armed ethnic militias is a significant challenge for centralised security. This chapter asks a simple question: How did South Sudan come to be in this situation? This project posits that the externally imposed lens of DDR suffered from many limitations. As presented in the introduction, security was "the main pillar of international support aimed at preventing the relapse to war" (Fiedler *et al.*, 2016, p. 2). The architects of this idea misplaced their belief in a state monopoly of force as an idea for the DDR in South Sudan. If the monopoly of violence is attributed to the state, it is essential to remember that the Republic of South Sudan was not a state before 2011. The use of force was held by different armed groups intent on projecting political and military advantage. Non-State Actors (NSAs) are "organised armed entities that are involved in armed conflict, which are motivated by political goals and which operate outside state control" (Barreau, 2016, p. 9; also, Call, 2016). These include armed ethnic youths and the Janjaweed in Darfur, which may differ in size, capabilities and motivation. The pursuit of political aims is critical, and has been excluded in the design and execution of DDR in South Sudan.

Thus, NSAs cooperation to be disarmed depends on their interests. Violent ethno-political groups in South Sudan can act against the interests of the embryonic state, particularly in "a state-and-peacebuilding process when the structure of the state is at its weakest" (Barreau, 2016, p. 9). This makes sense considering Vince's argument that "armed groups are principally focused on the maintenance of their autonomy, which is the root of their power" (2008, p. 300). The capacities of armed groups in South Sudan are variable. For example, insignificant guerrilla cells rely on a state to survive hidden. In the other hand, other groups, such as the SPLM/A, can acquire authority and legitimacy over large parts of territory and people. When it comes to power, security and the recourse to war, these groups are empirically sovereign. Such unrestrained behaviour leaned towards the "outsourcing of state functions typifies the steady erosion of the state monopoly over all forms of organised violence" (Small, 2006, p. 4). This complicated political and security situation requires recognition in DDR, but it is, unfortunately lacking.

The literature about the impacts of civil war stressed state collapse associated with internal violence. That analysis failed to explore the complexity of political orders at local level. Arguing that armed conflict in South Sudan created a fragmented politico-military order can provide a critical framework beyond institutional approaches (Arjona, 2009; 2016). While one of the urgent goals in a post-war situation is to "keep the (presumed) sources of post-conflict violence and insecurity at bay" (Muggah, 2009, p. 2), DDR in South Sudan failed to become a precondition for making a permanent peace. The reason for that failure, according to liberal ideals, was the lack of institutional traditions to restrain violence (Roberts, 2011; Mac Ginty, 2006). Such a conception, though correct, misses the underlying pattern of political organisations upon which South Sudan's groups based their violence. I argue that the liberal peace approach failed to define South Sudan as a situation where multiple armed actors with intersecting influences oversee the use of force. Instead of adhering to these concerns, international responses focused on the state, ex-rebels' security agencies, and establishing democratic control over the state's security forces (Deng, 2017).

This approach does not include the micro impact of violence on society (Justino, 2013; 2016). The point to stress, therefore, is that the decentralisation of violence in South Sudan resulted in the establishment and reproduction of hostile socio-political orders that have not been taken seriously in DDR. For years, liberal scholars have applied the security-development nexus without reflecting on whether that approach converges with armed actors' dilemmas. Jok stressed how groups' security demands pull in opposite directions from imagined objectives of DDR (Jok, 2017). Jok presented how such a contradictions lies in the fact that the South Sudanese state is too weak to fulfil its functions as the sole legitimate guarantor of security. Thus, this chapter seeks to highlight the limitations of the liberal peace argument through the examination of DDR. This emphasis is essential for reviewing the evolution of DDR and provides the opportunity to gather context-based deficit in the liberal peace-driven practice of the DDR. While South Sudan has received international aid, the DDR has not prevented relapse to civil war.

Almost a decade after seceding, South Sudanese state has collapsed, hence, ceased to accomplish minimal duties of the state because of political violence. This violence created uncertainties, which increases inter-groups' strategic dilemma (Sandler, 2000). While a strategic dilemma is used in the international relations, troubling political orders of South Sudan allowed those designated for the DDR to question the motive of the disarming authority, and resist. Given the violence in South Sudan, one could argue that armed groups are functioning as competitive firms. Such competing relationship arises because the behaviour of armed actors toward the DDR depends on the perceived choice or intentions of South Sudanese state. We can see resistance to the DDR as centred on OAGs' security needs versus the sovereign right of the state to dominate these groups. For liberal scholars, state security remains the core reason for justifying the DDR. As previously stated in Chapter One, the concept of security is ambiguous in South Sudan. For this chapter to analyse deficits of the liberal peacebuilding approach, there must be an emphasis on whether the term 'national' refers to the state and its institutions or the nation.

In the context of South Sudan, a nation could be a Dinka or Nuer, with a strong sense of identity - an "imagined community" (Anderson, 1991). The Dinka, for instance, have a claim to self-rule, but that does not mean group are a state of its own. National, on the other hand, is typified by a shared belief or language, to name a few. If the first meaning is intended, then strengthening national security through DDR becomes synonymous with the defence of sectional interests. If the second meaning is preferred, problematic questions arise in using force, as who or what the nation is, and what kind of security we envisage for groups who are part of that nation. South Sudan is a nation as per its sovereign status, but it lacks cohesion, organising principles and institutions. Its capacity to provide public services, including law and order, is almost non-existent (Wight, 2017). This argument will form the basis of Chapter Four, which focuses on the effects of the limitations of the state and emphasising that the South Sudanese government remained irreverent to some groups and powerless in forcing belligerents to conform to the DDR.

Significant bodies of knowledge informing the liberal peace thesis concentrated on fragility or extreme failure of the state and how that destroyed the states' monopoly of force. This project analyses how liberal peacebuilding became entangled in the reproduction of armed

113

violence in post-war/secession South Sudan. This project contends that the dream of the state's institutionalisation of security failed in South Sudan as violence and security governance took a hybrid form or the decentralisation of violence. This argument suggests that more consideration needs to be aimed at armed actors and violent political situation in which DDR occurred. The adaptation of the "hybrid peacebuilding" framework for this project does not intend to dwell on the failures of liberal approaches. However, it is beneficial for investigating the effects of South Sudan's competing factions on the DDR. De Waal alludes to context by emphasising how the battlefields of North and South Sudan have never resembled "conflict between two readily identifiable, internally coherent parties" (2017, p. 182). De Waal (2017) linked the challenge of the DDR with the failure to figure out who governed the use of force.

This deficiency arises due to mediators' overestimation of the capacity of the new system in South Sudan, ignoring the fact that "the SPLM had never succeeded in developing a national ethos" (Young, 2012, p. 323). There is a need to understand a connection between the absence of the state and the prevalence of self-mobilised violent organisations that are more than the sum of their parts (Cramer, 2010). Any rule of the state that distributes costs to citizens is absent in South Sudan. Thus, the hybrid framework provides an optimal understanding of how irregular tools of warfare and the contradiction in the exercise of public authority affected the disarmament. Hoffmann (2014) questioned the power-based approach, whereby the state is entangled in a web of self-perceived systems that behave like a state. Before

Hoffmann's thesis, Reno described the Democratic Republic of Congo as a "paradigmatic case of state failure", with the country's political system operating "outside conventions of the state sovereignty" (2006, p. 147). He argues that when self-security takes hold, resistance to disarmament becomes an obligation. This argument problematised the liberal-driven DDR because it promotes the tunnel-vision of post-war states. Thus, the next section will argue that peace is not necessarily the outcome of a liberal approach.

2.1 The Conceptualisation of Liberal Peacebuilding in Post-War Societies

The concept of liberal peacebuilding has spurred a debate within policy circles regarding its efficacy, and what it takes to (re)build post-war societies (Richmond, 2006). Most of the debate is centred on building peace, establishing who owns the peace, and determining how to engage local actors (Mac Ginty, 2006). These concerns are prudent in the DDR, as some scholars raised questions about how externally driven strategies do not move beyond a narrowly conceived institutional analysis (Doyle and Sambanis, 2000). For proponents of liberal peacebuilding, peace and security are by-products of an open political and economic system (Fukuyama, 2004). Since liberal strategies have propelled the West into prosperity, it is argued that transplanting them in fragile states can deliver sustainable peace through democracy (Messner *et al.*, 2016). These arguments form the basis of the *Fragile States Index* report every year.

This report focuses on the presence or absence of liberal peace strategies, seen as the panacea to the challenges of failing states

(Messner, 2019). Such an approach allowed the proponents of liberal peace to develop a system with instruments to rank countries along a spectrum from most stable to fragile (Brooks, 2005). This convention is challenged in South Sudan. After the ending of the war between North and South, the accord "paved the way for the replacement of the state-imposed political, economic and social order" with a more liberal regionally based system (Ylönen, 2012, p. 28). This power-sharing was based on a territorial dimension, "policies aimed at placing institutional limits on state centralisation through a constitutionally entrenched system of multi-tiered government" (Wight, 2017, p. 3). Instead of producing sustainable peace, "the CPA entrenched South Sudan as a one-party state" (Wight, 2017, p. 3). In this situation, the CPA failed to address the SPLM/A's fundamental nature "as a forum for a variety of competing individuals or groups interested in controlling the resources and clientelist structures associated with state power" (Wight, 2017, p. 3).

Some blamed the 2010 election for all the debacles facing South Sudan, arguing that it "left the SPLM/A politico-military elite with little choice but to struggle from within the SPLM for control" (Kisiangani, 2011, p. 10). However, it can be argued that the historical power contest within the SPLM/A, as well as between factions, affected the DDR. This long-lasting hostile relationships among different political players, in both North and South, lead to the creation of political and security hybridisation that increase the risk for violent opportunism and a sense of insecurity and instability in the socio-political interaction (Muncie, 2013; Gebrehiwot, 2007). In a theoretical context, liberal peacebuilding is guided by liberal norms (Zaum, 2012). Liberal scholars do not only see political liberalism "as the final form of human government", but they believe it creates a secure foundation for durable peace (Annan, 1999; 2000; citing Fukuyama, 1989, p. 4). However, there are questions about how liberal peacebuilding programmes arrives at success.

Liberal scholars argue that the promotion of a consensual political discourse would thus be a remedy for war as it is unlikely that states with the consensual politics will wage war against each other (Paris, 2004). Duffield (2001, p. 11) explicates how the liberal political and economic tenets would lead to policy preference that could end wars and contributed to societal reconstruction in the global South. Duffield's argument echoes the widespread agreement that armed conflict in the fragile countries is best approached through various political and economic transformative procedures. Hence, Duffield's argument has become the instrument of post-war interventions in war-affected states without a precise assessment of their politics and logic of civil war (Richmond and Franks, 2009). These objectives failed because the use of force shifted from centralised state-oriented systems towards OAGs. This study suggests that not only is the assumption that liberal agenda would deliver "long-term peace (...) largely illusionary" (Paris and Sisk, 2009, p. 1), but the standard security templates employed in the DDR had limited applicability. Munive (2013, p. 6), argues that security in South Sudan would depend on:

Serious engagement with the following twofold task: to comprehend and eventually change the basic structures and mechanisms of armed mobilisation prevalent and to understand and adapt SSR to a political environment that is constructed in terms of potential for violence and threats of destabilisation.

Based on Munive's analysis, the universal ambitions of liberal solutions discounted growing assertiveness among violent NSAs. My thesis problematises the liberal-driven DDR with an eye to the political dimensions of this process in terms of reintegration. While the aim of reintegration has increasingly expanded in recent years, "it is an area that mostly suffers from being under-conceptualised: reintegration is singularly under-conceptualised in policy, research and practice" (Muggah, 2009, p. 6). This emphasis echoed the argument that "there have been few attempts to generate a coherent and an understanding of what reintegration means, how it might be implemented and appropriate indicators and means of monitoring them over time" (Muggah and Baaré, 2009, p. 228). Most of the interviewees stressed the need to revisit the DDR. The basis of this criticism is that it has insufficient actor-oriented analysis.

Liberal peace relies heavily on an institutionalist approach rather than examining post-war situations, as demonstrated by Boutros-Ghali's definition of peacebuilding as "action to identify and support structures which will tend to strengthen and solidify peace in order to avoid a relapse into conflict" (1992, p. 104). In this view, DDR included "rebuilding the institutions and infrastructures of nations torn by civil war and strife; and building bonds of peaceful mutual benefit among nations formerly at war" as well as addressing "the deepest causes of conflict: economic despair, social injustice, and political oppression" (Boutros-Ghali, 1992, p. 102). Boutros-Ghali also argues that peacebuilding must include "disarming the previously warring parties and the restoration of order, the custody and possible destruction of weapons, advisory and training support for security personnel" and strengthening governmental institutions (1992, p. 115). These actions sought to build stable post-war entities. Since the days of Boutros-Ghali, an effort to solidify peace has shifted to "a new paradigm for international engagement in war" built on concepts of peace, democratisation liberalisation, rule of law, and human rights (Richmond and Frank, 2009, p.138). This framework has given way to a more bureaucratic focus on institutional structures, to ensure that post-war states assume control over legitimate means of violence. In South Sudan, the Weberian view of the state as an omnipotent entity with a monopoly of violence requires a degree of functionality of the state institutions and legitimacy that has never been existed where OAGs besiege dominant of the state as the organisational structure. The proliferation of armed groups embodies a dispersion of authorities. This situation created the crisis of legitimacy for the central authority, and that bred a political system sustained by violent patron-client relations (Richards, 2004). These challenges did not deter some scholars from advocating the importance of "bringing the state back" (Evens *et al.*, 1985, p. 3). This approach in other countries failed to assess the impact of negotiation with OAGs, including their political and economic situation, into the operation of the DDR (Wennmann, 2009, p. 1130). This unconventional approach suggests that OAGs must have an interest in creating a capable state to support the DDR.

Since they are rational groups motivated by political/economic goals, it is possible to discuss their expectations for the future state. By including OAGs, it is possible to prevent any relapse into war. In contrast, those calling to "bringing the state back" (Evens *et al.*, 1985, p. 3), peddled the state dominant; a model based on the state as a supreme structure in a given territory. While the rationale behind the supremacy of state is visible in the international politics, the contrast of that rationale to be made about countries whose sovereignty ceased to function, and the legitimacy of their governments is challenged by internal violent atmosphere comprise of different characteristics. The political wars and other violence which have engulfed South Sudan demonstrated that the supposedly supreme state has failed to reign over Non-State Actors. When conducting DDR in such a situation, where the state is not in control, the armed actor's motivation for war and interest should be taken into consideration in order to undertake the DDR. The next section will highlight the essence of this concept and argue that there is a recognised need to improve conceptualisations of the capacities of the state. This shift seeks to explain, not just the deficiency in the monopoly school, but more adequately how fragile states are reorganised, and to explore in many settings how that affects the DDR.

2.2 Monopoly School

Based on the earlier definition of in this chapter, security scholars regarded the DDR as "a set of activities that forms part of the strategies for peacebuilding" (Verkoren *et al.* 2010, p. 1). The relationship between the DDR and the monopolists' school lies in an attempt to promote national security (Coletta and Muggah, 2009). This approach derived from the perception of the state as "an ultimate authority with claims over the monopoly of the legitimate use of physical force within a given territory" (Weber, 1981, p. 158; 1946; 1978). Those who expanded Weber's argument recognise that states differ significantly "in their capacities and the extent to which they monopolise violence" (Acemoglu and Robinson, 2012, p. 6). While the state's monopoly of force is significant for peace, this project argues that such perception has a naïve view of the world.

This argument suggests that post-war intervention processes disregarded the history of the people and their modes of institutions and governance. The intention of this argument is not to deride the essence of the state; it is to raise a concern about how the liberal agenda is continuing to be implemented as a securitised process seeking to "create a state defined by the rule of law, markets and democracy" (Barnett *et al.*, 2007, p. 88; also Barnett, 2011). One would like to know why South Sudan still struggling with violence despite investments in peace support? The answer is that the ethics of violence monopolisation need to be analysed where the state is suffering from an anomaly of contested legitimacy. These contesting authorities create obstacles for the DDR. The reason is that, when the security providers at the grassroots are OAGs, then people will be unable to abandon the system that protects them.

In Buzan *et al.*'s (1998, p.24) emphasis, "security is the move that takes politics beyond the established rules of the game and frames the issue either as a special kind of politics or as above politics. Securitisation can thus be seen as a more extreme version of politicisation". When that is the case, the response to the DDR became politically driven. "…The reason why arms spread across South Sudan lies with the fact that state ceases to function" (P37/10/01/2018). This participant identified that South Sudanese conflicts are securitised because the groups believed their threat required measures outside the bounds of ordinary politics. Despite these concerns, the bulk of the DDR tends "to be externally run, biased, short-sighted, and implemented in artificial isolation from each other" (Dudouet, 2011, p. 4). Thus, the DDR, even when it is successful, does not address local security. When local security becomes the aim of the group, then it opens questions about whether standard DDR is an appropriate strategy. At best, DDR can be part of an extensive peacebuilding strategy, which also involves informal authorities (Lund, 2006). Regardless of these views, Annan (1998) proposes a more developmental idea, aimed at promoting peace through accountability in public administration. Annan advances the state-centric political philosophy that prioritises state survival (Mearsheimer, 1994; 2001).

While domestic politics have different context and players, it is defined by inter-group self-interests and fear similar to that of the society of states (Jackson, 2015). Thus, the state monopoly of force will depend on whether armed groups feel that the DDR would not hinder their security. This practice of self-protection draws on the language of state-like behaviour among the group. As noted by a participant in this study: "Bandits attacked us. They came at night and raided our cattle and [were] killing anyone. Now we have acquired more arms, and we will not give them up" (P2/07/07/2017). It is easy to predict the problems of the DDR in South Sudan based on this argument. As such, much of South Sudanese political trajectories unfold in the spaces created by continuous violent negotiation between actors. Here, the impact of standard DDR incentives can be blunt. To disarm the fearful group, one must recognise "abiding fear, strategies and local social practices that have developed during the conflict" (Arnold and Alden, 2007, p. 5).

It is relevant to say that South Sudanese violent entities resist DDR in pursuit of power. Power, in its abstract term, "is the ability to exercise one's will over others" (Nordstorm, 2004, p. 72). Of course, exercising one's will over others will involve exerting control, the very definition of power. For the most part, the ethno-political elites control the means of power. However, informal armed actors project their definition of power based on their daily activities. According to one participant, the informal armies that exist alongside the formal institutions "run everything". "We protect ourselves, collect the taxes to buy ammunitions and feed the youths in charge of our security" (P3/24/07/2017). This statement epitomises that power is contested by groups. However, my thesis suggests that the power is far more contested than this participant acknowledged. If the distance between state institutions and the manifestation of power is significant, the notion that power is contested takes on an inherent irony. This study argues that "power is not a monolithic construct" in South Sudan because it is "continuously challenged, subverted; negotiated and renegotiated over time, space and interaction" (Nordstrom, 2004, p.

72). Here, the rebuilding of a stable political order became a challenging problem in South Sudan.

As stated in Chapter One, not only is the South Sudanese state reduce to the level of another actor among many other actors but those actors, including the state, are engaging in political, economic and security interactions based on each actor's strategic focus. When that political system is defined by violent competition as it has been the case in South Sudan, the legitimacy of one actor to monopolise the use of force is discarded in favour of a multiplicity of contending sources of power. This meant that groups viewed their security the same way realists talk about how states' decision to increase military spending lies at the heart of how they perceive their surroundings. One may ask what would have been a preferable alternative for peacebuilding in South Sudan. This research moves beyond liberal conceptualisation to draw the factors causing war and resistance to the DDR into the debate. Based on the World Bank's (2017) report, South Sudan had over 40-armed groups since the CPA. Such violence is rooted in the power diffusion, triggered by the absence of a centralised socio-political and security mechanisms for adjusting the protection of citizens. This project suggests that the informality of authorities is not peculiar.

In that case, decentralised violence is perhaps one of the best terms that can be used for describing the distance between DDR and those who resist it. Based on the empirical data collected for this thesis, this project noted that understanding the disjuncture between state and the use of force is essential for an accurate analysis of the failure of the DDR. As several studies have confirmed, armed groups dominate politics in South Sudan (Laudati, 2011; Young, 2003; Jok, 2012). That condition allows this research to focus on the problems leading to the establishment of armed groups, and their impact on the DDR. Moreover, examining the nature of these problems requires a theory more in tune with the changing nature of organised violence (Sedra, 2013). One of the issues leading to war in South Sudan lies in what a participant described as "an effect of re-implementing a violent pyramidal SPLM/A system of hierarchy" (P3/24/07/2017).She blamed the resistance to the DDR on the structure of relationships between the government and groups as well as relationships that connect all actors in the conflict.

As South Sudan violently fragmented, it is crucial to focus on these relationships to assess the impact of the array of coalitions and conflicts as one of many reasons for the failure of the DDR. This argument assesses the bureaucratic nature of the liberal peacebuilding agenda. This analysis allows scepticism towards liberal democratic peace, and the presumed dividends of peace agreements, questioning the essential arguments underpinning the notion of post-war recovery concepts. This questioning is essential in presenting an alternative conceptual platform for analysing the liberal peace essentials (DDR included). Furthermore, this research argues that these liberal peace essentials do not sufficiently capture South Sudan's internal estrangements and factions that wield far more power than the post-secession state. This argument clears the path to critique the compatibility of the liberal peace model against the history and context of South Sudan (Mac Ginty, 2010b). One of the main issues rarely discussed in liberal peace, or emphasise during the design and application of the DDR, is the idea of "contact interventions".

Contact interventions refer to the tailoring of disarmament procedures according to the state in question, violent actors, and their motives (Green *et al.*, 1998). Due to high levels of political hostility among South Sudanese, it could be argued that liberal peace interventions are not designed to encourage inter-group contact and dialogue to improve inter-group relations. This argument is liable for criticism given the fact that the CPA was based on inter-group dialogue, but that criticism can be discounted by the fact that only two armed factions (GoS and SPLM/A) among many were engaged and agreed on the presumed dividends of the peace. Thus, the collapse of the DDR in post-war South Sudan is not because of the liberal peace procedures as such, but the way they were implemented. This argument is confirmed by the reality that the CPA-DDR was designed to strengthen the capacity of the SPLM/A to disarm competitors, in order to remove obstacles to domestic supremacy. This lens ignored the fact that South Sudan was not a state before 2011. Moreover, even if it was a state, liberal scholars forget how the ex-rebel government always operated through tensions with a bureaucratic system of governance.

Clapham (2012, p. 5) described these tensions as the "curse of liberation" citing how ex-liberators "bring into government the ideals that shaped the struggle". This thesis takes the stance that the SPLM came to power with more than the curse of liberation. South Sudan seceded in 2011, meaning the liberating elites were tasked with the challenging role of state formation and nation-building. My thesis argues that the liberal peace focuses on how the entire system of South Sudan derived from the informal armed and traditional system of adaptation and security in response to the protracted dearth of a central government. While South Sudan is not exempt from a perceived curse, conflict with armed actors could have been avoided if political elites had prioritised national interests. The South Sudanese state, despite its sovereign credentials, remained a repository of violent factionalism. The flows of power between armed factions rise and fall as various factions "gain and lose the capacity to institute order" (Hoffmann *et al.*, 2016, p. 1434).

The argument that liberal tactics cannot address this debacle is not an attempt to benchmark South Sudan against every programmed criterion of ascertaining the triumph and failure of the DDR. It is to privilege a process-oriented method of research, and to show that political interaction is more complicated than a weakness of the state in South Sudan. The resumption of war in South Sudan can cause stunned liberal practitioners to ask: how can this be? A question not satisfied by political analysis of post-war states in Africa. Given this gap, my thesis argues that the dynamics of war in South Sudan do not necessarily follow liberal peacebuilding's predictable linear trajectories. This argument is captured in Jok Madut's description of armed factions "as living under conditions of political conflict where fighting and defending one's family and the property is a major preoccupation" (Jok, 2005, p. 145). The position my dissertation takes on this argument is that it brings us to the limitation of the liberal peace, and the failure of liberal scholars' imagination about how the causes of violence might change everything. As an attempt to downgrade the scepticism emanating from this critique, some scholars propose the use of the "good enough" approach.

This approach moves away from an expectation that DRR will result in an idealistic Weberian state, to realistically seek "a mediated good enough state that meets the minimum criteria of statehood" (James and Oplatka, 2014). Thus, good enough advocates for a positive state that leaves a space between OAGs' expressed demands, and the state's demands (Wallis, 2017). This context is reflected in the English School's middle-ground approach, which is not the space between either liberal or absolute realism (Dunne, 2005; Linklater and Suganami, 2006). English School combines realists' claims of the primacy of state with the slight conciliatory approach of liberalism. This approach does not address what happens when the domestic sphere is fragmented and violent. This uncertainty allowed some to devise a middle-ground approach, as an attempt to avoid "long-term strategic planning by opting instead for incremental, iterative programming that favours short-and medium-term interventions as means to build momentum for more conventional reform strategies" (Sedra, 2013, p. 371).

This slight shift does not explore how the impact of the long-term absence of the state and informal armies embedded in local villages and how they are connected to power struggles. If the relationship among armed groups in South Sudan is based on fear and competitions, as it seemed to be the case, it is relevant to argue that both peace-and statebuilding procedures, including the disarmament of Ex-Combatants, would ultimately fail. No peacebuilding process, DDR or otherwise, is an island. This argument indicates that post-war states and international organisations involved in DDR needs a sustainable, peaceful interaction between the atomistic violent actors, which does not exist in South Sudan. Hence, the DDR might not be possible because of failure to digress from a "focus on (re)building the state as a central feature of peace" (Ylönen, 2012). While the liberal approach and its branches have good intentions, it does not address the violence that emerges from particular socio-political contexts. The crisis lies in the emergence of legitimised ethno-political factions, and non-state violent actors as security providers, apart from the state.

2.3 Crisis of Liberal Peace Approach in Africa: Analysis in the Context of South Sudan

While most of the ethno-political violence has occurred in Africa in recent decades, most studies do not concentrate on the context of African cases (Shaw and Mbabazi, 2007; Castaneda, 2009). Abrahamsen stressed that post-war policies emphasised a blurred agenda of "democracy and peace: development is dependent on democracy, and democracy supports peace and stability, further encouraging development" (2001, p. 80). Abrahamsen notes that the context of development through has "remained elusive in Africa because the context ignore[d] crucial features of the power structure in African states, and entailed an assault on existing relations and forms of power and legitimacy" held by non-state actors (2001, p. 80). Further, other scholars have stated that efforts to build liberal democratic states where none had existed, contributed to devastating violence (Williams, 2004). For example, since the advent of democratic processes in Kenya in 1992, electioneering processes have been characterised by violence (Rasmussen, 2018).

While it is misleading to describe attempts to create democratic government as "the legalisation of oppositions" (Barkan, 1993, p. 90), it is vital to point out the difficulties surrounding the creation of democracy in states where "nationalities are organised into quasi-states with traditional leadership and quasi-armies of their own" (Zambakari, 2014, p. 4). Sometimes, the notion of quasi-states is taken to mean sovereign states that fail to develop the necessary state institutions and structures of governance to function as "real" states (Jackson, 1990). This study argues that South Sudan emerged as a "quasi-state" because it seceded from Sudan, by laying claim to the territory and peoples therein, but no control over the sovereign territory and use of force. The above emphasis about the crisis of liberal peace is not an attempt to excuse the reign of tyranny or inaction in the face of raging violence. Instead, it counsels modesty of approach and acute sensitivity to the prospect of peacebuilding toward ethno-political armies that have evolved into dominant power brokers. Liberal peace, particularly democracy in fragile states, is criticised for leading to "the politicisation and the instrumentalisation of ethnic identities" (Mueller, 2008).

The politicisation of ethnic identities has been the core component of war in South Sudan. Deng (2005) argues that the former Sudanese State, as well as post-independence South Sudan, share the same challenge, that is to build a cohesive nation-state. Whether both phases for DDR succeeded or not, Deng noted that South Sudan was destined to struggle with the difficulty of building "a more inclusive political community that upholds unity in diversity, maintains the rule of law, and practices democracy in governance" (Zambakari, 2015, p.75; citing Deng, 2005). Deng attempts to make a case about the impact of ethno-political groups which are deeply involved in the war. In Zambakari's view, these armed groups have become an integral part of national power dynamics, and the impact is what this project describes as the militarisation of fragmented public space and socio-political order. Without a cohesive state, politics become a tool of deception, a competition or interaction concerned with beating the opponent by any means, frequently for personal or group gain. When this situation unfolded in South Sudan, the rights of political communities outlined by territorial sovereignty were torn apart.

As the state tore apart, the people who were supposed to defend the country and respect its legitimacy resorted to the reverse: a defence of ethno-political homelands, properties and micro political rights. In this situation, the state ceased to be a supreme authority as ethno-political groups controlled local armies. This process of governance disregarded the supremacy of the state. Thus, when ordinary men did not accept the state's protection, its right to monopolise the violence succumbed to the dynamics of militarisation. As emphasised in previous chapters, the higher the stakes in political competition and group security, the more likely the proliferation of arms. In such a scenario, it is impossible to 'buy peace' through DDR incentives where groups perceive existential threats. Such concerns arrest the state of

South Sudan at its infancy. South Sudan ascended into statehood as one of the weakest states in Africa. Hence, it found it difficult to control the use of force, mainly struggling to broadcast its power beyond the capital and strategic locales. Struggles to control state institutions in South Sudan overshadowed essential contents of the SSR.

When war erupted in 2013, it was "a signal that the centre can no longer hold" (Zambakari, 2015, p.71). This situation requires peacebuilders to make an observed assessment of the field of play and re-enter with strategy and resolve. Still, that is not historically how the U.N.'s interventions work. The so-called post-war securitisation approaches are based upon a fundamental misreading of the incentives driving conflict, and the idea that a dose of political liberalisation can act as a barrier to conflict is equally ill-conceived. There is adequate evidence to highlight the conflict-producing potential of rapid democratisation. Taylor argues that "the notion of the liberal peacebuilding as a representation of an internationalised neo-liberal hegemony depends in part upon the existence of a domestic hegemony", which does not exist in South Sudan (Tom, 2011, p. 112; citing Taylor, 2007). The idea of hegemony refers to "a dynamic lived process in which social identities, organisations, and structures based on asymmetrical distributions of power and influence are constituted by the dominant classes" (Mittelman and Chin, 2005, p. 18).

In liberal mindsets, hegemony belongs to the state, and that has an influence on the DDR. While no state has an ultimate hegemony, South Sudan did not achieve any level of hegemony because that "can only be achieved within the realm of Civil Society which gives meaning and organisation to everyday life resulting in the elimination of the need to use force" (Mittelman and Chin, 2005, p. 18). Achieving hegemony requires consent. The absence of hegemony at the domestic level in South Sudan allows the dominant group to resort to violence to control the state. As stated above, Taylor (2007; cited in Tom, 2011) rebuke liberal peace scholars, describing them as "naïve" in their understanding of the dynamic of politics and the political organisation in Africa. These arguments challenge the idea that the Western type of state's institutions can be transferred to non-Western states in their organic forms without considering political dynamics in those non-Western states. The near absence of the state in South Sudan calls for the need to reconsider liberal processes of the disarmament programmes. My thesis argues that, while South Sudan became a state through civil war and diplomacy, it emerged as a state that could not fend for itself.

Hence, it has disintegrated, although it still appears on the world map. I will argue in Chapter Four that, while South Sudan continues to exist as a state, the state monopoly of violence collapsed because of the absence of vital sovereign attributes deemed indispensable for statehood. This argument may promote criticism of the dominant political economy theory that describes the liberal peace strategy as "the software that drives the hardware of intervening actors because it is the dominant framework for peace operations championed by international actors" (Simangan, 2017, p. 36). This project's criticism of liberal peace comprises of two main arguments: "the biased conceptualisation of liberal peace and the flawed implementation of liberal peacebuilding" (Simangan, 2017, p. 37). The persistence of liberal peace solutions ignores difficult discussions about how sustainable peace may depend on local perceptions of legitimacy and security (Cooper, 2007; Cooper et al., 2011). I will argue that South Sudan existed by leaning on international legitimacy, but not on its internal structure of institutions and the rule of law.

Richmond, (2009a, p. 324) echoed this criticism saying: "corridors of power have so far failed to deliver on their promise of a liberal peace for all the citizens of the states that have been recipients of peace operations". The liberal peace approach at the policy stage failed to appreciate the political dimension of the post-war situation adequately. The whole context of the DDR sought to dissolve or return ex-fighters to their communities. However, other states in which this bandage security strategy is thought to have been successful "have become mere shells of a liberal state, lacking the potential for emancipation" (Simangan, 2017, p. 37). For example, DDR in Eritrea is described as "one of the best-planned programmes of its kind" (UNDP, 2006b, p. 1). Despite this, those who have studied Eritrea believed there was a sizeable variance between what was planned and what has been executed. In Eritrea, those who were demobilised were either disabled or nursing women. In response, the Eritrean military recruited "nearly the same number of youth" to its army (Mehreteab, 2007, p. 34). Since the political will is essential, Eritrea interest in maintaining large militaries depended on the political environment (Mehreteab, 2007). Another criticism of the hybrid approach asserts that the stance of liberal peacebuilders is destructive in the African context, where the central authority of most states is fragmented. This argument locates the causes of problems in the institutional legacy of colonial statecraft, and rigid institutionalisation that forms the basis of peacebuilding. So, despite efforts to prevent war and build a stable state, South Sudan is currently hosting different rebellions. This breakdown of the state suggests a constitutive basis for analysing the role of NSAs in the proliferation of arms. This study emphasises the impact of how informal armies institutionalise governance and the use of force by emphasising primacy in three contexts: coercive violence, social legitimation, and economic security (Mamdani, 2016). The point here is that the 'tectonic plates' underpinning war have barely moved in the domestic sphere over recent years. Because of that scenario, the challenge facing the DDR is the rise of various authorities with intersecting influences on security and war. This project demonstrates how state-and-peacebuilding arguments translate into practice.

However, this thesis argues that the practice of peace and statebuilding proceeded with limited understanding of "how the people of South Sudan can actively adapt and make use of such discourses for their own ends" (Aeberli, 2012, p. 1). Academics blamed the failure of the DDR in South Sudan on uncertainties unleashed by these structures (Knopf, 2016). Nonetheless, they fail to emphasise how such uncertainties lead to a mindset of seeking military advantage (Cooper et al., 2011). In this case, there is a need to recognise the rules governing the use of force when the state is not in charge of "command-and-control" (Kettl, 2000). All the armed groups in South

Sudan need to be conceived as relational actors, and that is what the hybrid approach provides: an emphasis on the lack of the historical continuity of centralising institutions. The hybrid concept is hence of interest to further analyse the nature of South Sudanese politics to provide a conceptual foundation between violent competition and the proliferation of arms.

2.4 The Conceptualisation of Hybrid Peace Approach

The concept of hybrid political orders has become widespread in the debate around peace and state building, and to some extent, counter-insurgency in post-civil war transitions (Marshall and Cole, 2008). While the theory emerges as "response to the failure of Western-style institutions" the concept itself is not new (Brown, 2018, p. 26). Young traces the roots of a hybrid approach to biology, citing the Latin definition as "the progeny of a tame sow and wild boar and for human beings, a progeny of human parents of different races" (1995, p. 6). In post-Cold War civil war situations, the hybrid theory has become a theme in debates on governance and security in places where NSAs have rebelled against the state (Brown *et al.*, 2009). Such a political system is different from an outright liberal idea of peace based on legitimate democratic institutions (Le Belloni, 2012). During the colonial periods in Africa, hybridity was applied as a form of "the resilience of the colonised and as the contamination of imperial ideology, aesthetics, and identity, by the natives who are striking back at imperial domination" (Kraidy, 2002, p. 319).

For Kraidy, local identities who encountered both colonial and post-colonial authorities found themselves caught in the middle of two systems; their own and one imposed on them. As seen in South Sudan, local systems negotiated continuously, struggled and re-appropriated the state dominance of violence for survival. For scholars of African politics, the waves of democratisation paid limited attention to the specific historical challenges that democratisation faces in Africa (Diamond, 2002; 2002; 2008). The hybrid theory allowed this project to attribute the challenge facing security and democracy in Africa to a deficiency of grounding the discourse in African political thought, and an unsuccessful mimicry of Western approaches. One of the most crucial elements to emphasise in this chapter is that the hybrid model encourages researchers to identify "the analytical subordination of the African experience to the experiences of others as another important factor" in the failure to design and implement successful DDR (Olukoshi, 1999, p. 464).

The flaws of globalising peacebuilding at the expense of domestic considerations become even more apparent when DDR and SSR are related to development. The designers of the DDR failed to recognise the historical imperative of the hybrid nature of African states because they take their "cues from the developmental democracy framework in which development and liberal democracy are assumed to be two sides of the same coin" (Osaghae, 2005, p. 4). What the globalists failed to see is that peace in South Sudan is mainly a socio-political action, rather than a mechanistic process. This research argues that the idea of a top-down approach to the DDR is contested and requires a more conscientious approach. This argument criticises an approach where international organisations see security in terms of the "use of organised force to establish and maintain social orders and to protect them from external and internal threats" (Luckham and Kirk, 2013, p. 2). In a fragmented state, security is about how each ethno-political group protected itself from violence.

So, understanding of the failure of the DDR hinges on the deep tensions between armed actors and perceived threats. Combining fear and mistrust is appropriate in the hybrid political order where the state's monopoly of force is contested. This study asks what security in this hybrid context looks like from the perspective of armed political groups opposing the state. As the term infers, 'hybrid' approaches represent interaction among multiple actors. In South Sudan, the making, experience and interests of non-state armed allowed them to engage in violent interactions with state or each other (Albrecht and Buur, 2009; Johnson and Hutchison, 2012). This contradictory political claims by the South Sudanese government and OAGs eroded the state's status. The emergence of NSAs activities represented a violent typology of ethno-political governance in rural areas, devised to fill the void of state. That, in itself, created a condition that the liberal peace approach failed to contextualise during the CPA and state formation in South Sudan. As this project discusses the notion of hybrid peace, the core emphasis lies with the purpose of hybrid institutions in war-torn states. In South Sudan's context, hybrid governance is ingrained into their socio-political system due to a prolonged lack of a functioning state.

This fragility led to the development of functioning informal systems, often recognised by the public as a representative of their interests (Jok, 2017). This situation reflects what Boege *et al.*, (2008, p. 6) described as a "hybrid political order" where various power claims and "logics of order overlap and intertwine". This environment has also been described as one of "institutional multiplicity where different sets of rules of the game, often at odds with one another, coexist in the same territory" (Richmond, 2011, p. 18). A functioning state hardly exists in this situation; hence, the post-war semi-autonomous government of the southern part of Sudan emerged as a political entity that did not resemble the Western-style model of the state. The involvement of OAGs in public life is the outcome of South Sudan's lack of capacity to overwhelm alternatives. These alternative systems did not emerge because of the collapsed state, but in part, because of engrained traditional structures of governance. This situation reflected Stringham and Forney's (2017, p. 178) argument that "it takes a village to raise a militia". This argument raises important questions linked to the failure of the DDR: Who raised the militia, and for what reasons? As argued earlier, political interaction in divided states are subjective because groups' stance is conceived in the view of the stakeholders. This flexibility of security renders DDR vulnerable to various OAGs in war-torn states. Given the lack of centralised protection in South Sudan, each groups' concerns surround threats posed to their respective objectives; a point missed entirely by liberal theorists who still believe the state's security reigns supreme, even in situations where the state is not the only ruler. As violence ensues between and within the groups, one would argue that South Sudan has a parallel security provision where different authorities "are part of more authentic processes of statebuilding rather than symptoms of criminality and state failure" (Boege *et al.*, 2008, p.7). The observation is that such hybrid violence is likely to create a political situation whereby armed actors resist and modify the liberal peace procedures. Despite the prominent role of OAGs in South Sudan, international scholars have consistently mentioned them but avoided analysing how to deal with them (Kimenyi, 2012).

While some have previously hinted a combination of methods in peacebuilding (Fortna, 2003), they fall short of calling for situating hybridity in peacebuilding. Richmond observed the "existence of resistance to the liberal peace" in war-affected states (2010b, p. 669). Richmond presented the inclusion of subaltern agencies in processes like the DDR. He used a hybrid peace model to explain violent interactions between and within groups, and to highlight the gap between liberal ideals of DDR and the kind of peace desired by other armed actors by focusing on the struggles, and sometimes deeply different logics of post-war political order, with different sources of influence and legitimacy. The focus on different logics political order in South Sudan draws to "the obvious but often overlooked observation that local communities are not passive in the face of state failure and insecurity, but instead adapt in a variety of ways to minimise risk and increase predictability in their dangerous environments" (Menkhaus, 2007, p. 75). What contributed to the shortfalls of the DDR in South Sudan requires an understanding of the context of the historical structures of governance and the new dimension of political orders.

This project argues that the new dynamic of war emerged because the state formation process failed to build the capacity of the state to self-govern. The CPA and peacebuilding processes created a phantom state "that depends largely external support and lacks political legitimacy" (Chandler, 2006). This project justifies this argument by analysing the weakness of South Sudan in the context in which the state negotiated the use of violence with other end-users. The thesis points to the significance of unsecured borders, where South Sudanese state is "violently challenged by alternative claimants to power or providers of security" (Luckham and Kirk, 2013, p. 2). The securitised policy approach by international organisations becomes vulnerable in those areas where the state is suspended or absent. Some may argue that the violence resulted from the interaction between the status-quo and OAGs reflects mutual dependency between the two in the formation of a security context (Schmeidl, 2009). The meaning of 'mutual dependency' appears to be a positive force as it may create space in which actors can enhance inclusivity.

South Sudan had group cohesion during the North and South war, only to collapse as new peripheral groups resisted the new dominance. While the hybrid peace model can sometimes ignore disproportionate power relations among identities, this study argues that recent efforts at establishing liberal state institutions in South Sudan created a hybrid state in which tribal elites command more power than the state. It is apparent that, due to the nature of politics in South Sudan, the hybrid theory remained a viable analytical approach to explore the impact of the dynamic of internal division on the DDR (Mehler, 2009). As stated before, the DDR was designed in favour of macro-security. The traditional and the new liberal approach, which defines security through the prism of the state, while still immensely influential, has lost its argument couched on the state monopoly over a legitimate means of force. In South Sudan, requesting consideration of the dynamics of violence does not imply a call for a return to the pre-colonial era. This research recognises that post-war societies experience conflicting political interests.

These interests "must function as sources from which to extract elements that will help in the construction of an emancipative epistemological paradigm relevant to the conditions in Africa at this historical moment" (Ramose, 1999, p. 130). A hybrid approach, thus, called for the myriad actors in post-war situations to understand conflict case by case and identify appropriate strategies for peacebuilding (Chandler, 2006). Thus, a hybrid concept holds that "effective SSR-DDR needs to be based on a realistic assessment of how existing forms of security function at the local level" (Andersen, 2011, p. 444). This chapter criticises the liberal approach for its reliance on Weber's view of the state (Ball and van de Goor, 2013). On the surface, this commitment can be viable where the centrality of a state's authority was once prominent (Chetail and Jütersonke, 2015). However, the history of the Sudanese state is characterised by conflict, especially in Southern Sudan and various regimes, where identity politics and economic exclusion has fuelled opposition to the centre, a notion violently manifested in South Sudan (Daly, 2007; Sørbø, 2010;

Adeba, 2019). While De Waal, (2017b, p. 3) does not blame the current situation on the CPA, he argues that:

South Sudan's political market had high barriers to entry. This was a recent and transient development-during the 1983-2005 civil war; the barriers to entry had been low. Oil riches had changed this. No alternative source of political finance could compete with oil, and entry through mutiny was risky-though successfully tried by some mid-level members of the SPLM/A. Control over violence-with-impunity was widely distributed: the SPLM/A conglomerate's 'monopoly' over legitimate violence was, at best, held by tenuous bargain, in which others also assumed that entitlement to kill.

Others contend that the socio-political and economic powers in South Sudan were difficult to allocate because there were many demands from political factions, which caused uncertainty (Idris, 2001; 2005; 2010). Instead of understanding the roles of factionalism, South Sudan approached the DDR according to the 'security-development nexus' and did not foresee inevitable socio-political pitfalls (Narayan *et al.*, 1999). Where violent factionalism is the norm, systemic theft of national resources and proliferation of arms are unavoidable as corrupt governing networks profited from war. This context is similar to Collier and Hoeffler's (2005, p.564) description of rebellion as 'similar to murder', in that it "needs both motive and opportunity". My thesis argues that motive does not have to be economical. The motive could be an abuse of civil rights.

So, basing the DDR entirely on Collier and Hoeffler's economic motive leads to SSR agenda concentrated on the capability of the state but not on accountability in security governance. "We (SPLA) were preparing for war with the North but also working hard to avoid conflict among southern rivals. Our policy was to accommodate all armed actors" (P16/19/09/2017). This participant statement supports the two main arguments presented in Chapter One: warring parties lack the political will to conduct honest DDR, and the SPLA seeks to maximise their military power. What the researcher of this thesis has learned during the fieldwork is that OAGs were treated as secondary actors in the DDR. Further, the effort to give the SPLA monopoly of violence over OAGs delivered poor results because such an approach was not coordinated with a good understanding of security and attitude. Attitude is a term used daily to describe many factors depending on the perspective. This thesis considers attitude in the context of South Sudanese's socio-political psychology, where groups view of each other lead to cooperation or struggle.

The formation of the South Sudanese state did not address groups' attitude and perception. This view contradicts Tilly's (1985, p. 171) description of states as "quintessential protection rackets with the advantage of legitimacy". This observation sees organised groups as state-like units that try to "regulate and control the production and distribution" (Varese, 2010, pp. 14). Because the South Sudanese state shares the stage with OAGs, most of them are not just criminal groups, but they filled the void of state absence. In contrast to South Sudan, the states of ex-Yugoslavia featured favourable conditions for DDR (Sedra, 2013). Most states, following the disintegration of Yugoslavia, were already featuring incentives for the security in the form of NATO

(Glaser, 1993). When Sudan disintegrated, South Sudan inherited an open space suitable for multi-layered security. It may be conceivable to apply a formulaic strategy where armed groups believe that the DDR is destined to end in mutual security, which is not the case in South Sudan.

Both advantages of the remnant of state institutions and security grantee were absent during the CPA-DDR in South Sudan. As mentioned by one participant: "the building of our nation was not started properly, and for that reason, it has led to major drawbacks in the process of trying to establish real peace" (P23b/23/12/2017). This participant alluded to political missteps of former rebel elites when it came to governing. The issue stressed above highlights how the peripheries' feared that DDR was a platform to support the tyranny of reckless dominant groups. Together, these fears created "a toxic brew of distrust and suspicion" (Lake and Rothchild, 1996, 42), where groups cannot entrust the state with a monopoly of force because of the sharp contrast between OAGs' security concerns and the fuzzier effects of state capacity to ensure overall protection. What emerged after independence was a ceremonial state crowned with the prestige of sovereignty, but unable to assert control over its violent internal dynamics (Wassaraa, 2015; Toft, 2003; 2007; 2010). When that is the case, it becomes difficult to build a classical state with the "manifestation of supreme material force necessary to (re-)establish a (new) political order" as ethno-political elites hijack the state and stoke violent power-struggles (Knotter, 2019, p. 119).

These understandings criticise how DDR is designed without

understanding the "genealogy of state"; a belief in the state as a supreme authority (Hindess, 1996). As presented in the introductory chapter, some ethnic and political groups believed that the CPA and secession had given ways to a despotic and ethnic dominated authority in South Sudan. This assumption resulted in a contest over the state's power and distribution of resources. As such, a fulsome DDR for those who wish to leave military service can be thwarted by armed groups thinking about the future of the irresponsible state domination on the use of violence (Baker and Scheye, 2007). These arguments imply that "the real centre of gravity of war" (Kaldor, 2006, p. 3; also 1999; 2001; 2009) has transformed and is neither valid for the analysis of the failure of the DDR. Herbst (2000) presents how this context obstructed peace, arguing that "African states have never had the security imperative to physically control the hinterlands". It means armed groups are un-paternalistic systems which are unbounded, and hybrid in nature and functions (Clements *et al.*, 2007). Although armed informal structures do not replace the state, they undermine state authority.

This argument emphasises the presence of violent veto powers whose agreement or objection is necessary for the success or failure of DDR (Tsebelis, 2000; 2002; Sesay *et al.*, 2009). These views reflected Cowan's (1964) reference to the nature of post-colonial African states where rapid modernisation created contradictions between traditional and modern states. Such contradiction existed in South Sudan where "tribal authorities still dominate as a response to the government's inability to maintain security" (Ottaway and El-Sadany, 2012). As South Sudan fell apart, vulnerable political identities homogenised their security within the weaker state system, obscuring the state hierarchy that makes them insecure. This context provides a unique case to explore unforeseen contradictions between the DDR and the complex relations between OAGs. That contradiction brings about the question of why the hybrid approach is an alternative framework where security is based on violent actors with unpredictable capabilities to influence, positive respond or resist the disarmament and demobilisation.

2.5 Hybrid Approach as an Alternative Framework

It has been argued that the experience of post-war "interventions shows that the expectation that the liberal agenda delivers sustainable long-term peace is largely illusionary" (Paris and Sisk, 2009, p. 20). It could be equally illusionary if I thought of having absolute peace in South Sudan. What dominates the peacebuilding discourse is, a more technical and toolkit discourse, based on the belief that substantial "change within a system can be achieved" from the outside if only the right means are adopted (Körppen, 2011, p.78). The meaning of 'the right means' is for international organisations to focus on visible and stable outputs: from a large peacekeeping mission to the building of political and economic infrastructure whose effects are assumed to be positive. Such an approach emphasises governance issues as concomitant with liberal peacebuilding. While the CPA transformed South Sudan "into new ground for post-war intervention" (Ylönen, 2012, p. 29), such support has failed to enhance political viability. The reasons why South Sudan emerged fragile and descended into war rest on political and security components of the OAGs.

Understanding the effects of these components on the DDR requires systemic thinking. The socio-political and security components of the OAGs or NSAs require recognition of armed groups' flexibility and what fuels their hesitation for the DDR. Understanding why groups resisted such a programme must not be based on the flaws of liberal peace. It requires a hybrid framing, an inward-looking analytical lens. Critics of the hybrid approach may argue that focusing on informal structures untenably widens the scope of peacebuilding. Hughes *et al.*, (2015, p. 818) warn of unbridled romanticisation of localised approaches, claiming that such practices downplay the "despotic tendencies that are endemic in some local states". Such a tendency can become troubling, where the Dinka ethnic majority stand accused by other identities of possessing despotic tendencies. While Mac Ginty agrees with Hughes's insinuation that local peacebuilding needs to be scrutinised, he argues that the liberal processes failed to address the "socio-psychological consequences of violent conflict" in the post-war states (2008, p. 158).

Thus, the hybrid peace model pushes for the introduction of hybrid intellectualism "suppressed under the material power held by the mainstream" (2008, p. 173). Despite these concerns, the post-war intervention in South Sudan is underpinned by the liberal approach. The fact that many NSAs regarded the states as an enemy or unable to protect their interests demonstrated that the socio-political procedures of the game guiding group's behaviours are not found in the formal system alone. This argument implies that the resistance to the DDR stemmed from numerous overlapping contradictions. Thus, understanding the impasses of the DDR need more than a re-assessment of the basic traditions of state-favouring approaches, and where they fell apart (Jackson, 2015; De Heredia, 2018). The question is where the hybrid framework deviates from other state-favouring concepts. I argue that the hybrid model deviates from the liberal peace model because it emphasises the role of non-state armed groups in shaping the outcome of the DDR. The proposal to have the local–turn in DDR is not an assault on liberal peace, but a necessity buttressed on the fact that those structures proliferate in states of war. Proponents of the inclusive DDR agrees with the hybrid position, and stress how peacebuilders in the post-war situation are "duty-bound to (re)orient local institutions and mores towards Westernisms" (Richmond and Mac Ginty, 2014, p. 178). This argument accused the liberal scholars of focusing on individual freedom and an effort to build structural functionalism of the post-war states. Perhaps the most criticised aspect of this approach is an oversimplification problem and exclusion of all the actors when attempting to building peace. The liberal peacebuilding processes are state-centric, which, in the case of South Sudan, aggravate rather than improving dystopic state. Thus, a hybrid framework criticises the institutionalisation process because it is the precursor to liberalisation. The local turn in DDR hints a study of the local context in its various forms to assess its capacity to hybridise the liberal peace (Tadjbakhsh, 2011b). Mac Ginty's hybridisation theory considers the negotiation of oppositions, where the compliance and incentivising powers of an international organisation are met by local resistance (2011, p. 78).

Mac Ginty is clear that the hybrid model "is not the grafting together of two separate entities to make a new, third entity" (2011, p. 89) yet it is unclear what else it can be if one builds a conceptual framework based on the existence of oppositional structures. The basis for applying the hybrid model to South Sudan is to understand how informal actors influence DDR. This argument holds that "effective SSR (…) needs to be based on a realistic assessment of how existing forms of security and justice are provided at the local level rather than on a normative idea of how it sought to be provided" (Andersen, 2011, p. 444). South Sudan is a fragile and fragmented state; hence, security institutions oriented who take part in violence. In 2011, Cubitt, of *The Africa Peace and Conflict Journal,* asked why state-based approaches produce unsustainable peace in Africa. In this, she questioned state-approaches that posit peace and stability should base on some socio-political proximity between the state and OAGs. Despite being shaped by civil wars in South Sudan, identities have exerted substantial determination and continue to "operate in parallel" with state institutions during the war with the North and after the secession (Connor, 1994).

Hence, despite the presence of international peacekeeping and other considerable material, liberal peace approaches have not "enforce compliance among local recalcitrant" (Mac Ginty, 2010, p. 399). This has forced some scholars to admit that DDR is faced with significant challenges when exogenous and endogenous factors do not operate in isolation (Tarimo, 2010; Gurr, 1994; Sharkey, 2007). The problem with the state-based approach is that it forgets that post-war states lost their exclusive rights to rule legitimately. The hybrid approach encourages building upon existing local institutions and customs. South Sudan suffers from "regulative redrawing of stateness" (Mastropaolo, 2012, p. 109). A regulative redrawing of stateness implies how the hierarchical power of the state may have lost control. DDR specialists often emphasised how unchecked use of force create weak institutions, without presenting other drivers of violence and fragility. The regulatory agencies that define state functions become attributed to the private use of force. This system is continued by rising violence among different authorities (Jabri, 2007).

This situation leads to the notion of "ungovernability" in the liberal sense of state. In the late 20th century, Foucault ushered in the idea of 'governmentality', referring to the procedures in which "the state exercises control over, or governs the body of its populace" (1980, p. 52). Foucault's work was based on two disparate projects: his concern with political reasons and the notion of the "genealogy of the state" emphasised earlier. He shows a focus on the ethical questions of states and the 'genealogy of the subject'. The missing link between the state and the genealogy of the subject to the state is the conundrum of government. This matter is an issue because Foucault utilises it to evaluate the contrasts between what he identified as "technologies of the self and technologies of domination" (1997b, p. 67; also, 1997a). This view lessened the state's status as a unique institution to govern people in societies subject to different means of regulations. One could argue it is helpful to try another approach due to an indication that peace depends on specific relations between the institutionalisation of armed actors.

The root of the hybrid school's critique of conventional theory is centred on state functionality. Baker and Scheye (2007, p. 505), emphasise two of the main proponents of the hybrid concept: "SSR is typically premised on two fallacies, which are the product of its state-centric approach. The first fallacy is that the nature and resources of the post-war and fragile state are capable of delivering the reforms proposed. The second is that the post-conflict and fragile state is in practice, the main actor in security and justice". Contrary to ideas of 'statism', many informal structures that provide security, legitimacy and justice exist within post-war societies (Sedra, 2013). This is mostly true about South Sudan, as argued by one participant: "somebody feels [more] strongly about being a Dinka than being a South Sudanese. We remained as an arena of competing tribal groups bunched together in one territory" (P3/04/09/2017). The informal structures the above participant referred to do not recognise the South Sudanese state as a mechanism for the definition and generation of legitimacy as well as the organisation that accumulate resources to enforce that claimed legitimacy. It is a country without a state.

In that way, the public withdraws from such a state. When there is conflict, these groups fall back to the confines of their identities and refuse to give up arms to an imaginary entity. This situation is contrary to the liberal peace argument that all ex-combatants and groups would be disarmed and converted into legitimate socio-political groups (Jütting, 2003). Blinded by liberal idealism, SSR-DDR designers tend to discount these informal security providers whose appeal stems from their "physical, linguistic and cultural accessibility; legitimacy; efficacy; and restorative justice" (Baker and Scheye 2007, p. 512). By presenting an account of resistance, the hybrid approach envisages the creation of co-governance measures between the state and informal actors. In a sense, the hybrid theory brings DDR back to its human security roots. South Sudan emerged from the war of the state. The rivalries between political factions reinforced the idea that non-state groups identified more with their OAGs than with the state (Smith, 2000).

It is evident in South Sudan informal actors could justly exercise "coercive force or claim for themselves an authority to use force to impose obedience to laws and policies" (Brady, 2016, p. 78). Hence, the rampant use of force and factional armies has proved that "the state is not a unique tool to govern human beings, which are subject to many other regulation and control techniques, while the state does not have a unique essence and a unique way to operate" (Mastropaolo, 2012, 102). This argument emphasises that the essence legitimacy to governance and force is not anchored only on the Republic of South Sudan, as a sovereign state. OAGs constrain the viability of the state. In this situation, the conventional approaches concerning the use of force no longer apply. One participant attributed the war in South Sudan to "a suspension of the state" and wondered how to assert state rule when state supremacy is challenged (P17/10/01/2018). The hybrid approach is suitable for analysing these challenges because it recognises other regulatory techniques. As such, the section below answers the question: What happens to a Weberian idea of the state when introduced into a fragmented South Sudan?

2.6 The Challenges of Multi-Layered Security on DDR in South Sudan

Political observers hint that the era of states as dominant political entities has ended, and been replaced by multi-layered political, economic and security governance, which will be difficult to reverse (Fahey, 2013). Mathews has argued that the world is witnessing "a novel redistribution of power among states, markets, and Civil Society" (1997, p. 50). Mathews' argument hinges on the impact of globalisation with little emphasis on post-war societies where informal armies pose risks to internal security. As argued in this chapter, South Sudan is characterised by the near absence of the state. These issues are worsened by OAGs' distrust in the state and legitimacy of the state's control over the use of force. In this case, the South Sudanese state is locked in a system of incessant violent negotiation with armed factions at several territorial tiers where the use of force is dispersed vertically between levels of informal actors, but also horizontally across several avenues of political interest and spheres of influence. In South Sudan, the state loses its powers to non-state actors by virtue of not meeting its sovereign obligations (Scheye and McLean, 2006).

South Sudan faces challenges exerted by armed multi-layered organisations that have eroded state supremacy from below. It has been argued that "the rampant unprofessional behaviour of uniformed personnel is partly responsible for the drive within many communities in South Sudan to acquire small arms and light machine guns for their protection" (Kuol, 2018, p. 2). Kuol argues that while South Sudan's police are alleged to have committed gross violations, including wrongful detentions, South Sudan National Security (NSS), "has a reputation of being the political police of the President" (2018, p. 2). This agency has been linked to extrajudicial killings and disappearances of the regime's critics. When citizens fear their government, it becomes harder to disarm the non-state armies erected for self-defence. This culmination of the weak state, OAGs' fear of the state, and OAGs' fear of each other reveals that authority and governance are multidimensional. Given the current situation, there is a retreat of the state's authority in South Sudan; thus, a supposed sovereign government remains irrelevant.

"South Sudan has been a fragmented front where ethno-political dimension causes a violent split" (P2/14/09/2017). This argument reflects a simmering view that South Sudan is an instrument of extortion, where competing groups use their position for protection and private gain. Johnson (2016) has depicted the rationale for the situation as a "business of violence", a reflection of the rationalist explanations for the war that often concentrate on economic power trajectories (Powell, 1999; 2004; 2006). Johnson's emphasis presented a paradox of violent transition that, while armed groups organise themselves in opposition to the state and each other, individuals have sought ties with elites deeply in the centre of the state. This situation may appear to be a state of chaos, but South Sudan is not in anarchy. The weak formal authority is replaced by fluid networking among distrustful violent actors. This argument is unlikely to convince state-driven theories, but the benefit of this emphasis is that its links the failure of the DDR with an understanding of armed groups' intentions in war. Informal security structures, although they are part of informal governance, are deeply interlaced with formal authorities (Jok, 2017).

It shows that leaders of armed factions can instigate violence with little or no constraint from the central government. This dispersal of power and the use of force by South Sudanese armed actors challenged a conceptual framing of state-based peacebuilding. It might be interesting to observe the need to re-examine to what extent South Sudan still worthy of a legitimate sovereign monopoly of force when it barely fulfilled its functions. While abuses committed by informal armies, such as the Janjaweed, typically garner most public attention, the expansion of these informal structures has had more impact on the DDR. This is because these structures are based on the elite's ability to create grassroots support, and mostly dependent on these informal armies for political survival. As noted by one participant, "across much of the country, everyday security is increasingly in the hands of ethnic armies, and these armies have become a ubiquitous feature of daily life" (P27/21/12/2017). This argument implies that governance of the use of the force is not confined to either the state or the NSAs in South Sudan (Spear, 2002).

Curiously enough, the critique of the state-based approach presents an examination of the post-war state that defies consensus (Fritz and Menocal, 2006; 2007). The analysis requires reflection on Goetze and Guzina's (2008) argument that mocks liberal peace as a process where one type of construction is believed to proceed to another. The critical problem emphasised below is that the conventional peacebuilding agenda in Africa, with its concentration on the stability of post-war states, has not made a substantial breakthrough. Both peace and statebuilding processes failed to convince Ex-Combatants and informal armies to abide by their states' formalised processes and respect the political, economic and security laws enshrined in post-war constitutions. Understanding the impact of this violent struggle requires a research method that will help this study examine the role of armed structures, agency, and processes related to armed conflicts, and how these factors fuelled a perpetual proliferation of small arms and armies.

2.7 Conclusion

A hybrid approach sees the concentration on rebuilding post-war states as anachronistic and encourages addressing localised courses of action (Steele, 2005). This view implies that the DDR applies liberal peacebuilding approach, which sanitises history and disregard imposed international constraints as well as ascribing democratic features to fragmented states. A breakdown of the central authority defines South Sudan. Hence, the state does guarantee not just essential services to its citizens, but also a well-ordered collective life. Thus, the resistance to the DDR comes down to the lack of collective protection and the motivations of OAGs. Regardless of decades of peace intervention and "notwithstanding the considerable enthusiasm for such activities, there is thin evidence that DDR yields effective outcomes during the transition from war to peace" (Colletta and Muggah, 2009, p. 446). While the DDR is technically practical, it may not be possible where a claim to legitimacy and the use of force is dispersed. This situation has led to the reality that recipients of the DDR often do not want what donors are selling (Ball and van de Goor, 2011).

The theoretical approach detailed in this chapter offers radical diagnoses and remedies for the problems hindering DDR. While the DDR is a vital aspect of peacebuilding, the hybrid concept sees the orthodoxy of the SSR model as too state-centric and normative. Instead of seeking to impose institutional approach in states with divided sources of legitimacy, the process should "work with multiple authorities in order to maximise their strengths and weaknesses" (Baker, 2007, p. 217). In many ways, the future of DDR boils down to two issues: the responsibility of the state and the capacity of the external agencies to actualise transformative change in line with liberal peace. The question that remains unanswered is: what happens when the state is not the sole actor providing stability, security and good governance? This is an open and controversial question. As Jackson (2011, p. 1818) states, "critics of the liberal peace approach, and by implication, the orthodox approach to SSR, concede that what is required is a rebalancing of external regulation and internal voice that could lead to an effective state that is locally accountable".

There is, though, the great division among critics on what role violent NSAs should play in this rebalancing. What has become less contentious in the last decade is the reality that the international community via Western donors have limited capacity to transform post-war states and re-make them in the liberal, Western image. Not only did the international community stand arm-folded and allow the pogroms in Rwanda and Darfur, but the interventions in Afghanistan,

Iraq, and Libya ended in disaster. These outcomes contradicted the intended purpose of re-branding dictatorial states into democracies and rebuilding war-affected states into stable authorities. South Sudan is not exceptional. The nascent state is a contrast of Annan's (2006, p.685) argument that "states are now widely understood at the services of their people and not vice versa". The South Sudanese state remained a quasi- or imaginary state, where security and freedom of individuals enshrined in the Charter of the UN are consigned to the papers on which they are written. As a weak and predatory state, South Sudan fall shorts of Deng's *et al.*'s (1996, p. 1) argument that "legitimate sovereignty required a demonstration of responsibility".

The growing cynicism of these Western peace approaches is no longer confined to academic discourse, but has gained momentum in mainstream policy circles, restraining enthusiasm in Western capitals for protracted overseas activities. As Ignatieff has observed about today's international state-builders: "no imperialists have ever been so impatient for quick results" (2003, p. 115; also 1996). Further, Western exasperation, cost and risk aversion appears set to increase in this era of financial difficulty. This project applies the hybrid model to emphasise how a "fend-for-yourself" security attitude among South Sudanese has shifted the idea of security away from a public authority. As the state disintegrates, the net result of violence is not just the plundering of state resources, but the undermining of rule-based use of force. To argue that the current violent turmoil in South Sudan is the result of defunct political institutions, this thesis will utilise a qualitative approach in the next chapter to understand conflict issues and interpret meaning from these data about the causes of conflict and its effect on the DDR.

Chapter Three: Paradoxes of Perception in Qualitative Research: An Assessment of the Effects of Violent Actors on DDR in South Sudan

After over four decades of civil war, the state of Sudan broke apart in 2011, and a cycle of organised violence started in South Sudan. Although different areas are affected by different degrees of violence, others were and are still exposed to the cruel effects of factional wars. South Sudan suffers from the consequences of these wars. The previous chapter argued that the legitimacy upon which the state monopoly of violence is based is contested in South Sudan. Hence, a hybrid framework helps this project analyse factors affecting the DDR by studying the nature of armed conflict among South Sudanese ethno-political groups and their attitudes and perceptions of political authority, leadership, and institutions. This understanding seeks to reframe the post-war intervention debate through fresh theoretical lenses, which view the situation in South Sudan as highly contested. South Sudan lacks a legitimate monopoly over the use of force as well as lacking effective administrative control (Lamoureaux and Sureau, 2019).

In the absence of a functioning state system, ethno-political groups organised themselves around armed factions, which protect them against their adversaries. Hence, the case study is how self-security mindset among South Sudanese encroached on "the ability of the state to command public loyalty to the governing regime" (Opongo, 2018, p. 3). This type of study suggests moving beyond the ordinary effects of civil war and focus on the legacy of civil war and groups' behaviour. To analyse the effects of these debacles on the DDR, this chapter applies a case study method that will include the perspectives of violent stakeholders. Utilising a qualitative approach helps identify the causes and motives of those engaging in violence. This insight is achieved by mapping the views of actors engaged in processes of transition during the CPA and renewed violence. A qualitative approach is appropriate because it allows the project to explain the challenges facing DDR through a group's context of security and political contest with another group. Thus, a qualitative methodology is appropriate for this study because it will help me ascertain the preferences, capacities, responses and agency of violent stakeholders in South Sudan.

The bulk of the research about the impact of small arms in South Sudan utilised quantitative comparative analysis focusing on the destructive nature of arms (ICG 2011; Garfield, 2007; Munive, 2013a). To obtain a nuanced interpretation of the circumstances affecting the DDR in South Sudan, it is vital to examine armed actors' interests in arms, and the direct and indirect consequences of their presence to the DDR. Answering the question about the negative impacts of armed actors' maximisation of force on the DDR requires a qualitative method because this project does not consider armed groups as objects of research, but as subjects. Finding out why Ex-Combatants and OAGs resisted the DDR in South Sudan requires an approach that enquires into the direct experience of armed groups. The insights generated from this approach may establish peacebuilding programmes. However, this effort to fully grasp the challenges of the

DDR from the participants' perspective recognises the legacy of perpetual armed conflicts in South Sudan and its devastating consequences on the formal authority and its capacity to govern.

This notes that the influence of war has eroded a civil procedure of dialogue and ushered in violence that has left behind considerable arms and those trained in their use (Meek and Malan, 2004). Thus, the qualitative approach enables this project to access right informants and acquire in-depth information, not just about the effects of war on the South Sudanese, but also on local armed actors' beliefs and feelings about DDR as a process of post-war intervention. Questions relating to individual or groups' subjective security perceptions cannot be properly addressed through a quantifiable or numerical approach since such approach stress the quantification of information and analysis (Bryman, 2004). The strength of a qualitative method lies in its capacity to provide/deliver multifaceted textual explanations of how groups' experience informs their activities and relationships with each other (Pelto and Pelto, 1997). This project will analyse the data gained from participants by answering the 'why' and 'how' questions.

Instead of relying on the emphasis of institutional deficits as the only factor forcing the failure of DDR, I will argue that there are structural problems in South Sudan where armed political identities have a tendency of violent autonomy. This research will present an assessment of how groups' contradictions overwhelm the transition and force South Sudan back into the war (Schirch 2008; Wood, 2008; Parkinson, 2013). Understanding the effect of violent contradiction among South Sudanese will largely depend on an understanding of "the purposeful behaviour of political elites" (Nordlinger, 1972, p. 4). The resistance to the DDR and violent conflict might be due to "conflictual relations", but also because of socio-political and ethnic binaries, which offer firmly unalterable settings (Guelke, 2012, p. 178). All these problems lead to self-mobilisation, as was the case in Rwanda (Weinstein, 2007). In effect, scholars have emphasised how sufficient knowledge of why armed groups mobilise can help in devising effective "post-conflict reconstruction" (Brown and Wycoff, 1987). Since the CPA, the U.N.'s initiative to keep peace and strengthen statehood has faltered in South Sudan, as the ethno-political groups collided.

This violent collision brought an essential change in the conflict dynamic by introducing a new perspective of security thinking. What is needed is an understanding of South Sudan's political terrain through analysing how armed structures affect conflicts related to a public authority and the impacts of an armed ethno-political group on state monopoly of violence. This type of questioning "reject[s] the practices and norms of the natural scientific model and of positivism in particular in preference for an emphasis on the ways in which individuals interpret their social world" (Bryman, 2001, p. 20). To appreciate the risks fractured security poses to the DDR, this thesis will use in-depth interviews, which are ideal for obtaining data on individuals or groups' histories and interpretation of their social world. South Sudan is a fragmented state where armed groups share control and governance of ethnic territories with state's weak central authority (Young, 2016). Under these conditions, it is necessary to examine the link between the proliferation of arms and how these factions interact. The question of who rebels against whom and why requires an emphasis on armed groups' behaviours and desires.

That approach exemplifies "a view of social reality as constantly shifting emergent property of individuals' creation" (Bryman, 2004, p. 20). Armed actors in South Sudan clash with the government, while some groups often fight on its behalf (De Waal, 2017). This situation requires understanding the overarching political condition of these groups through the analysis of the contexts of violence, to explain mobilisation. This framework is underpinned by the idea of 'widener' and 'traditionalist' perceptions of security based on the international relations theory of security. The distinction between the wideners' and the traditional approaches of security is in the choice. The wider emphasise the multi-sectoral and the traditionalist is based on a narrow agenda. Thus, "the traditionalists equate security with military issues and the use of force, while the wideners suggest broadening the legitimate agenda of the discipline to at least four other sectors: political, societal, economic and environmental" (Pupinis, 2011; citing Buzan, 1991, p. 6).

Such debate is important in the civil war context because of the question of who governs the use of force and whose security is contested (Booth, 1991; 2007). If South Sudanese factions dissident against the political system executed by the state or other militant groups, then rebellion and the proliferation of arms could be conceived as a relational decision based on armed groups' desires to control aspects of daily life in areas under their jurisdiction (LeBrun and Jonah,

2014). "We have nothing to do with the government", said the leader of armed youth (P26b/23/09/2017). To him, a tribal chief is an equivalence of a president. He can order the war. In this case, these armed groups determined threats and the security measures necessary to counter those threats. The impact of situations where factions objected to the state and function as the state is not examined as a reason leading to the failure of the DDR in South Sudan. This project stresses that the average South Sudanese lack trust in the post-secession state and unwillingness to conform to the rule of an entity unable to provide security (LeRiche and Arnold, 2012).

Despite these challenges, international actors ignored the fact that South Sudan is symbolically a state, but practically incapable of meeting the task of eliminating lacerating socio-political grounds for tension and violence. Today, nearly a decade into peace and state-building projects, the realities of war and violence on the ground seem to confirm my argument that those projects have failed. Finding out why the peacebuilding and war preventions measures failed requires the researcher of this project to explore the rhetoric of the armed actors and other stakeholders in South Sudan. Once the state as an institution for managing the affairs of the public security had collapsed, the ability to satisfy the interests of all citizens also suffers. Therefore, we need to find out how the fragmentation of South Sudan's socio-political cohesion, and between the various levels of social formation affected the DDR.

Anyone talking of re/building state to control a legitimate monopoly of violence in South Sudan is mistaken. There has never been a state in South Sudan. What emerged in 2011 remained fragile. In the recent conflict (2013-), even village chiefs commanded their armies. These are not regular armies, but tribal armies, which dispersed to their villages once the intensity of conflict waned (P37/10/01/2018).

The interpretation of this argument is that the legacy of war in old Sudan damaged the central structures and replaced them with hybrid structures. Violent actors gained legitimacy based on acceptance by their political groups, which are linked to customary institutions. This study characterises the war in South Sudan as a mixture of violent informal socio-political orders and a fragile central authority that seems to be collapsing. So far, instead of aiming to identify the origins of war and search for a remedy to the resistance against DDR, the debacles of South Sudan's war continue to be perceived as a tragedy of the weakness of the state. As the armed groups grew stronger, the outcome became a situation of security negation "where those interested in keeping central government institutions weak and ineffective have been placed in positions of authority over the state institutions that needed to be strengthened" (Fischer and Schmelzle, 2009, p. 7). This thesis argues that instead of describing the whole challenge of the DDR based on the fragility of state, it would be helpful to consider challenges in term of hybrid violent socio-political orders (Snowden, 2012). These problems require a reflective method to comprehend and interpret the impacts of armed groups' grievances (Gurr, 2015).

What is critical in this case study, is how the stances of armed groups can affect the concept of the state as a "superior and ultimate form of political order per se" (Boege et al., 2009, p. 88). Thus, the scope of this research covers the post-CPA setting between North-South Sudan and will draw on historical contexts that have led to various violent actors vetoing successful DDR in independent South Sudan. As argued in the last chapter, a violent network in fragmented states and their influence regularly change, which means that their functions and responses to the conflict and peace of the issue will vary over time. Hence, linking the behaviours of armed factions and the failure of the DDR in South Sudan requires a qualitative approach to understands and analyse the activities carried out and the roles played by the armed actors in relation to the collapse of the DDR. Such an approach will help in developing a research paradigm that will lead to an exhaustive view of the war in South Sudan in terms of "security-seeking motives" (Kalyvas, 2001, p. 99; 2006).

3.1 Paradigm of Research

Research must be guided by a paradigm (Makombe, 2017). Kuhn, (1962 cited in Brown *et al.*, 2019, p. 545) define paradigm "as the set of common beliefs and agreements shared between scientists about how problems should be understood and addressed". Thus, a paradigm of research is a system that directs the researchers, "not only in terms of choices of the method but in ontologically and epistemologically fundamental ways" (Guba and Lincoln, 1994, p. 195; also, 1981). This thesis seeks for explanations about the challenges facing the DDR and factors influencing its failure. This project seeks answers about what constitutes the violent reality on the ground in South Sudan, particularly when it comes to its nascent state institutions. This chapter will ask whether these institutions were very weak or subordinate to the violent politics pursued by elites in charge of various factions, and it explores how this possible weakness affected the DDR. Hence, the case study is the evaluation of the challenges of the DDR in South Sudan.

This assessment aims to find out why the SPLA [South Sudan armed forces] and other armed actors in the country were deeply reluctant to adhere to the procedure of the DDR. What the factors affecting the Ex-Combatants and armed tribal armies to commit to the DDR? This project will use the case study as a methodology, as the present study focuses on an examination of all armed groups' opinions, feelings, experiences and inner thoughts. Studies of civil wars raise concerns about bias because of the researchers' beliefs (Edward and Holland, 2013; Jensen *et al.*, 2014; Hammersley, 1993). These concerns are highlighted in this chapter through the emphasis of how the CPA obliged donors to fund projects that will encourage the unity of Sudan over secession (Bennett, 2010). Because of this mindset, external scholars report the situation according to the donors' preferences. To present the local version, I recognise that ethnic militias "embody a special dimension in warfare that transcends the classic inter-state and intra-state disputes of the past" (Arnold and Alden, 2007, p. 1). The point this thesis stresses is that compliance with the DDR cannot be reduced to the capacity of the state to restraints or incentives.

Instead, the path to compliance should base on "the logic of appropriateness", a notion that these armed actors or groups "make decisions based on their identity and on the perception of what is considered appropriate" (Costantini, 2015; citing March and Olsen

1998, p. 952). So, this research will strive to present how "individual strategies of status accruement, the pursuit of security and income enhancement can all serve as motivations that can challenge the effectiveness of the DDR" (Arnold and Alden, 2007, p. 5). Arriving at this point is exhausting; one must know by what logic armed groups pursue their political interests. So, the reason for using a qualitative approach is to build "a way of understanding and to explain how we know what we know" (Crotty, 2003, p. 3). This explanation provides "a philosophical grounding for deciding what kinds of knowledge are possible and how we can ensure that they are both adequate and legitimate" (Maynard, 1989, p. 10). This emphasises will allow the project to question how DDR sought to address post-war challenges and its limitations, caused either by the challenge of building a new state, and efforts exerted by the international community. These factors seek to contribute towards filling a gap in the literature on conflict and its effects on peacebuilding efforts in South Sudan.

3. 2 Quantitative and Qualitative Approaches

Positivism and post-positivism are two common theoretical perspectives in the social sciences (Kumar, 1996; 1998; 1999). In application, the former is used for scientific inquiry where the researchers arrive arguable at their conclusion, whereas the latter more typically takes a subjective qualitative stance. Qualitative researchers might ask questions to investigate how violent interactions among groups in South Sudan affect the processes of peacebuilding. The basis of that enquiry focuses on forming a holistic picture of an issue, such as armed conflict, and aims to construct a comprehensive account of behaviours, political norms, group attitudes towards the government, or social practice in a specific natural or political setting (Thompson, 2012). This contradiction between approaches has developed due to essential variances that "relate to the truth and value-free or value-laden research" (Denzin and Lincoln, 1994; 2000, p. 17).

Proponents of quantitative models have advanced specific processes for understanding phenomena that differentiate each model within the research. Quantitative researchers stress a need for measurable truth (Abbott, 2001; 2004), while qualitative researchers address why and how armed groups behave (Berg, 2004; Koenig, Spano and Thompson, 2019). The distinction between "causes versus searching for happenings" underpins how an investigator's method impacts what is being studied and but how the problem is being studied (Stake, 1995, p. 39; also 1978; 1998). Thus, the primary objective of this thesis is not only to provide a detailed consideration of the links between assessments of the quality of information and the epistemological positions that underpin the research. Despite this emphasis, some have argued for a "best of both worlds" approach, suggesting both quantitative and qualitative methods should be applied as mixed methods (Bryman, 2006, p.111; also 1988). This suggestion has deemed the knowledge acquired in the scientific format as an imperialist means of subjugating knowledge that can be reconstructed carefully while keeping sight of broader structural-discursive context (Sekaran, 1992; Clarke, 2003).

In post-war reconstruction literature, beneficiary states and international organisations applied a narrow focus on institution building. Based on this approach, the measurements of successes or failures are based on the centrality of liberal concepts in theoretical debates on post-war intervention. As argued before, that concept raises vital questions hinged around the effects of an externally driven effort to re-build the post-war state. This question is vital for this research because it emphasises how quantification of the challenges to security has "overlooked the tight interlace between institutions and organisations" as well as the fact that violent armed actors "can refer to alternative rules of the game" that can affect the DDR (Costantini, 2015, p. 36). This argument requires an interpretation of the impacts of different forms of conflicts in South Sudan, which do not often confine themselves within the normal procedures of conflict resolution. This situation needs rich information that presents armed actors' perspectives. To arrive at this position, this project will explain the interaction between armed actors and the institutions sustaining them.

Having a clear sense of these contexts helps understand the failure of the DDR. The notion of institutions refers to the rules of the game in society whereas "organisations are the players: groups of individuals bound by a common purpose to achieve objectives" (Costantini, 2015; citing North *et al.*, 2009, p. 23). In South Sudan, institutions and organisations include various armed groups. As it has been said, without procedures of the game, players cannot play; however, the existence of rules of the game alone may not make the game fairer. Due to the growing development of DDR challenges, the focus needs to shift from institutional capacity, which the conventional DDR inspired to achieve, to violent organisations, in order to understand the effect of the actor-shaped approach. Instead of refuting the basic tenet of institution building, a qualitative approach allows this research to seek a deeper way of knowing (Clarke, 2003). This approach requires information based on interactions with actors. It also reflects critical security studies, which infers the importance of placing the experience "for whom the present world order is a cause of insecurity rather than security at the centre of the agenda" (Jones, 1995, p. 309).

This argument revives the classical idea of philosophy "that was directed towards understanding, evaluation, and practice" (Shapcott, 2004, p. 328). Understanding what contributed to the failure of DDR requires the incorporation of the dynamic of "interaction and mutual influence between three layers: social forces, forms of state, and world orders" (Kellner, 1989, p. 13; also 1990). This context builds on Cox's (1989b, p. 38) argument that "the structural approach is not so much an alternative to the actor-interactions approach as a logical priority to it". Thus, the challenges of DDR cannot be based on academic objectivity, but an in-depth examination of the challenges in light of social realities (Leysens, 2006; Morrow and Brown, 1994). This project's choice of a qualitative method is founded on an outlook that exposes the "different truths and realities held by different individuals and groups" (Stringer, 1999, p. 41). As the situation in South Sudan shows, actors embody the principles of institutions, and they legitimise them by making them function (Thomas, 2000; Hurworth, 2003).

Despite qualitative researchers' attempts to transcend the "limitations of generalisation" (Fay, 1987), they are liable for criticism from those who question the reliability and inclusiveness of information when the research site happens to be a war-zone (Golafshani, 2003). South Sudan is not just a war-zone, but it is characterised by the multiplicity of violent institutions. This situation can make it hard to access the research site and bring in critical informants with the right information that can help in understanding the problems through interpretive validity. Maxwell argues that "interpretive validity captures how well the researcher reports the participants'" meaning of events and behaviours (Maxwell, 1992, p. 49). The main emphasis here is that the interpretations of events are not established on the academics' view, but the researched or participant. With that, "interpretive validity is inherently a matter of inference from the words and actions of participants in the situations studied" (Maxwell, 1992, p. 49). An interpretive validity describes the examiner's position and the potential bias investigator may have in the analysis of the issues causing war and resistance to the DDR in South Sudan (Hayashi *et al.*, 2019).

Interpretive validity can be affected by the following: the researcher, the subjects participating in the research, and the situational context. The effects of these problems will be discussed later in the section explaining how my relationship with the research topic hampered my role as an independent observer. Those who control access to information viewed me with suspicion because of my ethnic affiliation. It takes an effort to convince armed actors to answer questions about whether the proliferation of arms is a strategy for coping with socio-political and economic competition or as a way to provide "localised community contracts" (Pugh, 2011, p. 3). Despite these problems, this project focused on qualitative data because "the development of empirically-based knowledge about the causes, dynamics and resolution of armed conflicts are contingent on researchers' ability to gather useful information" (Höglund and Öberg, 2011, p. 4). Such types of data are backed up by the secondary data that includes a range of books, academic journals, government reports and correlative sources available on the internet.

Because this research seeks to explore the effect of conflict on socio-political behaviour in South Sudan, it "sees human beings as co-creating their reality through participation" (Denzin and Lincoln 1994, p. 206). In the section below, the thesis will describe the essence of qualitative methodologies, their usefulness and the criticism libelled against qualitative data and the methods of obtaining them. I will briefly overview the qualitative methodologies and present why all, except a case study approach, are not suitable for this study.

3.3 Qualitative Methodologies

Qualitative approaches can be separated into five categories: ethnography, narrative, phenomenology, grounded theory, and case study (Brannen, 1992; Creswell, 2003; 2007; 2009). While the methods mostly use similar data collection procedures, the purpose of the research differentiates them. The ethnographic approach allows researchers to immerse themselves in the participants' environment to observe, live, and understand their situation. "When used as a method, ethnography typically refers to fieldwork conducted by a single investigator who lives with and lives like' those who are studied, usually for a year or more" (Maanen, 1996, p. 263). Ethnography is presented as "a portrait of a people a description of a particular culture -the customs, beliefs, and behaviour" (Harris and Johnson, 2000).

Instead of relying on observation, ethnographic researchers experience the environment first-hand through observation. There are some problems of why ethnographic research is not suitable for this research. First, South Sudan is a war-zone state. Hence, the long period needed for the researcher to observe meaningful information about the actor's behaviours and impact of those behaviours on the DDR can be very costly, and potentially dangerous. Second, while ethnographic research a particular form of qualitative investigation, it is not qualitative enough. Ethnographic research and the data obtained through that process is "seen as a specific form of qualitative inquiry, to be compared or contrasted with others, for example, with life history work or discourse analysis" (Hammersley, 2006, p. 4).

Therefore, ethnographic research comprises of the "use of quantitative data and analysis, so that it may not be purely qualitative in character" (Hammersley, 2006, p. 4). Any slight content of quantitative data will allow this thesis to produce knowledge according to socio-political education that glorifies the prominence of acquiring first-hand information about what South Sudanese armed groups do and say in particular contexts. As an effort to transcend the ethnographic approach, some researchers applied the narrative methods to weave together a sequence of issues and events, usually from a few individuals or groups to form a cohesive story. The "narrative analysis treats stories as knowledge per se which constitutes the social reality of the narrator and conveys a sense of that person's experience in its depth, messiness, richness and texture, by using the actual words spoken" (Etherington, 2007, p. 81). This approach requires in-depth interviews. As the narrative approach involves an in-depth exploration into participants journeys (Josselson (1996, p. 9) highlights the importance of establishing a warrant for the research to ensure that the interference in participants' lives is 'justified from the interviewee's perception'.

It is hard for me to distil reliable information from armed groups or war-affected participants without exploring interviewees' standpoints to provide insight into their motivations (Davidsen, 2010). Like most other qualitative approaches, the interview starts with well-formed research questions, to build an adequate dataset to highlight universal themes and strengthen researchers' findings. Although this approach is essential, there is still the question of how researchers engage with the topic. Such an approach comes with its weaknesses because the terms used are obtuse. In focusing on a detailed description of experiences, researchers may not adequately describe the process that led to that experience (Polit and Beck, 2014). While a phenomenological approach could help describe the essence of armed groups' activity and the lived experience of being a member of an armed group, grounded theory collects data in a more open-minded way and then allows the data to speak for itself, rather than being guided by hypotheses (Bryant and Charmaz, 2007).

Some academics criticise a grounded theory, arguing that it produces substantial volumes of data, which is often overly complex to manage (Timonen et al., 2018). As such, grounded theory requires high levels of researcher skill. In order to explore the factors affecting the DDR, this thesis embraces a case study approach. The rationale for adopting the approach is not so much about what literature says about the civil war in South Sudan, but why individuals resorted to war? While the DDR aimed at addressing macro security issues, this project argues that less is known about the challenges at local levels. Hence, the next section will provide the critical components for analysing the challenges of consolidating political order in post-war states.

3.4 Analysis of Qualitative Research

Qualitative researchers pay analytic attention to in-depth interview stories as a way to assemble critical facets through questions (Riessman and Speedy, 2007). There are various kinds of interview in which the researcher records the experiences of participants (Creswell, 2007). The rationale for in-depth interviews in this project is founded on the premise that people "give meaning through stories" (Andrew *et al.*, 2008, p. 17). Therefore, interviews are a form of qualitative research methodology for gathering information in textual forms. The researcher of this project, for instance, will find out through interviews the causes the civil war in South Sudan, the actors, and the reason why they are engaging in war, and resisting the DDR.

The conceived meanings of stories are interpreted to provide an insight into the world of the researched. It is through this interpretation that researchers can gather "knowledge from the past and not necessarily about the past" (Bochner, 2007, p. 203). While it is common to read from the reports that "there are more guns in the hands of civilians in South Sudan than cell phones" such analogies failed to emphasise how "every gun possessed by civilians and every bullet fired goes beyond the potential loss of life" (Small Arms Assessment, 2016, p. 5). While these claims may not be authentically verified, alarming statistics highlight the proliferation of arms and the pressures those arms places on security and stability.

Some of the reports about the proliferation of arms can never be precisely due to the lack of concentration on OAGs. In response, I noted the lack of systematic studies on the issues of South Sudan, and that demanded a thorough investigation of what makes the armed groups engaged in violence, and how does an unchecked exercise of armed conflict sharpen political and inter-communal conflict? Thus, accessing the information through interviews will allow this project to contracture knowledge based on real-life experience (Bochner, 2007). The merit of concentrating on the actors' conflict lies in the notion that "knowledge is a belief" about a segment of truth (Bochner, 2007, p. 203). Due to the intricacy of the situation in South Sudan, interviews will provide a method for collecting in-depth information on individual or group's experiences and feelings about their motivation for war and possession of arms. This thesis deemed interviews useful because the inquiry relates to conflict require complex questioning and considerable probing. Interviews will provide "a set of empirical observations about the local environment, and a system of self-management that governs resource use" (Davis, 2001, p. 107).

Thus, acquiring information about the factors of violence requires interviews with local decision-makers and observers with knowledge about these actors (Byrne, 2009; Senehi et al., 2009). This research intends to understand internal complexities and their role in hindering the DDR. Such understanding required direct or indirect learning through organisations or political groups' perception of their observed indicators, such as political, economic and security interest. The strengths of interview stories, in this case, are their ability to tap into the knowledge of what led to war and how peace and security may be sustained (Ljungberg *et al.*, 2005). In South Sudan, however, war is prevalent, and that led to the corrosion of the state's central authority. As this project contends that the enduring consequence of civil war leads to the rise of violent informal authorities as a method of protection or resistance to the dominant political orders, it is essential to know how these violent armed groups interact, their interest and motivation, and how they create a space in which the rules of the state as a dominant authority can be suspended.

The basis of this inquiry lies in this study's identification of the lack of a constructive societal relationship in South Sudan. The research also examines the lack of inclusive political practices, the presence of which could enable state-society cooperation and build the state's capacity to carry out its duties. The aim is for the research to build a collaborative interpretive process based on the information drawn out from active engagement with post-war society via critical informants. This project will collect data in the form of stories, primarily as a way of recounting the historical facts influencing the present proliferation of arms. Stories are useful in understanding positive and adverse effects of "real" and "imaginary" aspects of politics, ethnic relations, and other elements, which may be significant to understanding why South Sudan has failed to conduct a successful DDR and neutralise the menace that war poses to stability. Such understanding can uncover "invisible issues" that are beyond the common assumption that a lack of institutions is the major challenge (Clandinin *et al.*, 2000; Thompson, 2011).

Qualitative stories can offer a helpful reflection of societal realities (Freire, 1974; 2005). As presented in Chapter Three, this method of enquiry transcends functional-institutionalist myopia and provides a lens for contextualising the extent to which violent post-war transition determined the outcomes of the DDR. The project may assume the lack of political will, but that cannot clarify the problems facing the DDR unless there is an understanding of the configuration of authorities, and related issues of legitimacy (Daly and Sarkin, 2007). Peacebuilding processes are envisioned as pathways to shape Ex-Combatants and agencies of violence in local spheres. Nevertheless, this vision has occurred in South Sudan. "What is DDR?" the leader of armed cattle-keeping youth asked. They have collected our arms [referring to South Sudan's army], but they did not tell us who will protect our cattle" (P14/03/08/2017). Protecting your cattle from who, I asked. However, this participant stressed how the armed conflict had been a character in South Sudan, and state become consigned with a long-lasting absence of central authority, and that heightened the risks of political wars and inter-ethnic violence.

This emphasis introduces a twist that can account for the advent of informal power, use of force and security in post-war states, including South Sudan. Hence, the importance of qualitative enquiry in understanding the challenges of the DDR lies in the collaborative construction of meaning. This context enhances a "deeper understanding of the process of war and peacebuilding both among elites and different groups of the population" (Brounéus, 2011, p. 130). Brounéus claims "in-depth interviews can be applied inductively to produce new hypotheses or used deductively to examine whether a theory based on results from previous studies at the nationwide echelon is appropriate" (2011, p. 130). Primary data expose the researcher to the situation and help recognise "what theories within peace research have missed" (Brounéus, 2011, p. 131). It is not just raw information that matters, but how the researcher orders data into themes. The themes can be a unifying concept that help the researcher to characterise the group's pattern of behaviours and perceptions of the war in the state (Cherry, 2009).

Since there is a scarcity of data on the DDR in South Sudan except for the description in the CPA, the choice is to go through an inductive process to describe the participants' views, interpret ideas and theorise them requires an inductive approach. These approaches are labelled as positivism and post-positivism approaches. For this project to produce an inductive finding, [unpacking what happened], it employs interpretivist and critical approaches. Accurately elucidating the positivist approach is challenging, for there are infinite distinctions between settings in which it is applied. As a system of research, positivism observes that only "factual information" extracted through objective experimental methods is reliable (Collins, 2010). The analysis focuses on quantifiable and objective methods (Crowther *et al.*, 2008). Besides, positivism depends on measurable interpretations that lend themselves to numerical emphasis (Collins, 2010, p. 38). Because positivism is based on testable results, there is no little interaction between the researcher and the study object. The proliferation of arms needs to be assessed based on how areas of limited statehood are governed (Fortna, 2004; Mansfield and Snyder, 2002; 2005).

When attempting to build knowledge, empirical observation and interpretation of the relevant issues become a necessary procedure. Crowther and Lancaster, (2008) emphasise that the positivist approach embraces a "deductive" method, while "inductive" studies focus on the detailed account of conscious experience. The point of positivism is a researcher's concentration on facts, while inductive methods focus on the meaning interlaced with human interest. In Fearon and Laitin's (2003) study, they report the main results of a cross-states statistical analysis of factors that distinguish the countries that have descended into a civil war since 1945. In this approach, factors such as fear and exclusion are considered. This research is cautious about the interpretivism because it is not independent. Independence means "that you maintain minimal interaction with your research participants when carrying out your research" (Wilson, 2010, p. 10). The positivist research is built on "facts" that can be "observed and described" objectively (Levin, 1988).

Morgan and Olsen (2007, p. 107) argue that "objectivity is a bridge between the subjectivities of subjects and the rest of the real world". Objectivity is considered as the vital principle of "research, and it is best understood in relation to the concept of subjectivity since we often think that some sorts of claims are less objective than others"

(Miller, 2005, p. 751). A research object is put to experimental practice to transform into measurable facts, but facts are not always realistic in a civil war situation (Osuala, 2001). Webb emphasises a lack of precision in these experimental practices because human characters and motives are unpredictable. Webb argues that "no objective analysis of social reality can be made because life with its irrational reality and its store of possible meanings is inexhaustible" (Webb, 1995, p. 98; cited in Omosulu, 2013). In agreement with Webb's idea, the issues of conflict and resistance to the DDR in South Sudan are not static but interlaced with various economic and socio-political factors. With these factors, it is impossible to conduct an objective inquiry in South Sudan without an individual or group's subjective interpretation of both history and state fragility (Kuhn, 1970; Andersen, 1985; Remenyi and Williams, 1996).

3.5 The Interpretive Approach

The interpretive approach is based on the philosophical and human sciences (Bryman, 1988; Gephart, 1988). It does not explore what is, but it challenges existing literature about current post-war states (Morrow, 2005). Because the interpretive is based on the incorporation of participants' perceptions, as well the complexity of whole settings, its approaches are interlaced with critical processes "concerned with the issue of power relations within the society and interaction that contribute to a social system" (Asghar, 2013, p. 313). This exploratory questioning seeks human emancipation by explaining "what is wrong with current social reality" and providing both explicit norms for criticism and transformation (Horkheimer, 1982, p. 244). The obstacles confronting South Sudan are complex. This multiplicity of actors means that little is known about players, and their motives, both of which are important in the abundance of light weapons. Thus, the implementation of the DDR in this context is hindered by the lack of state capacity to enforce central decisions (Risse, 2013). Here, the exploratory nature of the critical approach makes it open in the sense that it embraces constructive possibilities and empirical techniques (Richards, 2003). In contrast, this thesis will approach South Sudan as full of different systems founded on moral-psychological assumptions. In this sense, participants' reactions to research questions were "context-dependent and value-laden" (Kim, 2007, p. 369; 2003; Merriam, 2009).

3.6 Case Study as Research Design

Despite its ubiquitous use in academic inquiries, there is a lack of clarity surrounding the case study approach (Tellis, 1997). George and Bennett (2005, p. 6) contradict this sentence, arguing that "scholars have formalised case study methods more completely and linked them to underlying arguments in the philosophy of science". Case studies allow researchers to "describe a phenomenon using a variety of data sources" (Baxter and Jack, 2008, p. 544). Hence, case study situates the researcher in a world of objects of research. In the context of South Sudan, it is foreseeable that groups cannot settle their grievances through the barrel of the gun.

This argument was a key pillar of both CPA and post-secession DDR in South Sudan; to reduce the incentives to possess and use small arms. To understand how those arms fuelled the conflict, we need stories from stakeholders involved. Hence, a case study will help this project to explain how or why groups use their arms. This approach is essential in explaining the challenges of the DDR in South Sudan because it will illustrate what this project has found, and not just an explanation of what has happened (Miles and Huberman, 1994; 1984). Thus, South Sudan's politics of DDR is the unit of inquiry. Gerring (2007, p. 19; 2004; 2006) refers to the case study as "a spatially delimited phenomenon observed at a single point in time". Moreover, the case study is "an empirical inquiry that investigates a contemporary phenomenon within its real-life context; when the boundaries between phenomenon and context are not evident; and in which multiple sources of evidence are used" (Gerring 2007; citing Yin, 1984, p. 23). Yin argues that "case studies examine the operation of causal mechanisms in individual cases in detail" (2005, p. 21).

This approach implies that if the researcher is interested in exploring the armed group's stance, then a holistic approach would allow exploration of the case while studying the impact of the different political dimensions and related behaviours on ethnic decision-making. This approach to the case under investigation associated with numerous comparisons. Researchers could explore the differences between ethnic violence in South Sudan and Kenya, for example, with the hope of identifying the influence of the political context on the subject of the research. Most studies on similar topics are presented as comparatively. Thus, the application of multiple case studies "predicts similar results or predicts contrasting results but for predictable reasons" (Yin, 2003, p. 47). This project is a single case with embedded units because it explores South Sudan's socio-political decision-making as the central unit and assesses the impact of violent actors' interaction as sub-units. The research is designed in this manner to include the emerging centres of power outside the state domain. With these actors in the play, the use of force became an effort to address a hitch of alterity limited to the situation in which the calamity of war manifests (Mouton, 2010).

3.7 Data Collection Methods (Qualitative Interviewing)

Qualitative data collection can be time-consuming and expensive (Altshuld and Witkin, 2000; Kidder and Fine, 1987). Given that this research seeks to answer what and how questions as previously stated, it is crucial that the information/data collected will respond to the research questions and matching the context of analysis. Hence, interviews will be approached holistically to unpack the lived experiences of participants. Most of us have been interviewed for jobs. The routine questioning implies that our world has been the interview (Altshuld and Witkin, 2000). Most job interviews are qualitative, where two people engaged, with one person asking questions (Qu and Dumay, 2011). Depending on the topic, the interview can differ in its approach, from the confidential probing of the individual issue to the publicity-oriented interviewing of celebrities, to the aggressive questioning of political leaders (Mason, 2002).

As this project is academic research, it needs to move from the routinely imagined sense of the interview, like a job interview into its application as a practical tool. This idea reflects the theory of "communicative action" based firmly on the link to "identity and community" (Jones, 2001, p. 168). Informed by this argument, Cox and Sinclair (2002) proposed a leap beyond "inter-state relations' into a world order". Cox and Sinclair's (2002) argument seeks to avoid 'the state-centrism of the discipline' by not emphasising the significance of internal features shaping their outer reaction and behaviour. Thus, qualitative interviews applied the context of the domestic issues: a notion that raised questions regarding who the specific players are in a qualitative interview (Mason, 2002). I mentioned earlier that the interview participants would include public officials and NGO staff. These players will contribute to an understanding of elements of the study and their impact on the conditions that influence people's reactions and actions in South Sudan.

3.8 Advantages of Qualitative Interviewing

The personal, historical, and secretive phenomenon can be difficult or impossible to investigate through observation, and that makes asking participants the only viable method of finding information on the issue. That does not mean the viewpoint provided through interviews address all the questions. The participant can be deliberate in their choice of words, and leave things unsaid or ambiguous. Yet, viewpoints are significant as they come from people with a great experience of the phenomenon. To access/reach what (Habermas, 1984) describes as an ideal speech situation requires asking questions and examining the conditions facing various armed contenders (Jok, 2015). A theme that arises from this emphasis is the degree to which participants and researchers produce knowledge as opposed to quantitative finding. Interviewing South Sudanese people can provide extensive knowledge of the violent factionalism that affected the DDR by excavating the conflictual trends buried in community perceptions (Kymlicka, 1995a; 1995b).

It is not practical to carry out an observation about something which is highly vested with feelings without asking questions and getting answers from those with lived and varied experience. It is essential to seek understanding about what an individual or group is feeling about a specific issue and situate that feeling into current contexts. This project used the interview as a mechanism for obtaining people's feelings about their experience. Expressed experiences allow researchers to view phenomena through the prism of participants' environment and describe the meanings in the lifeworld of the subjects (Kvale, 1996). Such a strategy is captured in Smith's (1999) thesis on Indigenous knowledge, where she highlighted her desire to produce scholarship in line with the interests and wishes of those communities. Asking questions about increased violence in South Sudan, for instance, will contribute to an appreciation of the multitudes of problems connected to the entrenched causes of the conflict to facilitate deconstruction of taken-for-granted realities. In this research, local South Sudanese respondents will be drawn from diverse settings to establish the conditions inherent to conflict and the actors' substantive grievances.

3.9 Disadvantages of Qualitative Interviewing

The interviews facilitate what Geertz (1973a, p. 454; also, 1973b; 1967) calls thick description, meaning, "paying attention to contextual detail in observing and interpreting social meaning when conducting qualitative research". However, listening and hearing the meanings shaped by words can be prejudicial; hence, criticised for subjectivity (Patton, 1987; 1990; Powney and Watts, 1987). Critics see the interview data as untrustworthy, imprecise, and bias (Mishler, 1991). In comparison to casual discourses, that often situated the interviewees on a similar path, "interview can be described as an asymmetry of power in which the interviewer is in charge of questioning an interviewee" (Denzin and Lincoln, 2000, p. 12). Despite this view, Beckker (1970, p. 30) pointed to "incompleteness of interview data" when compared to the data obtained through observation. Furthermore, Scheurich, (1995, p. 260), also argues that "what occurs in a specific interview is contingent on the specifics of individuals, place, and time".

Mishler stated that the "relationship between language and meaning is contextually grounded, ambiguous, and subject to endless reinterpretation" (Mishler, 1991, p. 260). While it may seem that the nature of our daily life is an interview, quantitative researchers argue that qualitative interviews are conducted casually with little preparation (Hannabuss, 1996). Some critics argue that it is never easy to understand another person's motives unless we can understand their "stream of consciousness and subjective understanding and experience what they experience" (Schultz, 1967, p. 11). These critics attack the wisdom associated with knowledge gained through the interviews (Qu and Dumay, 2011, p. 239). As I study the motivations for war, proliferation arms and behaviours of violent groups, it is beneficial to use sampling procedures techniques to reach hard-to-reach stakeholders in South Sudan's violent politics. The aim is to conduct qualitative interviews and focus on the contexts to explain the significant challenges brought by such violence towards the DDR (Hooks, 1989; Walsham, 1993; 1995).

3.10 Sampling Procedures

Sampling enables researchers to acquire representative or appropriate units from the population under study, for example, senior members of South Sudan's government and armed groups (Field, 2005). The units selected for participation provide information about, or representative of, the population under investigation (Rubinstein, 1990). However, sampling indicates the "selection of subjects in research that has as its goal the understanding of individuals' naturalistic perceptions of self, society, and the environment" (Luborsky, 1995, p. 89; citing Williams, 1984, p. 175). The meaning of what is being studied "is defined as the process of reference and connotation, undertaken by individuals, to evoke key symbols, values, and ideas that shape, make coherent, and inform experience" (Luborsky, 1995, p. 89). This thesis understands decisions surrounding the sampling technique as crucial for gaining information about violent negotiation of power in order to gauge the effects of such interaction on security governance and security reform.

I also note the importance of remaining mindful about essential questions regarding what type of sampling is appropriate and how a sample is selected from the entire population under investigation. It is also essential to ask how the resulting sample information will be analysed, and whether the findings will provide statements applicable to the whole population. The conventional sampling methods are probability and non-probability. In probability, all the aggregates (members of the population under study) have an equal opportunity of inclusion in the research sample, whereas, in non-probability, the item of the sample is selected deliberately, also known as purposive sampling (Suri, 2011). As a qualitative assignment, this study does not aim to produce statistically generalisable knowledge (Glasser and Strauss, 1967). It seeks to explore the problems of South Sudan by sampling a subset of the units from different armed actors. Thus, the sampling was purposively based on character and information applicable to the context and practical difficulties of the DDR. Patton emphasises that "the logic and power of purposeful sampling lie in selecting information-rich cases for study in-depth" (Patton, 2002, p. 230).

Because this in-depth formation is obtained from a segment of the people in the country in question, I utilise snowball sampling, where participants are referred by other participants, to identify information-rich interviewees (Atkinson *et al.*, 2001). This method offers critical benefits for researchers who seek to access hard-to-reach and hidden populations (Noblit *et al.*, 1988; Sudman, 1985; Goodman and Smyth, 2011). In South Sudan, getting well-informed participants involved referral. This chain-link referral is where ethical issues arise. There is often an argument that a 'bond' or 'link' between the first sample and a would-be the next research sample in the same target aggregate allows a series of referrals that could lead to skewed data because if participants are referring participants, they may have a similar point of view politically or otherwise (Berg, 2004; Hendricks and Singhal, 2005). I believe there is a risk that could emanate from hearing similar views, but this project addresses that concern. First, I am a South Sudanese; hence, I also had first insight about the issues. Second, participants were mostly public officials, recruited through formal procedures, such as an introduction letter, and I met them in person, via scheduled appointments at agreed venues and times to facilitate confidentiality.

3.11 The Responsibility of the Interviewer/Researcher and Limitations

The responsibility of the researcher is distinctive because it is defined. In effect, the researcher conducts a diligent search of what is, or what has been, with the aim of the discovery and interpretation of facts behind the issue (Webster, 1985). The quest for discovery warrants the deployment of the human instrument, instead of scientific analysis. Thus, my first task is to facilitate the research by defining the research objectives and informing participants of their role. Conducting a qualitative study is challenging in any situation but can be extremely dangerous in violent environments, necessitating careful risk assessment and mitigation strategies (Goldstein, 2014). Research situations prone to violence place researchers in a state of constant vigilance to threats to their safety and that of interviewees (Bloor et al., 2007; Marwick et al., 2016). As a result, I expected to encounter some difficulties during this research.

While some hazards are blatant, such as violent robbery, others may include more subtle things like "being in the wrong place at the wrong time, asking the wrong question of the wrong person" (Goldstein, 2014, p.1). In this case, extreme caution is essential, not only when the researcher is in the field, but also when he goes about his daily life. On top of this, I face extreme difficulty due to my citizenship. As a South Sudanese citizen, I was assigned socio-political identification by default. As a member of the Dinka ethnic majority accused of different atrocities, there was a risk of misrepresentation in the part of some people, and that adversely affect neutrality, and perhaps the reputation of the thesis. Some did not regard as an independent observer; hence, my requests to seek information was ignored in some instances. This mean thesis might not be free from "any biases, assumptions, expectations, and experiences" (Greenbank, 2003, p. 797). This is because researchers are expected to remain neutral and to gain the trust of participants. That, however, will be difficult in this case.

First, I will not be detached from a subjective appeal in term of the research, as well as because I am a part of a specific identity group among the warring South Sudanese (Bonner *et al.*, 2002). It will be hard to avoid biases due to my identity. Bias, according to the Oxford Dictionary 2019) is "an inclination or prejudice for or against one person or group, especially in a way considered to be unfair". Hence, bias is a systematic distortion of statistical results due to a factor not allowed for in their derivation. This condition is common when dealing with the chest-thumping groups who may want to deride others as a problem. It is not only subjective stances that are inevitable but also the interaction with a socio-politically divided society. I may be accused of cherry-picking the sampling as well as being prejudiced because I come from a defined ethnic group and am an obstinate critic of the situation in South Sudan. How did I overcome this bias; some may ask? To minimise both political and cultural bias, I adopted careful sampling by showing a positive attitude to participants of the different ethno-political groups and being cognizant of their own political and security assumptions (Groger and Mayberry, 1999).

Complete socio-political sensitivity, in a violent, divided state like South Sudan, is never 100 per cent achievable, but it reduces biases. The aim of reducing bias is not to make everyone consulted the same, but to make sure that questions are posed considerately, and the information obtained is analysed in a way that reflects participants emphasis or feelings without researcher-inferred distortion. Another factor that influenced the ability to conduct this research was due to the war in South Sudan. As such, Deakin University's Human Research Ethics Committee (DUHREC) deemed the country inaccessible as per the Australian Department of Foreign Affairs and Trade travel warning that places South Sudan on their 'do not travel' list. This restriction forced me to conduct the research in neighbouring Kenya, which presented its own challenges. While the security situation in Kenya was less risky than that of South Sudan, it is not free from danger, particularly in the regions bordering South Sudan.

Insecurity due to terrorist attacks in Kenya resulted in uncertainty and negatively impacted on my movements and interactions with different institutions. These clouds of insecurity confined me to Nairobi for over six months. Despite my inability to research South Sudan, I was nonetheless, able to interview thirty-seven participants from various backgrounds. Majority of the participant were South Sudanese, diplomats, and humanitarian leaders. My interaction with government thinks-tanks and academic researchers across different fields of politics and security studies added a valuable network that continued to funnel information into the research. Throughout the fieldwork, foreign missions and United Nations agencies consulted with me on the shifting political violence befalling South Sudan. These conversions shaped the information about armed actors reported, thus adding a deeper contextual understanding of security complexities and how its subjective operationalisation hampered the DDR. It became apparent that South Sudan is short of public organisation, and its security system is no more effective than other parts of the public sector.

3.12 Data Examination and Analysis

Qualitative data come in different shape and formats. In this thesis, data consist of interview transcripts (primary) and academic literature and secondary data. The question that follows is what to do with this data and how do we learn from the data. Thus, 'uncovering' meanings requires analysis of "how data were sorted, arranged, conceptualised and interpreted" (Thorne, 2000, p. 69). Most studies on South Sudan has applied constant comparative analysis, which emerged "out of the sociological theory of symbolic interactionism" (Glaser and Strauss, 1967; citing Blumer, 1969, p. 72). As Patton, (2015; p. 521; 2002 argued, "qualitative analysis transforms data into findings, but no formula exists for that transformation". The context of the information can offer direction, but each researcher knows the destination. This presents the importance of "qualitative analytic reasoning procedures" where researchers apply inductive reasoning to interpreting and construct the meanings of the data (Mayring, 2000). Qualitative analytic reasoning avoids reflexive interpretations but reads the text to construct meaning (Crabtree and Miller, 1999).

This thesis explores challenges to the DDR by constructing the meaning through an in-depth study of data without pre-set notions. The data analysis begins during the interviews, through the identification of problems and the organisation of the data into concepts (Miles and Huberman, 1984). Examination of the field notes has the benefit of letting the researcher improve the research by turning written data into the findings. There are no universal formulas with which to examine qualitative data (Altheide and Schneider, 2012). The first phase of data analysis started when a researcher questions and recorded the conversation. It is in this stage where the researcher could decide what to record, and what to discard. This analysis depends on the methodology of the research. In this case, this research will use the case study as a paradigm of analysis because of its proximity to the emphasis on the importance of personal view and interpretation (Strauss and Corbin, 1990). This concentration on the objects of direct experience is "treated as pure phenomena and represented as absolute data from where to begin" (Eagleton, 1983).

The purpose of applying phenomenology is "the return to the concrete", captured through the experience of researched actors (Moustakas, 1994). Capturing the experience of researched actors is useful in indicating the presence of factors and their effects on the multilayered case study. In this case, inductively coding the data will help identify critical thematic areas that link to the research questions (Bogdan and Biklen, 1982). The research questions frame the case study and determine what is in scope, but the findings are analysed inductively because a large section of the research is based on theories addressing formulation. Additionally, this project benefited from some level of deductive analysis in the initial phases of the research to explain the history of the crisis in South Sudan. By revisiting the history of violence in South Sudan, the researcher of this thesis cannot help but be struck by the seemingly symbiotic link between the spreading of arms and violent actors, and the long-term deficiency of the centralised security system. Behind every fragmented state stood an array of disgruntle and repealing identities. Access to such groups, to inquire about their course for violence proved crucial to understanding the contradiction between armed groups and centralising policies.

3.13 Conclusion

In South Sudan's system of violent fragmentation have arrogated the functions of state institutions, including forming large armies, and they have stoked the violent proliferation of arms. Amid the chaos of or unstable public authority, the competing elites and armed actors vandalised the state monopoly of violence. These contesting authorities have distorted the state's institutions, with catastrophic consequences on the national security creating an atmosphere in which too many groups are left to reach for arms with impunity. As public security remains absent, and the rule of law is undermined by OAGs, these problems require me to demonstrate genuine "respect for and curiosity about what people say, and a systematic effort to hear and understand what people tell" (Rubin and Rubin, 2004, p. 17). This chapter has introduced the research model, including the qualitative paradigm, case study and thematic data analysis.

Additionally, this chapter discussed notions of rigour, ethics, and researcher positionality. This chapter defines qualitative research in the context of the quote attributed to Cameron that "not everything that can be counted counts and not everything that counts can be counted" (Cullis, 2017, p. 506; citing Cameron, 1963). This quote suggests that some important ideas and information cannot be collected and reported through quantitative methods. For instance, a deep and complex question about how identity influences violence cannot be fully explored through numbers and statistics alone. A qualitative approach provides a unique contribution to research through meticulous and extensively accepted/recognised techniques for research design, selection of participants, data collection and analysis. These techniques could help to unravel the complexities of South Sudan and unpacking what already occurred and their impact on the DDR. In order to analyse the data collected, and transform it into research findings, the next chapter of this project will approach South Sudan based on the notion of limited/fragile statehood and assess its security and socio-political implications on the fragmented post-war political order.

This approach is expected to contextualise the "why and what" of this research project as presented at a theoretical level and ascertain pivotal understandings of the challenges encountered by the post-war intervention programmes. While South Sudan lacks a consolidated statehood, the challenge facing the DDR lies with the behaviours of the ethno-political identities. As such, determining the reason why armed groups resisted the DDR requires moving beyond the argument of the state fragility. Hence, in this situation, post-secession South Sudan lacked a practical domestic dimension of sovereignty or the state capacity to enforce central decisions. This challenge referred to the absence of the organisation of public authority within a post-war state. In volume two of this book, the study applies conceptualisation of political instability: defining South Sudan as a country where activities and pattern of violent behaviour change the political system of the nascent state into a chaotic scene of violent competition among factions.

References

All the interviewees are cited anonymously throughout this project. This application of anonymity is in line with the requirements of this project's ethic approval. I was born and raised in the Republic of South Sudan. Hence, I have both ethnic and political labels. I am also aware of the political and security sensitivity of the information collected during the field trip. The majority of interviews were conducted in Nairobi, Kenya, where I was confined due to the travelling restriction. Therefore, the anonymous nature of research allowed me to cite all the participants as P1 or P2, for instance, to protect their anonymity. All interviews were conducted by the author.

1.   A senior member of the ruling SPLM/A, (P3a/08/07/2017)

2.   A senior member of the ruling SPLM/A, (P3b/08/07/2017)

3.   A senior member of the ruling SPLM/A, (P3c/08/07/2017)

4.   A senior member of the ruling SPLM/A, (P3d/20/07/2017)

5.   A senior member of the United Nations in South Sudan, (P21/17/11/2017)

6.   A Senior SPLA Military Official, (P33/03/01/2018)

7.   Confidential document on the SPLA's Arms Shipment (P27/12/09/2017)

8.   Confidential insight about the SPLA's behaviour toward the DDR, (P20/13/09/2017)

9.   Discussion with senior with international advisers (P19/11/09/2017)

10.   Discussions with former IGAD official and international adviser (P26/08/11/2017)

11. Discussions with international advisers on South Sudan DDR (P19/17/11/2017)

12. Ex-SPLA General, (P26/23/10/2017)

13. High-Ranking Rebel General, (P5/04/08/2017)

14. High-ranking officer of the SPLA-in opposition, (P30/21/12/2018)

15. Informal, but confidential discussion with senior U.N. SSR adviser, (P23/21/11/2017)

16. Interview with a confidential source (P17/21/09/2017)

17. Interview with a confidential source (P26/14/09/2017)

18. Interview with a confidential source (P4/22/07/2017)

19. Interview with a confidential source, [Senior UN SSR adviser] (P26/23/10/2017)

20. Interview with confidential source [Academic] (P17/04/09/2017)

21. Interview with confidential source [One of the senior rebel generals] (P17/10/01/2018)

22. Leader of a local NGO, (P16/03/08/2017)

23. Leader of a rebel faction, (P21/21/07/2017)

24. Member of foreign mission, (P27/21/12/2017)

25. Member of South Sudanese Informal Army, (P16/19/09/2017)

26. Member of the Dinka Informal Armed Youth, (P23/21/09/2017)

27. Member of the Dinka Informal Armed Youth, (P26b/23/09/2017)

28.   Member of the foreign mission, (P12/04/09/2017)

29.   Member of the foreign mission, (P17/04/09/2017)

30.   Member of the foreign mission, (P17a: /14/09/2017)

31.   Member of the Nuer Informal Armed Youth, (P19/28/09/2017)

32.   Member of the Nuer Informal Armed Youth, (P26a/23/09/2017)

33.   Member of the SPLA ex-intelligence community, (P23b/12/2017)

34.   Political/military leader (P14/03/08/2017)

35.   Senior Clergy of South Sudanese Anglican Church, (P2b/07/07/2017)

36.   South Sudan's Government Official, (P6/24/08/2017)

37.   South Sudanese's expert, (P1/19/06/2017)

38.   South Sudanese's Member of Parliament Security Committee, (P17b/21/09/2017)

39.   South Sudanese's Political Leader (P26a/14/09/2017)

40.   The United Nation Member of Peacebuilding, (P19/17/11/2017)

41.   Youth leader and activist (P2a/07/07/2017)

Abbott, A. (2001) *Chaos of Disciplines'*, Chicago: University of Chicago Press.

Abbott, A. (2004) Methods of Discovery: Heuristics for the Social Sciences', In: W. Norton. Aiken, Scott, F., and Robert B Talisse, (Ed.), Pragmatism and pluralism, (pp. 17–26). *Revisited Political Studies Review*,

New York.

Abdel Salam, A.H. and De Waal, A. (2001) *The Phoenix State: Civil Society and the Future of Sudan'*, Asmara: Justice Africa and the Committee of the Civil Project', Lawrenceville NJ: Red Sea Press.

Abrahamsen, R. (2001) *Development Policy and the Democratic Peace in Sub-Saharan Africa'*, Conflict, Security and Development, Vol. 1, No. 3, pp. 79-103.

Abrams, P. (1988) Notes on the Difficulty of Studying the State', *Journal of Historical Sociology*, Vol. 1, No.1, pp. 58–89.

Acemoglu, D. and Robinson, J.A. (2012) *Why Nations Fail: The Origins of Power, Prosperity, and Poverty'*, Crown Business, New York.

Acemoglu, D. *et al.* (2001) The Colonial Origins of Comparative Development: An Empirical Investigation', *American Economic Review*, Vol 91, pp. 1369-1401.

Adams, K.R. (2000) *State Survival and State Death: International and Technological Contexts'*, PhD dissertation, University of California, Berkeley.

Addai-Sebo, A. (2011) How the U.N. Failed Côte d'Ivoire', New African, No. 503, pp. 16–19.

Addison, T. and Murshed, S.M. (2002) Credibility and Reputation in Peacemaking', *Journal of Peace Research*, Vol. 39, No. 4, pp. 487–501.

Adeba, B. (2015) *Making Sense of the White Army's Return in South Sudan'*, CSG Paper No. 1, Centre for Security Governance.

Adeba, B. (2019) A Hijacked State: Violent Kleptocracy in South Sudan', *The Enough Project*, https://enoughproject.org/reports/a-hijacked-state, [Accessed: 29/03/2019].

Adedokun, A. (2019) Transition from Civil War to Peace: The Role of the United Nations and International Community in Mozambique', *Peace and Conflict Studies*, Vol. 26, No.1, pp.2-25.

Adekanye, J.B. (1995) *Structural Adjustment, Democratisation and Rising Ethnic Tensions in Africa'*, Development and Change, Vol. 26, No. 2, pp. 355–74.

Aeberli, A. (2012) Decentralisation Hybridised', The Graduate Institute', *Graduate Institute ePapers*, Geneva, https://repository.graduateinstitute.ch/record/13629 [Accessed: 23/12/2019].

Afisi, O. T. (2009) Tracing Contemporary Africa's Conflict Situation to Colonialism: A breakdown of Communication among Natives', *Academic Journals, Philosophy Papers and Reviews*, Vol.1, No. 4, pp. 59–66.

Afolabi, B.T. (2009) *Peacemaking in the ECOWAS Region: Challenges and Prospects'*, In Conflict Trends. Durban: Accord, Vol. 2, p. 24.

Ahmed, E. (2009) *The Comprehensive Peace Agreement and the Dynamics of Post-Conflict Political Partnership in Sudan'*, Africa Spectrum, Vol.44, No. 3, pp.133-147.

Ake, C. (1993) *The Unique Case of African Democracy'*, International Affairs, Vol. 69, No, 2, pp. 239-244.

Albin, C. (2001) *Justice and Fairness in International Negotiation'*, Cambridge University Press, Cambridge.

Albrecht, P. (2015) *Building on what Works: Local Actors and Service Delivery in Fragile Situations'*, In: P. Jackson (Ed.). Handbook of International Security and Development, pp. 279-93. Danish Institute for International Studies, DIIS, Copenhagen.

Albrecht, P. and Buur, L. (2009) *An Uneasy Marriage: Non-State Actors and Police Reform'*, Policing and Society, Vol. 19, No. 4, pp. 390–405.

Alden, C., Thakur, M., and Arnold, M., (2011) *Militias and the Challenges of Post-Conflict Peace: Silencing the Guns'*, London: Zed Books

Alesina, A., Özler, S., Roubini, N. and Swagel, P. (1996) Political Instability and Economic Growth', *Journal of Economic Growth*, Vol. 1, pp. 189-211.

Alexander, J. (2006) *The Unsettled Land: State-making and the Politics of Land in Zimbabwe 1893-2003'*, Oxford: James Currey.

Ali, A. and Albadawi, I. (2002) Explaining Sudan's Economic Growth Performance', *AERC Collaborative Research Project on Explaining Africa's Growth Performance*, https://media.africaportal.org/documents/Sudan.pdf.

Ali, M. (2011) *Gender and State-building in South Sudan'*, Special Report, Washington: United States Institute for Peace.

Alier, A. (1990) *South Sudan: Too Many Agreements Dishonoured'*, Ithaca Press, Exeter, UK.

Alkire, S. (2004) *A Vital Core that must be Treated with the Same Gravitas as Traditional Security Threats, Security Dialogue'*, Vol. 35, No. 3, pp. 359-360.

AllAfrica.com, (2011) *Sudan: Joint Donors warn South government over Corruption'*, http://allafrica.com/stories/201104130175 html [Accessed 26/07/2018].

Allen, T. and Vlassenroot, K. (2010) Introduction: in Allen, Tim and Vlassenroot, Koen (Eds.), *The Lord's Resistance Army: Myth and Reality'*, London: Zed Books, London, UK.

Altbach, P. and Knight, J. (2007) The Internationalisation of Higher Education: Motivations and Realities', *Journal of Studies in International Education*, Vol.11, No.3/4, pp. 290-305.

Altheide, D.L. and Schneider, C. (2012) *Qualitative Media Analysis'*, 2nd (Ed.), Thousand Oaks, CA: Sage.

Altschuld, J.W. AND Witkin, B. R. (2000) *From Needs Assessment to Action'*, Thousand Oaks, CA: Sage.

Alusala, N., Gasana, J-M., Lamb, G. and Francis, G. (2012) *Rumours of peace, Whispers of War: Assessment of the reintegration of Ex-combatants into Civilian Life in North Kivu, South Kivu and Ituri Democratic Republic of Congo'*, Washington, DC: World Bank.

Andersen, L. (2011) *SSR and the Dilemmas of Liberal Peacebuilding'*, DIIS Working Paper, No. 31. Copenhagen: Danish Institute for International Studies.

Anderson, B. (1983) *Imagined Communities: Reflections on Origin and Spread of Nationalism'*, London: Verso.

Anderson, D.M. (2002) *Vigilantes, Violence and the Politics of Public Order in Kenya'*, African Affairs, Vol. 101, No.405, pp. 531-55.

Anderson, D.M. and Rolandsen, Ø. H. (2014) Violence as Politics in Eastern Africa, 1940–1990: Legacy, Agency, Contingency', *Journal of Eastern African Studies*, Vol. 8, No. 4, pp. 539–557.

Andeweg, R.B. (2000) Consociational Democracy', *Annual Review of Political Science*, Vol. 3, pp. 509–36.

Andreski, S. (1968) *The African Predicament: A study in the Pathology of Modernisation'*, Atherton Press, New York, pp. 108-9.

Andrews *et al.* (2008) *Doing Narrative Research'*, London: Sage.

Andrews, M. (2007) *Exploring Cross-cultural Boundaries'*, In D. Jean Clandinin (Ed.), Handbook of Narrative Inquiry: Mapping a Methodology (pp. 489-511). Thousand Oaks, CA: Sage.

Andrews, M., Pritchett, L. and Woolcock, M. (2012) *Escaping Capability Traps Through Problem-Driven Iterative Adaptation* (PDIA)', UNU-WIDER Working Paper.

Annan, K. (1999) *Preventing War and Disaster: A Growing Global Challenge'*, Annual Report on the work of the Organisation, (A/54/1, United Nations.

Annan, K. (2000) *The Question of Intervention: Statements by the Secretary-General'*, New York: United Nations Publications, We the Peoples: The Role of the United Nations in the 21st Century (A/54).

Annan, K. (2006) *Towards a New Definition of Sovereignty'*, In G.M. Reichberg, H. Syse, & E. Begby (ed.), The Ethics of War, (pp. 683-693). Malden, MA: Blackwell Publishing

Annan, K. (2014) Violent Conflicts and Civil Strife in West Africa: Causes, Challenges and Prospects, Stability', *International Journal of Security and Development*, Vol. 3, No. 1, pp. 1-16.

Ansorg, N. (2017) SSR in Africa: Donor Approaches versus Local Needs', *Contemporary Security Policy*, Vol. 38, No.1, pp. 129-144.

Ansorg, N. and Gordon, E. (2019) Co-operation, Contestation and Complexity in Post-Conflict SSR', *Journal of Intervention and Statebuilding*, Vol. 13, No.1, pp. 2-24.

Ansorg, N. and Strasheim, J. (2019) Veto Players in Post-Conflict DDR Programs: Evidence from Nepal and the DRC', *Journal of Intervention and Statebuilding*, Vol. 13, No, 1, pp. 112-130.

Anstee, M. J. (1996) *Orphan of the Cold War: The Inside Story of the Collapse of the Angolan Peace Process 1992–93*', London: Macmillan.

Antonioni, D. (1998) Relationship between the Big Five Personality Factors and Conflict management styles', *International Journal of Conflict Management*, Vol. 9, No.4, pp. 336-355.

Antrim, L.N., and Sebenius, J. K. (1992) *Formal Individual Mediation and the Negotiators' Dilemma: Tommy Koh at the Law of the Sea Conference*', Mediation in International Relations: Multiple Approaches to Conflict Management, (Eds), Jacob Bercovitch and Jeffrey Z. Rubin. New York: St. Martin's Press.

Arjona, A. (2009) Social Orders in Warring Times: Armed Groups' Strategies and Civilian Agency in Civil War', *Paper Presented at the Workshop Mobilisation for Political Violence*: What Do We Know? Oxford University Press.

Arjona, A. (2016) *Rebelocracy: Social order in the Colombian Civil War*', New York, New York: Cambridge University Press.

Arjona, A., Kasfir, N. and Mampilly, Z. (2015) *Rebel governance in Civil War*', New York: Cambridge University Press.

Arnold, M. (2007) The South Sudan Defence Force: Patriots, Collaborators or Spoilers? *Journal of Modern African Studies*, Vol 45, pp. 489–516.

Arnold, M. and Alden, C. (2007) This Gun is Our Food: Demilitarising the White Army militias of South Sudan', *Norwegian Institute of International Affairs,* (NUPI) Working Papers, Oslo.

Arnold, M. and LeRiche, M. (2008) *Allies and Defectors: An Update on Armed Group Integration and Proxy Force Activity*', Geneva: The Sudan

Human Security Baseline Assessment (HSBA).

Arrow, K. (1985) *The Economics of Agency'*, In: J. Pratt, R. Zeckhauser (Eds.), Principals and Agents: The Structure of Business, Harvard Business School Press, Boston.

Arthur, P. (2012) Reintegration and Reconstruction in Post-War South Sudan', *International Peace Support Training Centre.*

Arthy, S. (2003) *Ex-Combatant Reintegration: Key Issues for Policy Makers and Practitioners, Based on Lessons from Sierra Leone'*, Department for International Development, United Kingdom.

Asghar, J. (2013) Critical Paradigm: A Preamble for Novice Researchers', *Life Science Journal*, Vol.10, No. 4, pp. 3121-3127.

Assael, H. and Keon, J. (1992) Non-sampling Vs. Sampling Errors in Survey Research', *Journal of Marketing*, Vol. 46, No.2, pp. 114-123.

Assefa, H. (1999) *A Lack of Visionary Statesmanship and Democratic Leadership'*, In: Searching for Peace in Africa, Utrecht: European Platform on Conflict Prevention and Transformation.

Atkinson, P. and Coffey, A. (2003) *Revisiting the Relationship between Participant Observation and Interviewing'*, In Jaber F. Gubrium & James A. Holstein (Eds.), Postmodern is Interviewing, (pp. 109-122). Thousand Oaks, CA. Sage.

Atkinson, P. and Delamont, S. (2006) *Rescuing Narrative from Qualitative Research'*, Narrative Inquiry, Vol.16, No.1, pp. 164-172.

Atkinson, R. (2010) *The Realists in Juba?' An Analysis of the Juba Peace Talks'*, In A. Tim and K. Vlassenroot (eds.) The Lord's Resistance Army: Myth and Reality, (pp. 205-223). London: Zed Books.

Atkinson, R. and Flint, J. (2001) Accessing Hidden and Hard-to-reach

Populations: Snowball Research Strategies', *Social Research Update*, Vol. 33. Retrieved from http://sru.soc.surrey.ac.uk/SRU33pdf, [Accessed: 25/06/2019].

Auerbach, Y. (2009) *The Reconciliation Pyramid—A Narrative-Based Framework for Analysing Identity Conflicts'*, Political Psychology, Vol. 30, No. 2, pp. 291-318.

Awolich, A. (2014) *The Unwarranted Carnage in South Sudan'*, The Sudd Institute, Policy Brief, Juba.

Ayoob, M. (2007) State Making, State Breaking, and State Failure', In Crocker, C., F. Hampson, & P. Aall (eds.), *Leashing the Dogs of War – Conflict Management in a Divided World*, (pp. 95-114). Washington, DC: United States Institute of Peace Press.

Baas, S. (2012) *From Civilians to Soldiers and From Soldiers to Civilians: Mobilisation and Demobilisation in Sudan'*, Amsterdam University Press, Amsterdam.

Baaz, E. M. and Verweijen, J. (2013) *Between Integration and Disintegration: The Erratic Trajectory of the Congolese Army, Social Science Research Council: DR Congo Affinity Group'*, New York, USA: Social Science Research Council, Conflict Prevention and Peace Forum.

Babiker, M. and Ozerdem, A. (2003) A Future Disarmament, Demobilisation and Reintegration process in Sudan: Lessons learned from Ethiopia, Mozambique and Uganda', *Conflict, Security and Development*, Vol. 3, No. 2, pp. 211-232.

Badiey, N. (2013) The Strategic Institutionalisation of Land Tenure in State-building: The case of Juba, South Sudan', *Journal of the International African Institute*, Vol. 83, No. 1, pp. 57-77.

Baholzer, L. (2014) *When Do Disarmament, Demobilisation and Reintegration Programmes Succeed? Discussion Paper*', German Development Institute, No. 8, pp. 597-8. Deutsches Institut für Entwicklungspolitik (DIE), Bonn.

Bailey, P.H. and Tilley, S. (2002) Storytelling and The Interpretation of Meaning in Qualitative Research', *Journal of Advanced Nursing*, Vol. 38, No. 5, pp. 74-583.

Baker, B. (2008) *Multi-choice policing in Africa'*, Uppsala: Nordiska Afrikainstitutet.

Baker, B. and Scheye, B. (2007) *Multi-layered Justice and Security Delivery in Post-Conflict and Fragile States'*, Conflict, Security and Development, Vol. 7, No. 4, pp.503-528.

Baker, C.L. (2011) *South Sudan's enduring Secession Issues: is Peace Possible?* The Applied Anthropologist, Vol.31, No. 2, pp. 42-48.

Baldwin, D. (1997) The Concept of Security', *Review of International Studies*, Vol. 23, No. 1, pp. 5-26.

Ball, N. (1997) *Demobilising and Reintegrating Soldiers: Lessons from Africa'*, In Krishna Kumar, (Eds.). Rebuilding Societies after Civil War: Critical Roles for International Assistance, (pp. 85-105). Boulder: Lynne Rienner.

Ball, N. (2002) *The Reconstruction and Transformation of War-torn Societies and State Institutions: How can External Actors Contribute?* In: Debiel, T & Klein, A. (Eds). Fragile Peace: State Failure, Violence and Development in Crisis Regions', pp. 33-55. London: Zed Books in Association with the Development and Peace Foundation.

Ball, N. and Fayemi, K. (2004) *Security Sector Governance in Africa: A handbook'*, London: Centre for Democracy and Development (www.ssrnetwork.net/document_library/detail/3155/security-sector-governance-in-Africa-a-handbook).

Ball, N. and Goor, L. (2006) *Disarmament, Demobilisation and Reintegration: Mapping Issues, Dilemmas and Guiding Principles'*, Working Paper, August. The Hague: Netherlands Institute for International Relations (Clingendael) Conflict Research Unit.

Ball, N. and Hendrickson, D. (2006) *Trends in Security Sector Reform (SSR): Policy, Practice and Research'*, International Development Research Centre (IDRC), Ottowa.

Ball, N. and Van de Goor, L. (2013) *The Challenges of Supporting Effective Security and Justice Development Programming'*, Washington DC: Centre for International Policy.

Ballentine, K. and Nitzschke, H. (2005) *The Political Economy of Civil War and Conflict Transformation'*, Berghof Research Centre for Constructive Conflict Management, https://www.berghof-foundation.org/fileadmin/redaktion/Publications/Handbook/Dialogue_Chapters/dialogue3_ballentine_nitzschke.pdf. [Accessed: 06/09/2017].

Bankston, C.L, and Zhou, M. (2002) *Social Capital as a Process: The Meanings and Problems of a Theoretical Metaphor'*, Sociological Inquiry, Vol. 72, pp. 285-317.

Barash, D.P. and Webel, C.P (2014) *Peace and Conflict Studies'*, 3rd (Ed.), Thousand Oaks, CA. Sage

Barbier, E. B. *et al.* (2011) *The Value of Estuarine and Coastal Ecosystem Services'*, Ecology Monographs, Vol. 81, No. 2, pp. 169–193.

Barkan, J.D (1993) Kenya: Lessons from a Flawed Election', *Journal of Democracy*, Vol. 4, No. 3, pp. 85–99.

Barnett, M. and Zürcher, C. (2007) *The Peace Builders Contract: How External Intervention Reinforces Weak Statehood'*, Paper for the Research Partnership on Post-War Peacebuilding.

Barnett, M. *et al.* (2007) *Peacebuilding: What is in a Name?* Global Governance, No. 13, pp. 35-58.

Barnett, M. N. (2011) *Empire of Humanity: A History of Humanitarianism'*, Ithaca, N.Y. and London: Cornell University Press.

Barth, F. (1969) Introduction', In: F. Barth (Ed.), *Ethnic Groups and Boundaries: The Social Organisation of Cultural Difference'*, (pp. 9-38). Allen and Unwin, London.

Basedau, M. and Köllner, P. (2007) *Area Studies, Comparative Area Studies, and The Study of Politics: Context, Substance, and Methodological Challenges'*, Zeitschrift für Vergleichende Politikwissenschaft, Vol. 1, pp. 105–124.

Basedau, M. and Lay, J. (2009) Resource Curse or Rentier Peace? The Ambiguous Effects of Oil Wealth and Oil Dependence on Violent Conflict', *Journal of Peace Research*, Vol. 46, No. 6, pp. 757–776.

Bates, R.H. (1983) *Modernisation, Ethnic Competition and the Rationality of Politics in Contemporary Africa'*, In: D. Rothchild and V. A. Olorunsola (Eds.), State Versus Ethnic Claims: African Policy Dilemmas, (pp. 152–71). Boulder, Co.: Westview Press.

Baumann, M. and Kuemmerle, T. (2016) The Impacts of Warfare and Armed Conflict on Land systems', *Journal of Land Use Science*, Vol. 11, No. 6, pp. 672–688.

Baxter, P. and Jack, S. (2008) *Qualitative Case Study Methodology: Study Design and Implementation for Novice Researchers'*, The Qualitative Report, Vol. 13, No. 4, pp. 544-559.

Bayart, J.F. (1993) *The state in Africa: The Politics of The Belly'*, 2nd (Ed.). London: Longman.

Becker, H.S. (1970) *Sociology work: Method and Substance'*, New Brunswick, NJ: Transaction Books

Beckker, H.W. (1970) *Sociological Work'*, Chicago: Aldine.

Bell, C. and Pospisil, J. (2017) Navigating Inclusion in Transitions from Conflict: The Formalised Political Unsettlement', *Journal of International Development*, Vol. 29, No. 5, pp. 576-593.

Bell, C. and Watson, C. (2006) *DDR: Supporting Security and Development'*, The EU's Added Value, London: International Alert, http://www.international-alert.org/pdf/EU_DDR_Aug_2006.Pdf

Bellina, S., Darbon, D., Eriksen, S., and Sending, O.J. (2009) *The Legitimacy of the State in Fragile Situations'*, Organisation for Economic Cooperation and Development DAC; development and aid committee, Norwegian Agency for Development Cooperation, Oslo, Norway.

Benard, C., Jones, G., Oliker, O., Thurston, Q., Stearns, K., and Cordell, K. (2008) *Women and Nation-Building'*, Santa Monica, CA: RAND Corporation, at http://www.rand.org/pubs/monographs/2008/RAND_MG579.pdf [Accessed 14/04/2018].

Bennett, J. (2010) *Aiding Peace: A Multi-donor Evaluation of Support to Conflict Prevention and Peacebuilding Activities in Southern Sudan 2005–2010'*,

Brighton: ITAD.

Bennett, J., Pantuliano, S., Fenton, W., Vaux, A., and Brusset, E. (2010) *Aiding the Peace: A Multi-donor Evaluation of Support to Conflict Prevention and Peacebuilding Activities in Southern Sudan 2005—2010'*, Canadian International Development Agency (CIDA), Hove, East Sussex: ITAD. http://www.acdi-cida.gc.ca/acdi-cida/acdi-cida.nsf/eng.

Bercovitch, J. and DeRouen, K. (2005) *Managing Ethnic Civil Wars: Assessing the Determinants of Successful Mediation'*, Civil Wars, Vol.7, No. 1, pp. 98-116.

Bercovitch, J. and Gartner, S.S. (2006) *Is There Method in the Madness of Mediation? Some Lessons for Mediators from Quantitative Studies of Mediation'*, International Interactions, Vol. 32, No.4, pp. 329-354.

Berdal, M. (1996) *Disarmament and Demobilisation after Civil Wars: Arms, Soldiers, and the Termination of Conflict'*, Adelphi Paper No. 303. Oxford, UK: Oxford University Press.

Berdal, M. (2003) *How, New are New Wars? Global Economic Change and the Study of Civil Wars'*, in Global Governance, Vol.9, No.4, pp. 477-502.

Berdal, M. (2005) Beyond Greed and Grievance – and Not Too Soon', *Review of International Studies*, Vol. 31, No. 4, pp. 687-698.

Berdal, M. and Keen, D. (1997) *Violence and Economic Agendas in Civil Wars: Some Policy Implications'*, Millennium, Vol. 26, No. 3, pp. 795–818.

Berdal, M. and Malone, D. (2000) *Greed and Grievance: Economic Agendas in Civil Wars'*, Boulder, CO: Lynne Rienner.

Berdal, M. and Ucko, D.H. (2009) *Introduction: The Political Reintegration of Armed Groups after War'*, in Berdal and Ucko (Eds), Reintegrating

Armed Groups after Conflict: Politics, Violence and Transition. London:

Berg, B.L. (2004) *Qualitative Research Methods for the Social Sciences'*, Boston: Pearson.

Berger, P.L (ed.) (2010) *Between Relativism and Fundamentalism: Religious Resources for a Middle Position'*, Grand Rapids, Michigan: William B. Eerdmans Publishing Company.

Berlin, I. (2001) *Nationalism: Past Neglect and Present Power'*, In: Isaiah Berlin, Henry Hardy and Roger Hausheer (Eds.), Against the Current: Essays in the History of Ideas, (pp. 333-355). Princeton, NJ: Princeton University Press.

Berman, B. (1998) *Ethnicity, Patronage and the African State: The Politics of Uncivil Nationalism'*, African Affairs, Vol. 97, No. 388, pp. 305-341.

Beshir, M. O. (1968) *The Southern Sudan: Background to Conflict'*, New York: Praeger.

Beswick, S.F. (1991) *The Addis Ababa Agreement: 1972-1983 Harbinger of the Second Civil War in the Sudan'*, Northeast African Studies, Vol. 13, No. 2 & 3, pp. 191-215.

Beswick, S.F. (2004) *Sudan's Blood Memory: The Legacy of War, Ethnicity, and Slavery in South Sudan'*, University of Rochester Press.

Bhabba, H. (1994) *The Location of Culture'*, New York: Routledge.

Bickman, L. and Rog, D. (2009) *Applied Research Design: A Practical Approach'*, In: L. Bickman and D. Rog (Eds.), Handbook of Applied Social Research Methods, 2nd (Ed.), pp. 3-43. Thousand Oaks, CA: Sage.

Biel, M.R and Ojok, D. (2018) *IGAD, Political Settlements and*

Peacebuilding in South Sudan: Lessons from the 2018 Peace Negotiation Processes', Konrad-Adenauer-Stiftung report (KAS), https://www.kas.de/c/document_library/get_file?uuid=aa8118eb-f1b8-5845-b628-606fd3c17361&groupId=280229[Accessed: 20/08/2019].

Binder, I. (2013) *The Discourse of Ethnicity in Sociology of International Relation'*, History, Babeş-Bolyai, University of Cluj-Napoca, pp. 221-238.

Bindi, I.T. and Tufekci, O. (2018) Liberal Peacebuilding in Sierra Leone: A Critical Exploration', *Journal of Asian and African Studies*, No, 2-05, pp. 1-16.

Bior, K.B. (2018) *Evaluation of the implementation of the SA of the Agreement on the Conflict in South Sudan (ARCSS): Implications for the Security Sector Reforms'*, Policy Brief, The Sudd Institute, Juba. South Sudan.

Blanchard, L. P. (2016) *Conflict in South Sudan and the Challenges Ahead'*, Congressional Research Service, https://fas.org/sgp/crs/row/R43344.pdf.[Accessed: 26/09/17].

Bloor, M., Fincham, B. and Sampson, H. (2007) *Qualities (NCRM) Commissioned Inquiry into the Risk to Well-Being of Researchers in Qualitative Research'*, Cardiff ESRC National Centre for Research Methods, Cardiff University Wales.

Blumer, H. (1969) *Symbolic Interactionism: Perspective and Method'*, Berkeley: University of California Press.

Bochner, A.P. (2007) *Notes towards an ethics of memory in auto-ethnographic Inquiry'*, In: Norman K. Denzin & Michael D. Giardina (Eds.), Ethical futures in Qualitative Research, (pp.196-208). Walnut Creek, Ca: Left

Coast Press.

Boege, V., Brown, A. and Clements, K. (2008) *States Emerging from Hybrid Political Orders – Pacific Experiences Brisbane'*, The Australian Centre for Peace and Conflict Studies (ACPACS), Occasional Papers Series.

Boege, V., Brown, A., Clements, K., and Anna Nolan, A. (2009) *On Hybrid Political Orders and Emerging States: What is failing – States in the Global South or Research and Politics in the West?'* Berghof Handbook Dialogue Series, Vol. 8, pp. 15-35.

Boege, V., Brown, A., Clements, K., and Nolanet, A. (2009*) Building Peace and Political Community in Hybrid Political Orders'*, International Peacekeeping, Vol. 16, No. 5, pp.599-615.

Boege, V., Brown, A., Clements, K., and Nolanet, A. (2009a) *Undressing the Emperor: A Reply to our Discussants'*, In Martina Fischer & Beatrix Schmelzle (Eds), Building Peace in the Absence of States: Challenging the Discourse on State Failure, (pp. 15-31). Berlin: Berghof Research Centre.

Bogdan, R. C. and Biklen, S. K. (1982) *Qualitative research for education: An Introduction to Theory and Methods'*, Boston: Allyn & Bacon

Bohannan, P. (1963) *Social Anthropology'*, New York Holt, Rinehart and Winston.

Bohman, J. (2003) *How to Make a Social Science Practical: Critical Theory, Pragmatism, and Multiperspectival Theory'*, Millennium, Vol. 21, No. 3, pp. 499-524.

Boland, R.J. (1985*) Phenomenology: A Preferred Approach to Research in Information Systems'*, In: Research Methods in Information Systems, E.

Mumford, R. A. Hirschheim, G. Fitzgerald, and A. T. Wood-Harper (Eds.), (pp. 193-201). North-Holland, Amsterdam.

Boland, R.J. (1991) *Information System Use as a Hermeneutic Process'*, In: Information Systems Research: Contemporary Approaches and Emergent Traditions, H-E. Nissen, H. K. Klein, and R. A. Hirschheim (Eds.), (pp. 439-464). North-Holland, Amsterdam.

Bonner, G. *et al.* (2002) Trauma for all: A pilot study of the subjective experience of physical restraint for mental health inpatients and staff in the UK', *Journal of Psychiatric and Mental Health Nursing*, Vol. 9, pp. 465–473.

Booth, K. (1991) Security and Emancipation', *Review of International Studies*, Vol. 17, No. 4, pp. 313-326.

Borger, J. (2008) *War Crimes: General Consensus that Al-Bashir behind Genocide'*, https://www.theguardian.com/world/audio/2008/jul/15/borger.sudan:[Accessed: 30/04/2017].

Bossuroy, T. (2008) *Ethnicity as a Resource in Social Capital'*, Typescript, Paris School of Economics, DIAL.

Boswell, A. (2019) *Insecure Power and Violence: The Rise and Fall of Paul Malong and the Mathiang Anyoor'*, Geneva: Small Arms Survey, Briefing Paper, Graduate Institute of International Studies, pp.1-20. http://www.smallarmssurveysudan.org/fileadmin/docs/briefing-papers/HSBA-BP-Mathiang-Anyoor.pdf [accessed: 20/11/2019].

Boutros-Ghali, B. (1992) *An Agenda for Peace: Preventive Diplomacy, Peacemaking and Peace-Keeping'*, United Nations: New York.

Bozus, L. (2013) *Applying the Governance Concept to Areas of Limited*

Statehood: Implications for International Foreign and Security Policy', In Governance without a State? Policies and Politics in Areas of Limited Statehood, (Ed.), T. Risse, (pp. 262–280). New York: Columbia University Press.

Braathen, E., Bøås, M., and Saether, G. (2000) *Ethnicity Kills? The Politics of War, Peace and Ethnicity in Sub-Saharan Africa'*, McMillan Press Ltd.

Brady, M. (2016) *Neoliberalism, Governmental Assemblages, and the Ethnographic Imaginary'*, University of Toronto Press, Toronto, Canada.

Bragg, C. (2006) *Challenges to Policy and Practice in the Disarmament, Demobilisation, Reintegration and Rehabilitation of Youth Combatants in Liberia'*, Sussex Migration Working Paper', No. 29, pp.1-23.

Branch, A. and Mampilly, Z. (2004) Winning the War, But Losing the Peace? The dilemma of SPLM/A Civil Administration and the Tasks Ahead', *Journal of Modern African Studies*, Vol. 43, No. 1, pp. 1–20.

Brandt, P.T., Mason, D., Gurses, M., Petrovsky, N., and Radin, D. (2008) *When and How the Fighting Stops: Explaining the Duration and Outcome of Civil Wars'*, Defence and Peace Economics, Vol. 19, No. 6, pp. 415-434.

Brannen, J. (1992) *Mixing Methods: Qualitative and Quantitative Research'*, London: Routledge.

Brannen, J. (2017) *Mixing Methods: Qualitative and Quantitative Research'*, New York, N.Y.: Routledge.

Bratton, M. and Masunungure, E. (2008) Zimbabwe's Long Agony', *Journal of Democracy*, Vol. 19, No. 4, pp. 41-55.

Breidlid, I.M. and Arensen, M.J. (2014) *Demystifying the White Army: Nuer Armed Civilians involvement in the South Sudanese Crisis'*, Conflict

Trends, Vol. 3, pp.32–39.

Breitung, C., Paes, W., and van de Vondervoort, L. (2016) *In Need of a Critical Re-think: SSR in South Sudan*', BICC Working Paper, No. 6. https://www.bicc.de/publications/publicationpage/publication/in-need-of-a-critical-re-think-security-sector-reform-in-south-sudan-654/[Accessed: 20/03/2018].

Brethfeld, J. (2010) *Unrealistic Expectations: Current Challenges to Reintegration in Southern Sudan*', Small Arms Survey, Geneva: Graduate Institute of International and Development Studies, HSBA Working Paper, No. 21, pp. 4-45.

Brett, R. and Specht, I. (2004) *Young Soldiers: Why They Choose to Fight*', Boulder, CO: Lynne Rienner.

Brewer, C. (2010) *Disarmament in South Sudan*', Case study No. 7, Centre for Complex Operations, Washington, DC, National Defence University.

Brinkerhoff, D. W. (2005) *Accountability and Good Governance: Concepts and Issues*', International Development Governance, (Eds.), Ahmed Shafiqul Zafarullah and Habib Mohammad Huque. New York: CRC Press.

Britten, N. (1995) Qualitative Research: Qualitative Interviews in Medical Research', *British Medical Journal*, Vol. 3, No. 11, pp. 251-253.

Broch-Due, V. (2005) *Violence and belonging: Analytical Reflections*', In: V. Broch-Due (ed.), Violence and belonging: The Quest for Identity in Post-Colonial Africa (pp.1-40). London: Routledge.

Brosche, J. (2009) *Sharing Power-Enabling Peace? Evaluating Sudan's Comprehensive Peace Agreement 2005*', Uppsala: Uppsala University.

Brosche, J. (2014) *Masters of War: The Role of Elites in Sudan's Communal Conflicts'*, Uppsala: Uppsala University Press.

Brosche, J. and Höglund, K. (2016) Crisis of Governance in South Sudan: Electoral Politics in the World's Newest Nation', *Journal of Modern African Studies*, Vol. 54, No. 1, pp. 1–24.

Brosche, J. and Höglund, K. (2017) *Riek Machar: Warlord-Doctor in South Sudan'*, In Anders Themné, (Eds.), Warlord Democrats in Africa: Ex-military Leaders and Electoral Politics', (pp. 199-220). Nordic Africa Institute, Uppsala, Sweden.

Brown, J.A. (2014) *South Sudan's Slide into Conflict: Revisiting the Past and Reassessing Partnerships'*, Chatham House: The Royal Institute of International Affairs.

Brown, L.P. and Wycoff, M. A. (1987) *Policing Houston: Reducing Fear and Improving Service'*, Crime and Delinquency, Vol. 33, No. 1, pp. 71–89.

Brown, M.E. (1996) *The Causes and Regional Dimensions of Internal Conflict'*, In: Michael Brown, (Ed.), International Dimensional of Internal Conflict, pp. 571-602. Cambridge, MA: MIT Press.

Browning, C. S., (2018a) *Jesuis en terrase: Political Violence, Civilisational Politics, and the Everyday Courage to be'*, Political Psychology, Vol. 39, No. 2, pp. 243–226.

Brubaker, R. (2009) Ethnicity, Race and Nationalism', *Annual Review of Sociology*, Vol. 35, pp. 21-42.

Bryant, A. and Charmaz, K. (2007) *Grounded Theory Research: Methods and Practices'*, In: A. Bryant & K. Charmaz (Eds.), The Sage handbook of grounded theory (pp. 1-28). London, UK: Sage.

Bryden, A. and Hänggi, H. (2005) *Reforming and Reconstructing the Security Sector'*, In: Bryden, A., and Hänggi, H. (Eds.), Shaping a Security Governance Agenda in Post-Conflict Peacebuilding, (pp. 23-43). Geneva Centre for the Democratic Control of Armed Forces (DCAF).

Bryden, A. and Scherrer, V. (2012) *Disarmament, Demobilisation and Reintegration and SSR'*, Insights from U.N. Experience in Afghanistan, Burundi and the Democratic Republic of Congo', LIT Verlag Münster.

Bryden, M. (2014) *The Reinvention of Al-Shabaab'*, *Centre for Strategic and International Studies'*, https://www.csis.org/analysis/reinvention-al-shabaab[Accessed: 12/09/2016].

Bryman, A. (2004) *Social Research Methods,'* 2nd (Ed.), Oxford: Oxford University Press.

Bryman, A. (1988) *Quantity and Quality in Social Research'*, London: Allen & Unwin.

Bryman, A. (2001) *Social Research Method'*, Oxford: Oxford University Press.

Bryman, A. (2006b) Paradigm Peace and the Implications for Quality', *International Journal of Social Research Methodology*, Vol 9, pp. 111-126.

Burgess, S.F. (2008) *Fashioning Integrated Security Forces after Conflict'*, African Security, Vol.1, No. 2, pp. 69 – 91.

Bush, R.A. and Folger, J. P. (2005) *The Promise of Mediation. The Transformative Approach to Conflict'*, book San Francisco, CA: Jossey-Bass.

Butterfield, H. (1951) *History and Human Relations'*, London: Collins.

Buzan, B. (1981) *People, States and Fear: An Agenda for International Security*

Studies in the Post-Cold War Era', 1st (Ed) 1981, 2nd Edition. Hertfordshire: Harvester Wheatsheaf, 1991 and 2008 with a new preface from the author.

Buzan, B. (1991) *New Patterns of Global Security in the Twenty-First Century'*, International Affairs, Royal Institute of International Affairs 1944, Vol. 67, No 3, pp. 431-451.

Buzan, B. (1991) *People, States and Fear'*, Boulder, Colorado: Lynne Rienner Publishers.

Buzan, B. (1998) *Security, the State, the New World Order, and Beyond'*, On Security, (Ed.). Ronne D. Lipschutz. New York: Columbia University Press.

Buzan, B. (2006) *The War on Terrorism as the New Macro-Securitisation?* Oslo Workshop, pp. 1-25.

Byrne, A. (2009) *Experience and Content'*, The Philosophical Quarterly, Vol. 59, Issue 236, pp.429–451.

Cabestan, J. P. and Pavković, A. (2013*) Secessionism and Separatism in Europe and Asia: To have a State of One's Own'*, New York: Taylor and Francis.

Call, C. (2010) *Liberia's War Recurrence: Grievance over Greed'*, Civil Wars, Vol 12, No. 4, pp. 347-369.

Call, C. and Cook, S.E. (2003) *On Democratisation and Peacebuilding'*, Global Governance, Vol. 9, No. 2, pp. 233-46.

Call, C. and Wyeth, V. (2008) *Building States to Build Peace'*, Boulder: Lynne Rienner Publishers.

Call, C., and Cousens, E.M. (2008) *Ending Wars and Building Peace: International Responses to War-Torn Societies'*, Blackwell Publishing,

International Studies Perspectives, Vol. 9, pp.1–21.

Campbell, D.T. (1988) *Methodology and Epistemology for Social Science'*, (Ed.), E. S. Overman, Chicago: University of Chicago Press.

Campbell, D.T. and Stanley C. (1963) *Experimental and Quasi-Experimental Designs for Research'*, N.Y.: Houghton Mifflin.

Caplan, R. (2005) *International Governance of War-Torn Territories: Rule and Reconstruction'*, Oxford: Oxford University Press.

Carney, T. (2007) *Some assembly required: Sudan's Comprehensive Peace Agreement'*, Washington, DC: U.S. Institute of Peace.

Castaneda, C. (2009) How Liberal Peacebuilding Might be Failing Sierra Leone', *Review of African Political Economy*, Vol. 36, No. 120, pp. 235-51.

Chabal, P. and Daloz, J.P. (1999) *Africa Works Disorder as a Political Instrument'*, Oxford, James Currey. Indiana University Press.

Chambers, R. (1997) *Whose Reality Counts? Putting the First Last'*, London: Intermediate Technology Publications.

Chambers, R. (1998) *Challenging the Professions: Frontiers for Rural Development'*, London: Intermediate Technology Publications.

Chandler, D. (1999) *Bosnia: Faking Democracy after Dayton'*, London: Pluto Press.

Chandler, D. (2006) *Empire in Denial: The Politics of State-building'*, London. Pluto Press.

Chandler, D. (2010) *Race, Culture and civil society: Peacebuilding Discourse and the Understanding of Difference'*, Security Dialogue, Vol. 41, No. 4, pp. 369-390.

Chandler, D. (2013) *Promoting democratic norms? Social Constructivism and* the 'Subjective' Limits to Liberalism', Democratisation, Vol. 20, No. 2, pp. 215-239.

Chandler, D. (2015) Resilience and the 'Every day': Beyond the Paradox of 'Liberal Peace', Review of International Studies, Vol. 41, No. 1, pp. 27-48.

Chandra, K. (2001) Cumulative Findings in the Study of Ethnic Politics', Vol. 12, No.1, pp. 7-11.

Chandra, K. (2012) Constructivist Theories of Ethnic Politics', Oxford: Oxford University Press.

Chang, H. and Dodd, T. (2001) International Perspectives on Race and Ethnicity: Annotated Bibliography', the Electronic Magazine of Multicultural Education.

Chassang, S. and Miquel, G.P. (2008) Mutual Fears and Civil War', Bread Working Paper, 165. http://ipl.econ.duke.edu/bread/papers/working/165.pdf [Accessed: 27/07 2018].

Chazan, N., Mortimer, R., Ravenhill, J., Rothchild, D. (1992) The Diversity of African Politics: Trends and Approaches', In: Politics and Society in Contemporary Africa, Palgrave, London.

Chen, C. (2015) Negotiated Settlement and the Durability of Peace: Agreement Design, Implementation, and Mediated Civil Wars', Master thesis, Utah State University, pp. 1-44.

Chetail, V. and Jütersonke. (2015) Peacebuilding: A Review of the Academic Literature', Geneva: GPP. Conciliation Resources', The International Contact Group on Mindanao, http://www.cr.org/featured-work/international-contact-group-mindanao[Accessed: 13/5/2017].

Childress, S. (2011) *South Sudan Seeks Statehood'*, Wall Street Journal: Africa   News. https://www.wsj.com/articles/SB10001424052748704739504576067 790998188326(Accessed: 16/12/2017].

Chirban, J.T. (1996) *Interviewing In-Depth: The Interactive-Relational Approach'*, Thousand Oaks, CA. Sage Publications.

Chua, A. (2003) *World on Fire: How Exporting Free Market Democracy Breeds Ethnic Hatred and Global Instability'*, New York: Doubleday.

Civic, A. and Miklaucic, (2011) *The State and the Use of Force: Monopoly and Legitimacy'*, in Monopoly of Force; the Nexus of DDR and SSR', (Ed), by Melanne A. Civic and Miklaucic, M. Centre for Complex Operations Institute for National Strategic Studies, National Defence University Press. Washington, DC.

Clandinin, D.J. and Connelly, F.M. (2000) *Narrative Inquiry: Experience and Story in Qualitative Research'*, San Francisco: Jossey-Bass.

Clapham, C. (1982) *Clientelism and the State'*, In: C. Clapham, ed., Private Patronage and Public Power: Political Clientelism in the Modern State, (pp. 1-35). New York: St Martin's Press.

Clapham, C. (1996) *Africa and the International System: The Politics of State Survival'*, Cambridge: Cambridge University Press.

Clapham, C. (2012) *From Liberation Movement to Government: Past Legacies and the Challenge of Transition in Africa'*, The Brent Hurst Foundation, Johannesburg, Oppenheimer & Son (Pty) Ltd.

Clark, J.N. (2009) The Limits of Retributive Justice: Findings of an Empirical Study in Bosnia and Herzegovina', Journal of International Criminal Justice, Vol. 7, No. 3, pp. 463-487.

Clark, J.N. (2014) *International Trials and Reconciliation: Assessing the Impact of the International Criminal Tribunal for the Former Yugoslavia'*, New York: Routledge.

Clarke, D. (2003) *Research Methods in Education'*, unpublished manuscript, Melbourne.

Clarke, L. (1995) Nursing research: Science, Vision and Telling Stories', *Journal of Advanced Nursing*, Vol. 21, pp.584-93.

Cleaver, F. (1998a) Gendered incentives and Institutions: Women, Men and the Management of water', *Journal of Agriculture and Human Values*, Vol.15, No. 4.

Cleaver, F. (1998b) *There's a Right Way to Do It – Informal Arrangements for Local Resource Management'*, Waterline, Vol. 16, No. 4. pp. 12-14.

Clement, C. (2009) *SSR in the DRC: Forward to the Past'*, In: TK editors, SSR in Challenging Environments, Geneva, DECAF Annual Yearbook.

Clement, C. (2015) *Stepping beyond the Ideological Clash: A Window of Opportunity for Effective Peacebuilding in South Sudan'*, Presented at Wilton Park's Peacebuilding in Africa, Geneva Centre for Security Policy, pp.1-13.

Cockett, R. (2010) *Sudan: Darfur and the Failure of an African State'*, New Haven, CT: Yale University Press.

Cohen, A. (1969) *Custom and Politics in Urban Africa: A Study of Hausa Migrants in a Yoruba Town'*, London: Routledge & Kegan Paul.

Cohen, J.L. (1999) *Changing Paradigms of Citizenship and the Exclusiveness of the Demos'*, International Sociology, Vol. 14, No. 3, pp. 245-68.

Cohen, R. (1978) Ethnicity: Problem and Focus in Anthropology',

Annual Review of Anthropology, Vol.7: pp. 383-384.

Coleman J.S. (1958) *Relational Analysis: The Study of Social Organisations with Survey Methods'*, Human Organisation, Vol. 17, pp. 28–36.

Coleman, J.S. (1988) Social Capital in the Creation of Human Capital', *American Journal of Sociology*, Vol. 94, pp. 95-120.

Colletta, N. Kostner, J., Wiederhofer, M., and Kostner, M.(1996a) T*he Transition from War to Peace in Sub-Saharan Africa'*, Washington, DC: The World Bank.

Colletta, N., Kostner, J., Wiederhofer, M., and Kostner, M. (1996b) *Case Studies in War-to-Peace Transition: The Demobilisation and Reintegration of Ex-Combatants in Ethiopia, Namibia, and Uganda'*, Discussion Paper No. 331 (Africa Technical Department Series). Washington, DC: The World Bank.

Colletta, N.J. (1999) *The World Bank, Demobilisation, and Social Reconstruction'*, In: Jeffrey Boutwell and Michael T. Klare (Eds.), Light Weapons and Civil Conflict: Controlling the Tools of Violence, (pp. 203–214). Lanham: Rowman and Littlefield.

Colletta, N.J. and Cullen, M.L. (2000) *The Nexus between Violent Conflict, Social Capital, and Social Cohesion: Case Studies from Cambodia and Rwanda'*, Washington DC: The World Bank: Social Capital Initiative.

Colletta, N.J. and Muggah, R. (2009) Rethinking Post-War Security Promotion', *Journal of Security Sector Management*, Vol. 7, No. 1, pp. 1–25.

Collier, P. (1998) *On Economic Causes of Civil War'*, Oxford Economic Papers, Vol.50, No.4, pp.563-573.

Collier, P. (2000a) Rebellion as a Quasi-criminal Activity', *Journal of Conflict Resolution*, Vol 44, No. 6, pp.839-853.

Collier, P. (2000b) *Doing Well out of War'*, in Berdal, M. and D.M. Malone (Eds.), Greed and Grievance: Economic Agendas in Civil Wars, (pp. 91-111). Boulder: Lynne Rienner Publishers.

Collier, P. (2007) *The Bottom Billion: Why the Poorest Countries are Failing and What Can Be Done About It'*, Oxford: Oxford University Press.

Collier, P. (2009) *Wars, Guns and Votes: Democracy in Dangerous Places'*, London: Random House.

Collier, P. and Hoeffler, A. (2004) *Greed and Grievance in Civil War'*, Oxford Economic Papers, Vol.56, No.4, pp.563-595.

Collier, P. and Hoeffler, A. (2007) *Civil War'*, In: T. Sandler and K. Hartley (Eds.), Handbook of Defence Economics', (pp. 712–39). Elsevier, Amsterdam.

Collier, P., Hoeffler, A. and Rohner, D. (2009) *Beyond Greed and Grievance: Feasibility and Civil War'*, Oxford Economic Papers, Vol. 61, No.1, pp.1-27.

Collins, R.O. (2007) *Civil Wars in the Sudan'*, History Compass, Vol 5, No. 6, pp. 1778- 1805

Collins, R.O. (1983) *Shadows in the Grass: Britain in the Southern Sudan, 1918-1956'*, New Haven: Yale University Press.

Comaroff, J.L. (1996) *Ethnicity, Nationalism, and the Politics of Difference in an Age of Revolution'*, In: The Politics of Difference: Ethnic Premises in a World of Power, (Ed.). McAllister Patrick and Edwin Wilmsen, Chicago, University of Chicago Press.

Connor, W. (1994) *Ethnonationalism: The Quest for Understanding'*, Princeton: Princeton University Press.

Cooper, N. (2007) *On the Crisis of the Liberal Peace'*, Conflict, Security and Development, Vol. 7, No. 4, pp. 605-616.

Cooper, N., Turner, M. and Pugh, M. (2011) The End of History and the Last Liberal Peacebuilder: A Reply to Roland Paris', *Review of International Studies*, Vol. 37, No. 4, pp. 1995-2007.

Copnall, J. (2014) *A Poisonous Thorn in Our Hearts: Sudan and South Sudan's Bitter and Incomplete Divorce',* Hurst Publishers, Great Russell Street, London WC1B 3PL.

Coppieters, B. (2003) *War and Secession: A Moral Analysis of the Georgian-Abkhazian Conflict',* In Bruno Coppieters and Richard Sakwa (Eds.), Contextualising Secession: Normative Studies in Comparative Perspective. Oxford University Press.

Coser, L.A. (1967) Social Conflict and the Theory of Social Change', *The British Journal of Sociology*, Vol. 8, No. 3, pp. 197-207.

Cox, R.W. and Scechter, M.G. (2002) *The Political Economy of a Plural World: Critical Reflections on Power, Morals and Civilisation',* New York: Routledge.

Coyne, C. (2006) *Reconstructing Weak and Failed States: Foreign Intervention and the Nirvana Fallacy',* Foreign Policy Analysis, Vol. 2, No. 4, pp. 343-360.

Crabtree, B. and Miller, W. (1999) Doing Qualitative Research', 2nd (Ed.), London: Sage.

Cramer, C. (2006) *Civil War is Not a Stupid Thing: Accounting for Violence in Developing Countries',* London: Hurst & Co.

Cramer, C. (2010) *Unemployment and Participation in Violence',* Background paper for WDR 2011.Washington, DC: World Bank.

Creswell, J. (2003) *Research Design: Qualitative, Quantitative, and Mixed*

Method Approaches', 2nd (Ed.), Thousand Oaks, Calif.: Sage Publications.

Creswell, J. W. (2007) *Qualitative Inquiry and Research Design: Choosing Among Five Approaches*', London. Sage Publications.

Creswell, J. W. (2009) *Research Design: Qualitative and Mixed Methods Approaches*', London: Sage.

Crotty, M. (1989) *The Foundations of Social Research*', London: Sage.

Crotty, M. (2003) *The Foundations of Social Research: Meaning and Perspectives in the Research Process*', 3rd (Ed.), London: Sage Publications.

Crowley, J. (1999) *The Politics of Belonging: Some Theoretical Considerations*', In: Andrew Geddes and Adrian Favell (Eds.), The Politics of Belonging: Migrants and Minorities in Contemporary Europe Aldershot: Ashgate.

Crowther, D. and Lancaster, G. (2008) *Research Methods: A Concise Introduction to Research in Management and Business Consultancy*', Butterworth-Heinemann.

Crowther, D. and Lancaster, G. (2008) *Research Methods*', London: Routledge.

Cubitt, C. (2011) *African Peace and Conflict Journal*', Vol. 4, No. 1, pp.1-101.

Cullis, J.O. (2017) Not everything that can be counted counts... British Journal of Haematology', Vol. 177, No. 4, pp. 505–506.

Cunningham, D. E. (2013) Who Should Be at the Table: Veto Players and Peace Processes in Civil War', *Penn Journal of Law and International Affairs*, Vol. 2, No. 1, pp. 38-47.

Cunningham, D.E. (2006) Veto Players and Civil War Duration', *American Journal of Political Science*, Vol. 50, No. 4, pp. 875–892.

Dagne, T. (2011) *The Republic of South Sudan: Opportunities and Challenges for Africa's Newest Country'*, CRS Report for Congress. Congressional Research Service.

Dahl, R. A. (1989) *Democracy and its Critics'*, Yale University Press: New Haven.

Daly, M. W. (2007) *Darfur's Sorrow: a History of Destruction and Genocide'*, Cambridge: Cambridge University Press.

Das, T. and Teng, B. (1998) *Between Trust and Control: Developing Confidence in Partner Cooperation in Alliances'*, The Academy of Management Review, Vol. 23, No. 3, pp. 491-512.

Davidsen, A. (2010) *To Survive, General Practice needs a Reintroduction of the Psychodynamic Dimension'*, Psychodynamic Practice, Vol. 16, No. 4, pp. 451–61.

Davidson, B. (1992) *Man's Burden: Africa and Roots of State the Curse of the Nation-State'*, Cambridge: Cambridge University Press.

Davidson, B. (1992) *The Black Man's Burden: Africa and the Curse of the Nation-State'*, Oxford: James Currey.

Davies, J. (2001) *Review', Agriculture, Ecosystems and Environment'*, Vol. 86, No. 1, pp. 107–109.

De Herdt, T. and J.P. Olivier de Sardan. (2015) *Introduction: The Game of the Rules'*, In: T. De Herdt and J.-P. Olivier de Sardan (Eds) Real Governance and Practical Norms in Sub-Saharan Africa: The Game of the Rules, pp. 2–16. London and New York: Routledge.

De Heredia, M. I. (2018) *The Conspicuous Absence of Class and Privilege in the Study of Resistance in Peacebuilding Contexts'*, International Peacekeeping, Vol. 25, No. 3, pp.325-348.

De Maio, J.L. (2009) *Confronting Ethnic Conflict: The Role of Third Parties in Managing Africa's Civil Wars*, Lanham: Lexington Books.

De Soysa, I. (2000) *The Resource Curse: Are Civil Wars Driven by Rapacity or Paucity?*' In: Berdal, M. and Malone, D. Boulder, (Ed.), Greed and Grievance: Economic Agendas in Civil War, CO: Lynne Rienner.

De Soysa, I. (2002) Paradise is a Bazaar? Greed, Greed, and Governance in Civil War, 1989–99', *Journal of Peace Research*, Vol. 39, No. 4, pp. 395–416.

De Vries, L. and Schomerus, M. (2017) *South Sudan's Civil War Will Not End with a Peace Deal*', Peace Review, Vol. 29, No. 3, pp. 333-340.

De Waal, A. (2000) *Who Fights? Who Cares? War and Humanitarian Action in Africa'*, (Eds.), Africa World Press.

De Waal, A. (2007) *Sudan: the Turbulent State'*, In; Alex de Waal (Eds.), War in Sudan and the Search for Peace. Harvard University Press, Cambridge, MA.

De Waal, A. (2014) *When Kleptocracy Becomes Insolvent: Root Causes of the Civil War in South Sudan'*, African Affairs, Vol. 113, No. 452, pp. 347–369.

De Waal, A. (2017) Peace and the Security Sector in Sudan, 2002–11', *African Security Review*, Vol. 26, No. 2, pp. 180-198.

De Waal, A. (2018) *The Political Marketplace Framework: Framing Paper Prepared for the First Political Markets Workshop'*, May 30-31, Martin School, University of Oxford.

De Waal, A. (2019) Sudan', In: *Comparing Peace Processes'*, (Eds.), by Alpaslan Özerdem and Roger Mac Ginty, Routledge.

De Waal, A. and Abdul Mohammed, A. (2014) *Breakdown in South*

Sudan',   Foreign   Affairs,
http://www.foreignaffairs.com/print/137729[Accessed:
20/04/2017].

De Waal, A. and Pendle, N. (2018) *South Sudan: Decentralisation and the Logic of the Political Marketplace*,' In: Luka Biong Deng Kuol and Sarah Logan (Eds.) The Struggle for South Sudan: Challenges of Security and State Formation, London, IB Tauris.

DeNardo, J. (1985) *Power in Numbers: The Political Strategy of Protest and Rebellion'*, Princeton, NJ: Princeton University Press.

Deng, D. (2018) *Compound Fractures: Political Formations, Armed Groups and Regional Mediation in South Sudan'*, Institute for Security Studies, Vol. 21. pp. 1-24.

Deng, F. (1995) *War of Visions: Conflict of Identities in the Sudan'*, Washington, DC, Brookings Institution.

Deng, F. (2005) *Sudan's Turbulent Road to Nationhood'*, In: R.R. Laremont, ed. Borders, Nationalism, and the African State, Boulder: Lynne Rienner.

Deng, F. and Morrison, J.S. (2001) *U.S. Policy to end Sudan's War: Report of the CSIS Task Force on U.S.–Sudan Policy'*, Washington, DC: CSIS.

Deng, L.B. (2005a) *The Comprehensive Peace Agreement: will it also be dishonoured? Forced Migration Review'*, Vol. 24, pp.15-16.

Deng, L.B. (2005b) *The Sudan Comprehensive Peace Agreement: Will it be sustained?* Civil Wars, Vol. 7, pp. 244-257.

Deng, L.B. (2017) *Dinka Youth in Civil War: Between Cattle, Community, and Government'*, In: Madut, J.J, Schomerus M, Kuol, L.B, Breidlid, I.M, Arensen, M. J (Eds) Informal armies: community defence groups in

South Sudan's Civil War. Saferworld, pp 1–6. https://www.saferworld.org.uk/downloads/informal-armies-final.pdf.

Denzin, N. K. and Lincoln, Y. S. (2000) *Introduction: the Discipline and Practice of Qualitative Research*', In: N. K. Denzin and Y. S. Lincoln (eds) The Sage Handbook of Qualitative Research', London: Sage.

Denzin, N. K., and Lincoln, Y.S. (1994) *Handbook of Qualitative Research*', Thousand Oaks, CA: Sage.

DeRouen, K. and Chowdhury, I. (2013) *Mediation and Civil War Peace Agreement Implementation*', In APSA 2013 Annual Meeting Paper.

Di John, J. (2007) Oil abundance and Violent Political Conflict: A Critical Assessment', *The Journal of Development Studies*, Vol. 43, No. 6, pp. 961-986.

Diamond, L. (1996) Is the Third Wave Over?' *Journal of Democracy*, Vol.7, pp. 20–37.

Diamond, L. (2002) Thinking about Hybrid Regimes', *Journal of Democracy*, Vol. 13, pp. 21–35.

Diamond, L. (2008) *The Democratic Roll-back: The Resurgence of the Predatory State*', Foreign Affairs, Vol. 87, pp. 36–48.

DiMaggio, P.J. and Powell, W.W. (1991) Introduction. In W. W. Powell & P. J. DiMaggio (Eds.), *The new institutionalism in organisational analysis*, Chicago: University of Chicago Press.

Disarmament, Demobilisation and Reintegration- Fact Sheet. (2010) Report of the Secretary-General on the Sudan', United Nations (S681).

Dobbins, J. Dobbins, J., Jones, S. Keith Crane, K., Beth C.D. (2007) *Beginner's Guide to Nation-Building*', Santa Monica: RAND.

Dobbins, J., Jones, S. Keith Crane, K., Beth C.D. (2003) *America's Role in Nation-Building: From Germany to Iraq'*, Santa Monica, CA: RAND Corporation',

https://www.rand.org/pubs/monograph_reports/MR1753.html [Accessed: 06/03/2019].

Doki, C. and Ahmad, A.M. (2014) *Africa's Arms Dump: Following the Trail of Bullets in the Sudans'*, Guardian Africa Network Sudan, https://www.theguardian.com/world/2014/oct/02/-sp-africa-arms-dump-south-sudan [Accessed: 16/01/2020].

Dorman, S.R. (2006) *Post-Liberation Politics in Africa: Examining the Political Legacy of Struggle'*, Third World Quarterly, Vol. 27, No.6, pp. 1085-1101.

Dowden, R. (1993) *Reflections on Democracy in Africa'*, African Affairs, Vol. 92, No. 369, pp. 607-13.

Downes, A.B. (2004) *The Problem with Negotiated Settlements to Ethnic Civil Wars'*, Security Studies, Vol. 13, No. 4, pp. 230-79.

Doyle, D. (2011) *Ripe Moments for Exiting Political Violence, an Heuristic Model from Northern Ireland and its Application in Kashmir'*, Dublin City University: Centre for International Studies School of Law and Government.

Doyle, M. (1983) *Kant, Liberal Legacies, and Foreign Affairs'*, Philosophy and Public Affairs, Vol. 12, No.3/4, pp. 323–53.

Doyle, M. (2005) *Three Pillars of the Liberal Peace'*, The American Political Science Review', Vol. 99, No.3, pp. 463-466.

Doyle, M. W. and Sambanis, N. (2000) International Peacebuilding: A Theoretical and Quantitative Analysis', *The American Political Science*

Review, Vol. 94, No.4, pp. 779-801.

Doyle, M.D. and Sambanis, N (2006) Making War and Building Peace: The United Nations Peace Operations, Princeton University Press.

Drapeau, M.   (2004b) *Réflexion Épistémologique Sur La Recherche Qualitative E.T. La Psychanalyse: Refaire une place au rêve E.T. àl imaginaire [Epistemological reflection on qualitative research and psychoanalysis*, Redeeming the dream and the imaginary]. Le Coq-héron [The Rooster], Vol. 2, No. 177, pp. 124-129.

Drysdale, J. (1964) *The Somali Dispute'*, New York: Praeger Press.

Dryzek, J.S. (2005) *Deliberative Democracy in Divided Societies: Alternatives to Agonism and Analgesia'*, Political Theory, Sage Publications.

Du Toit, P. (1989) Bargaining About Bargaining: Inducing the Self-negating Prediction in Deeply Divided Societies—the Case of South Africa', *The Journal of Conflict Resolution*, Vol 33, No. 2. pp. 210–30.

Dudouet, V. (2006) *Transitions from Violence to Peace: Revisiting Analysis and Intervention in Conflict Transformation'*, Berghof Report No. 15. Berghof Research Centre for Constructive Conflict Management.

Dudouet, V. Civic, (2011) *Non-state Armed Groups and the Politics of Post-war Security Governance in Monopoly of Force; in the Nexus of DDR and SSR'*, (Ed.), In: Melanne A. Civic and Miklaucic, M. Centre for Complex Operations Institute for National Strategic Studies, National Defence University Press Washington, DC.

Duffield, M. (2001) *Global Governance and the New Wars'*, London: Zed Books.

Duffield, M. (2007) *Development, Security and Unending War, Governing the World of Peoples'*, Cambridge: Polity.

Dulic, T. (2011) *Peace Research and Source Criticism; Using Historical Methodology to Improve Information Gathering and Analysis'*, In: K. Höglund and M. Öberg (Eds.), Understanding Peace Research, Methods and Challenges (pp. 35-46). London/New York: Routledge.

Dunne, T. (2005) System, State and Society: How Does it All Hang Together? *Millennium-Journal of International Studies,* Vol. 34, No.1, p. 157-170.

Durkheim, E. (1973) Pacifism et Patriotism' translated', by N. Layne in, Sociological Inquiry, Vol. 43, No. 2, PP. 99–103.

Duursma, A. (2014) A current literature review of international mediation', *International Journal of Conflict Management,* Vol. 25, No. 1, pp. 81-98.

Eagleton, T. (1983) *Literary theory: An Introduction'*, Oxford: Basil Blackwell

Ebo, A. (2007) *The Role of SSR in Sustainable Development: Donor Policy Trends and Challenges'*, Conflict, Security & Development, Vol. 7, No. 1, pp. 27-60.

Egnell, R. and Haldén, P. (2009) *Laudable, a historical and Overambitious: SSR meets state formation theory'*, Conflict, Security and Development, Vol. 9, No. 1, pp. 27-54.

Eisenstadt, S.N. (1978) *Revolution and the Transformation of Societies: A Comparative Study of Civilisations'*, New York, N.Y.: Free Press.

Ekeh, P. (1975) *Colonialism and the Two Publics in Africa: A Theoretical Statement'*, Comparative Studies in Society and History, Vol. 17, No. 1, pp. 91-112.

El-Affendi, A. (2001) *The impasse in the IGAD peace process for Sudan: the limits of regional peacemaking?* African Affairs, Vol 100, pp.581–599.

Elaine, K. and Walters, B. (2014) Ethnicity and Civil War', Anniversary Special Issue, *Journal of Peace Research*, Vol. 51, No. 2, pp. 199–212.

El-Battahani, A. (2007) Tunnel vision or kaleidoscope: Competing concepts on Sudan identity and national integration', *African Journal on Conflict Resolution*, Vol. 27, No. 2, pp.37–61.

Elena, T. *et al.* (2011) Historical research in Archives: User Methodology and Supporting Tools', International Journal of Digital Library, Springer-Verlag.

Englebert, P and Tull, D.M (2008) *Post-conflict Reconstruction in Africa'*, International Security, Vol. 32, No. 4, spring 2008, pp. 106-139.

Eriksen, T. H. (2004) *What is Anthropology'*, London: Pluto Press.

Eriksen, T.H. (2002) *Ethnicity and Nationalism, Anthropological Perspectives'*, London: Pluto Press.

Eriksson, M. and Wallensteen, P. (2004) Armed Conflict, 1989–2003', *Journal of Peace Research,* Vol. 41, No. 5, pp. 625–636.

Esman, M. (1994) *Ethnic Politics'*, Ithaca, New York: Cornell University Press.

Esman, M. (2004) *An introduction to Ethnic Conflict'*, Polity Press, Ltd.

Etherington, K. (2006) *Chicken or Egg? An Exploration of The Relationships Between Physical and Psychological Symptoms with a Woman Diagnosed with Tourette's Syndrome'*, In: Counselling and Psychotherapy Research. Vol. 6, no. 2, pp138-146.

Etherington, K. (2007) *Ethical Research in Reflexive Relationships'*, Qualitative Inquiry, Vol. 13, No. 50, pp. 599 -616.

Evans, G. and Newnham, J. (1998) *Dictionary of International Relations'*,

London: Penguin Books

Evans, G. and Sahnoun, M. (2002) *The Responsibility to Protect'*, Foreign Affairs. Vol. 81, pp. 99–110.

Evans, P.B., Rueschemeyer, D. and Skocpol, T. (1985) *Bringing the State Back'*, Cambridge University Press.

Eyoh, D. (1999) *Community, Citizenship, and the Politics of Ethnicity in Post-Colonial Africa'*, in E. Kalipeni and P. Zeleza (Eds), Sacred Spaces and Public Quarrels, (pp. 271–300). Trenton, NJ and Asmara: Africa World Press.

Fahey, D. (2013) *Gold, Land, and Ethnicity in North-Eastern Congo'*, London: Rift Valley Institute.

Fay, B. (1987) *Critical Social Science'*, Cornell University Press, Ithaca, New York.

Fearon, J. (1998) *Bargaining, Enforcement, and International Cooperation'*, *International Organisation'*, Vol. 52, No, 2, pp. 269-305.

Fearon, J. (2004) Why Do Some Civil Wars Last So Much Longer than Others?' *Journal of Peace Research*, Vol. 41, pp. 275-302.

Fearon, J. (2005) Primary Commodity Exports and Civil War', *Journal of Conflict Resolution*, Vol. 49, No. 4, pp. 483–507.

Fearon, J. and David D. L. (2000) *Ordinary Language and External Validity: Specifying Concepts in the Study of Ethnicity'*, Paper Presented at the October 2000 meeting of LICEP, University of Pennsylvania.

Fearon, J. and Laitin, D. (2003 Ethnicity, Insurgency, and Civil War', *American Political Science Review*, Vol. 97, pp. 75–90.

Fearon, J. and Latin, D. (2000) *Violence and the Social Construction of Ethnic Identity'*, International Organisation, Vol 54, No. 4, pp. 845-877.

Fearon, J. D. (2004) Why Do Some Civil Wars Last So Much Longer than Others? *Journal of Peace Research*, Vol. 41, No. 3, pp. 275–301.

Fearon, J. D. and Laitin, D.D. (1996) Explaining Inter-ethnic Cooperation', *American Political Science Review*, Vol 90, pp. 715-735.

Fiedler, C. and Karina, M. (2017) *Post-conflict Societies: Chances for Peace and Types of International Support',* Briefing Paper, Bonn: German Development Institute/Deutsches Institutfür Entwicklungspolitik, Vol. 4. https://www.die-gdi.de/uploads/media/BP__4.2017.pdf.

Field, A. (2005) *Reliability Analyses',* In: Field, A. (Ed.), Discovering Statistics Using Spss, Sage, London.

Fischer, A. M. (2008) *Resolving the Theoretical Ambiguities of Social Exclusion with Reference to Polarisation and Conflict',* Working Paper No. 08-90. DESTIN, London School of Economics. http://www.lse.ac.uk/internationalDevelopment/pdf/WP/WP90.pdf.

Fischer, M. and Schmelzle, B. (2009) *Building Peace in the Absence of States: Challenging the Discourse on State Failure',* Berlin: Berghof Research Centre.

Fithen, C (1999) *Diamonds and War in Sierra Leone: Cultural Strategies for Commercial Adaptation to Endemic Low-intensity Conflict',* In: London: Department of Anthropology, University College, London.

Foley, D. (2003) *Indigenous Epistemology and Indigenous Standpoint Theory',* Social Alternatives, Vol. 22, No, 1, pp. 44-52.

Fortin, J. (2016) *Deadly Attacks Leave Victims Wondering Why',* New York Times 17 April, https://www.nytimes.com/2016/04/18/world/africa/deadly-attacks-in-ethiopia-leave-victimswondering-why.html.

Fortna, V.P. (2003) *Inside and Out: Peacekeeping and the Duration of Peace after Civil and Inter-state Wars'*, International Studies Review. Vol. 5, No. 4, pp.97-114.

Fortna, V.P. (2004) *Peace Time: Cease-Fire Agreements and the Durability of Peace'*, Princeton, NJ: Princeton Univ. Press.

Foucault, M (1991) *Governmentality'*, (trans. R Braidotti and revised C Gordon) In: Burchell G, Gordon C and Miller P (Eds) *The Foucault Effect: Studies in Governmentality*, (pp.87-104) Chicago: University of Chicago Press.

Foucault, M. (1980) *Power/Knowledge: Selected Interviews and Other Writings 1972-1977'*, (Ed.), C. Gordon. Brighton: Harvester.

Foucault, M. (1997a) *Ilfau défendre la société'*, *Cours au Collège de France 1976, Paris*: Gallimard/Seuil.

Foucault, M. (1997b) *Security, Territory, and Population'*, In: Michel Foucault, Ethics: Subjectivity and Truth', (Ed.), (pp. 67-71). By Paul Rainbow, New York: The New Press.

Frahm, O. (2012) *Defining the Nation: National Identity in South Sudanese Media Discourse'*, Africa Spectrum. Vol 1, pp.21-49.

Freire, P. (1974) *Education for a Critical Consciousness'*, New York, N.Y.: Continuum.

Freire, P. (2005) *Pedagogy of the Oppressed: 30th-anniversary edition'*, London, United Kingdom: Continuum.

Fritz, V. and Menocal, A.R. (2007) *Forthcoming Developmental States in the New Millennium: Concepts and Challenges for a New Aid Agenda'*, Development Policy Review. Vol. 25, Issue, 5, pp. 531-552.

Fritz, V. and Rocha Menocal, A.R. (2006) *(Re) building Developmental States: From Theory to Practice'*, Working Paper No. 274, London, ODI.

Fukuyama, F. (2004) *State-Building: A New Agenda'*, Cornell University Press.

Fukuyama, F. (2004) The imperative of Statebuilding', *Journal of Democracy*, Vol. 15, No. 2, pp. 17-31.

Fukuyama, F. and Levy, B. (2010) *Development strategies: Integrating Governance and Growth'*, World Bank Policy Research Working Paper, Washington DC: World Bank. https://openknowledge.worldbank.org/bitstream/handle/10986/19915/WPS5196.pdf?sequence=1.

Gabriele Pollini (2005) Socio-Territorial Belonging in a Changing Society, *International Review of Sociology*, Vol 15, No. 3, pp. 493-496.

Gadir, A. (2003) *Conflict Resolution and Wealth Sharing in Sudan: Towards an Allocation Formula'*, http://www.arab-api.org/jodep/products/delivery/wps0305.pdf. [Accessed: 20/02/2017].

Gadir, A., Ibrahim, A., and El-Batahani, A. (2005) *The Sudan's Civil War: Why has it Prevailed for So Long?'* in Collier, P. and Sambanis, N. (Eds.), *Understanding Civil War: Evidence and Analysis*, Vol.1, (pp.193-220). Africa, Washington, DC: The World Bank.

Galbraith, P. W. and Van Hollen, Jr. (1988) *Chemical Weapons Use in Kurdistan: Iraq's Final Offensive'*, Staff Report to the Committee on Foreign Relations, U.S. Senate, Washington, DC: U.S. Government Printing Office

Galbraith, P.W. (2003) *The Ghosts of 1991'*, Washington Post, 12 April,

Academic, Lexis-Nexis, University of Iowa Library, Iowa City, IA.

Gall, M.D and Borg, W. (2003) *Educational Research: An introduction*, 7th (Ed.), Boston, MA: A & B Publications.

Galtung, J. (1965) A Structural Theory of Aggression', *Journal of Peace Research*, Vol. 1, No. 2, pp. 95-119.

Galtung, J. (1976) *Three Approaches to Peace: Peacekeeping, Peacemaking, and Peacebuilding*, In: J. Galtung. Peace, War and Defence: Essays in Peace Research, Vol. 2, pp. 297-298.

Galtung, J. (1990) Cultural Violence', *Journal of Peace Research*, Vol. 27, No. 3, pp.291–305.

Galtung, J. (2001) *After Violence, Reconstruction, Reconciliation, and Resolution', Reconciliation, Justice and Coexistence'*, (Ed.), Mohammed Abu-Nimer, Oxford, England: Lexington Books.

Galtung. J (1985) Twenty-Five Years of Peace Research: Ten Challenges and Responses', *Journal of Peace Research*, Vol. 22, pp. 141–158.

Garang, A. (2015) *The impact of external actors on the prospects of a mediated settlement in South Sudan'*, Paper was Presented at the Academic Conference on International Mediation. The University of Pretoria, 2-4 June 2015, Pretoria, South Africa.

Garang, J. (1987) *The Call for Democracy in Sudan'*, London: Kegan Paul International.

Garang, J. and Khalid, M. (1987) *John Garang Speaks'*, London: Kegan Paul International.

Gates, S. and Strøm, K. (2008) *Power-sharing, Agency and Civil Conflict: Power-sharing Agreements, Negotiations and Peace Processes'*, Policy brief forms, pp.1-15.

Gazit, N. (2009) Social Agency, Spatial Practices and Power: The Micro-foundations of Fragmented Sovereignty in the Occupied Territories', *An International Journal of Politics, Culture and Society*, Vol. 22, No. 1, pp. 83-104.

Gebrehiwot, G. and Abeba, A. (2007) *Cross Border Cooperation in the IGAD Region: A study Commissioned by IGAD as Part of its Peace and Security Strategy Development Project'*, The Framework Vol. 1, pp. 2-62.

Gebreselassie, S. (2018) *Disarmament Process in the Greater Lakes Hampered by Availability of Guns and Lack of Trust'*, UNMIS News: https://unmiss.unmissions.org/disarmament-process-greater-lakes-hampered-availability-guns-and-lack-trust [Accessed 15/03/2018].

Geertz, C. (1967) *Old Societies and New States: The Quest for Modernity in Africa and Asia'*, New York: The Free Press.

Geertz, C. (1973) *The Interpretation of Cultures'*, New York: Basic Books.

Geertz, C. (1973) *Thick Description Toward an Interpretive Theory of Culture'*, In C. Geertz. Ed. The Interpretation of Cultures, New York: Basic Books.

Gellner, E. (1983) *Nations and Nationalism'*, Oxford: Basil Blackwell.

George, A.L. and Bennett, A. (2005) *Case Studies and Theory Development in the Social Sciences'*, The MIT Press.

Gephardt, R.J. (1988) *Ethno-statistics: Qualitative Foundations for Quantitative Research'*, Newbury Park, CA: Sage.

Gerrard, A.J. (2000) *What is a Mountain? Background Paper to Definition of Mountains and Mountain regions (English)'*, Washington, DC: World Bank Group. pp. 1-9.

Gerring, J. (2004) What is a Case Study and What Is It Good for?', *American Political Science Review*, Vol. 98, No. 2, pp. 341-354.

Gerring, J. (2006) *Case Study Research: Principles and Practices'*, Cambridge University Press: Cambridge.

Gerring, J. (2007) *Is There a (Viable) Crucial-Case Method? Comparative Political Studies'*, Vol. 40, No. 3, pp. 231-253.

Geschiere, P. (2009) *The Perils of Belonging: Autochthony, Citizenship, and Exclusion in Africa and Europe Chicago'*, University of Chicago Press.

Gettleman J (2012a) *Accounts emerge in South Sudan of 3,000 Deaths in Ethnic Violence'*, New York Times 5 Jan. http://www.nytimes.com/2012/01/06/world/africa/in-south-sudan-massacre-of-3000-isreported.html

Gettleman, J. (2008) *Anarchy-Cursed Nation Looks to Bottom-Up Rule,'* New York Times, August 18, p. A6, http://www.nytimes.com/2008/08/18/world/africa/18somalia.html
.

Gettleman, J. (2012b) *Born in Unity, South Sudan is Torn again'*, New York Times 12 Jan. http://www.nytimes.com/2012/01/13/world/africa/south-sudan-massacres-followindependence.html

Gettleman, J. (2013) *Quandary in South Sudan: Should it lose its Hard-won Independence?* New York Times, 23 January. https://www.nytimes.com/2017/01/23/world/africa/quandary-in-south-sudan-should-it-loseits-hard-won-independence.html

Ghani, A. and Lockhart, C. (2008) *Fixing Failed States: A Framework for Rebuilding a Fractured World'*, Oxford: Oxford University Press.

Ghobarah, H.P. and Russett, B. (2003) Civil Wars Kill and Maim People, Long after the Fighting Stops', *American Political Science Review*, Vol 97, No. 2, pp.189-202.

Gilley, B. (2004) *Against the Concept of Ethnic Conflict'*, Third World Quarterly, Vol. 25, No. 6, pp. 1155-1166.

Gilpin, R. (1981) *War and Change in World Politics'*, Princeton: Princeton University Press.

Ginifer, J. (2003) *Reintegration of Ex-Combatants'*, In Meek, Sarah, Thokozani Thusi, Jeremy Ginifer, and Patrick Coke (Eds.). Sierra Leone: Building the Road to Recovery. Institute for Security Studies Monograph No. 80. Pretoria, South Africa: Institute for Security Studies.

Glaser, C. (1993) *Why NATO is Still Best: Future SA for Europe'*, International Security, Vol. 18, No. 1, pp. 5-50.

Glasser, B. G. and Strauss A.L. (1967) *The Discovery of Grounded Theory: Strategies for Qualitative Research'*, Chicago: Aldine Publishing Company.

Glassmyer, K. and Sambanis, N. (2008) *Rebel—Military Integration and Civil War Termination'*, Journal of Peace Research, Vol.45, No. 3, pp. 365–384.

Glazer, N. and Moynihan, D. (1975) *Ethnicity: Theory and Experience'*, Cambridge, MA, Harvard University Press.

Gleditsch, K.S. (2004) *A revised list of Wars between and Within Independent States, 1816–2002'*, International Interactions, Vol.30, pp. 231–62.

Gleditsch, N.P., Wallensteen, P., Eriksson, M., Sollenberg, M., and Strand, H. (2002) Armed Conflict 1946–2001: A New Dataset', *Journal of Peace Research*, Vol. No, 39, pp. 615–37.

Glowacki, L. and Wrangham, R. (2015) *Warfare and Reproductive Success in a Tribal Population'*, Proceedings of the National Academy of Sciences, Vol 112, No. 2, pp. 348–353.

Goetze, C. and Guzina, D. (2008) *Peacebuilding, Statebuilding, Nation-building – Turtles All the Way Down?* Civil Wars, Vol. 10, No. 4, pp. 319-347.

Golafshani, N. (2003) *Understanding Reliability and Validity in Qualitative Research'*, the *Qualitative Report*, Vol. 8, No. 4, pp. 579-606.

Goldstein, D.M (2014) *Qualitative Research in Dangerous Places: Becoming an 'Ethnographer' of Violence and Personal Safety'*, The DSD Program is funded by the Open Society Foundations, The program is a partnership between OSF, the SSRC, pp. 21.

Gonzalez, M. (2009) *Local Histories: A Methodology for Understanding Community Perspectives on Transitional Justice'*, In: Van Der Merwe *et al.* Assessing the Impact of Transitional Justice. Challenges for Empirical Research. Washington, D. C: University of Peace Press.

Goodhand, J. (2006) *Working in and on War, Civil War, Civil Peace'*, Yanacopulos, H. and Hanlon, J., Open University in association with James Currey, Oxford and Ohio University Press, Athens.

Goodman, L. A. and Smyth, K. F. (2011) *A Call for a Social Network-oriented Approach to Services for Survivors of Intimate Partner Violence'*, Psychology of Violence, Vol. 1, No. 2, pp. 79–92.

GoS (2007) *The National DDR Strategic Plan 2007, Khartoum, Sudan Government of South Sudan (GoSS)-Approved Budget 2012-2013'*, Ministry of Finance and Economic Planning, Juba

Government of Sudan (2007) *The National DDR Strategic Plan'*,

Disarmament, Demobilisation and Reintegration Coordination Council, Khartoum.

Grafstein, R. (1981) *The Institutional Resolution of the Fact-Value Dilemma'*, Philosophy of the Social Sciences, Vol. 11, No. 1, pp. 1–14.

Graham, S. (1992) *Most of the subjects were White and Middle Class: Trends in Published Research on African Americans in Selected APA Journals, 1970-1989*, American Psychologist, No. 47, pp. 629-639.

Gramsci, A. (1971) *Selections from the Prison Notebooks'*, New York, N.Y.: International Publishers.

Grawert, E. (2010) *After the Comprehensive Peace Agreement in Sudan'*, Woodbridge, Suffolk; Rochester, N.Y.: Boydell & Brewer.

Green, D.P. and Seher, R.L. (2003) *What Role Does Prejudice Play in Ethnic Conflict?* Annual Review of Political Science, Vol. 6, pp. 509-531.

Green, D.P., Stolovitch, D. Z. and Wong, J.S. (1998) Defended Neighbourhoods, Integration, and Racial Motivated crime', *American Journal of Sociology*, Vol. 104, pp. 372–403.

Green, E. (2006) *Redefining Ethnicity'*, Development Studies Institute', London School of Economics; Paper prepared for presentation at the 47th Annual International Studies Association Convention, San Diego, CA.

Greenbank, P. (2003) The role of values in educational research: the case for reflexivity', *British Educational Research Journal*, Vol. 29, No.6, pp. 791-801.

Grieco, J, (1993) *Anarchy and the Limits of Cooperation: A Realist Critique of the Newest Liberal Institutionalism'*, In: David Baldwin ed., Neorealism and Neoliberalism: The Contemporary Debate.

Groger, L and Mayberry, P. (1999) *What We Didn't Learn Because of Who Would Not Talk to Us'*, Qualitative Health Research. Vol. 9, No. 6, pp. 829-835.

Grossman, H. (1999) *Kleptocracy and Revolutions', Oxford Economic Papers'*, No. 51, pp. 267-283.

Guba, E. (1981) *Criteria for Assessing the Trustworthiness of Naturalistic Inquiries'*, Educational Resources Information Centre Annual Review Paper, Vol. 29, pp.75-91.

Guba, E. G. and Lincoln, Y.S. (1994) *Competing Paradigms in Qualitative Research'*, In: N. K. Denzin & Y. S. Lincoln (Eds.), Handbook of Qualitative Research, pp. 105-117.

Gubrium, J.A. and Holstein, J.A. (2001) *Handbook of Interview Research: Context and Method'*, Thousand Oaks, CA. Sage Publications.

Guelke, A. (2012) *Politics in Deeply Divided Societies'*, Polity Press: Cambridge.

Guibernau, M. (2000) *Nationalism and Intellectuals in Nations without States: The Catalan Case'*, Political Studies, Vol.48, No. 5, pp. 989–1005.

Gurr, T. (1968) A Causal Model of Civil Strife: A Comparative Analysis Using New Indices', *American Political Science Review*, Vol 62, No. 4, pp. 1104–1124.

Gurr, T. (1970) *Why Men Rebel?* Princeton, NJ: Princeton University Press.

Gurr, T. (1993) *Why Minorities Rebel: A Global Analysis of Communal Mobilisation and Conflict since1945'*, International Political Science Review. Vol 14, pp. 161-201.

Gurr, T. (1994) *People Against States: Ethno-political Conflict and the Changing World System'*, International Studies Quarterly. Vol. 38, pp. 347-377.

Haass, R. (2014) *Tipperary International Peace Award'*, http://www.cfr.org/peace-conflict-and human-rights/richard-n-haasssremarks-upon-receiving-2013-tipperary-international-peace award/p33186.[Accessed: 07/04/2018].

Hagmann, T. and Péclard, D. (2010) *Negotiating Statehood: Dynamics of Power and Domination in Africa'*, Development and Change, Vol. 41, No. 4, pp. 539-562.

Hall, R. A. (2009) *From Rebels to Soldiers: An Analysis of the Philippine and East Timorese Policy Integrating Former Moro National Liberation Front (MNLF) and Falintil Combatants into the Armed Forces. SSRN Scholarly Paper'*, http://papers.ssrn.com/ abstract1450242 [Accessed 16/04/2017].

Hall, R. and Biersteker, T. (2002) The Emergence of Private Authority in Global Governance', *Cambridge Studies in International Relations*, Cambridge: Cambridge University Press.

Hambrecht, M. *et al.* (1993) *Evidence for a Gender Bias in Epidemiological Studies of Schizophrenia, Schizophrenia Research'*, No. 8, pp. 223-231.

Hamelink. C. J. (2002) Communication May Not Build Peace, But It Can Certainly Contribute to War', *Journal of Media Development*, Vol. 49, No. 2, pp. 36-37.

Hammersley, M. (1993*) What is Social Research?* Milton Keynes: Open University Press.

Hänggi, H., (2005) *Approaching Peacebuilding from a Security Governance*

Perspective, In Bryden and H. Hänggi, (Eds.), Security Governance in Post-Conflict Peacebuilding (pp. 3-19). Münster and New Brunswick, NJ: Lit Verlag and Transaction Publishers.

Hannabuss, S. (1996) *Research Interviews*, New Library World. Vol. 97, No. 5, pp. 22-30.

Hansen, T. and Finn, S. (2006) Sovereignty revisited', *Annual Review of Anthropology*, Vol. 35, pp. 295–315.

Hanson, S. (2007) *Disarmament, Demobilisation, and Reintegration (DDR) in Africa'*, Backgrounder, http://www.cff.org. Publication [Accessed 15/04/2016].

Hanzich, R. (2011) Struggles in South Sudan', *Harvard International Review*, Vol. 33, No. 1, pp. 38-41.

Harle, J. (2016) *Research and Knowledge Systems in Difficult Places, part 1, Research to Action'*, The Global Guide to Research Impact. http://ebn.bmj.com/content/3/3/68.full [Accessed: 20/06/2016].

Harris, M. and Johnson, O. (2000) *Cultural Anthropology*, 5th (Ed.), Needham Heights, MA: Allyn and Bacon.

Harsch, E. (2005) *Reintegration of Ex-combatants when War ends: transforming Africa's Fighters into Builders'*, Africa Renewal, https://www.un.org/africarenewal/magazine/october-2005/reintegration-ex-combatants[Accessed: 15/08/2019].

Hartzeil, C. and Hoddie, M. (2003) Institutionalising Peace: Power-Sharing and Post-Civil War Conflict Management', *American Journal of Political Science*, Vol 47, No. 2, pp. 318-332.

Hartzell, C, Hoddie, M. and Rothchild, D. (2001) *Stabilising the Peace after Civil War: An Investigation of Some Key Variables'*, International

Organisation, Vol. 55, No. 1, pp. 183–208.

Hartzell, C. A. and Hoddie, M. (2007) *Crafting Peace: Power-Sharing Institutions and the Negotiated Settlement of Civil Wars'*, University Park PA: Pennsylvania State University Press.

Haug, W. (2001) Ethnic, Religious and Language Groups: Towards a Set of Rules for Data Collection and Statistical Analysis', *International Statistical Review*, Vol. 69, No.2, pp. 303-311.

Hayashi, P., Abib, G. and Hoppen, N. (2019) Validity in Qualitative Research: A Processual Approach', *The Qualitative Report*, Vol. 24, No. 1, pp. 98-112.

Hazen, J. M. (2010) *Understanding Reintegration within Post-conflict Peacebuilding: Making the Case for Reinsertion' First and Better Linkages Thereafter,'* In: Monopoly of Force; The Nexus of DDR and SSR', (Ed.), by Melanne A. Civic and Miklaucic, M. Centre for Complex Operations Institute for National Strategic Studies, National Defence University Press Washington, DC.

Healy, S. and Plaut, M. (2007) *Ethiopia and Eritrea: Allergic to Persuasion'*, Briefing Paper, African Affairs, Chatham House, The Royal Institute of International Affairs. London.

Hechter, M. (1986) *A Rational Choice Approach to Race and Ethnic Relations'*, In D. Mason, and R. J, Theories of Race and Ethnic Relations (pp. 268-277). Cambridge: Cambridge University Press.

Hechter, M. (1987) *Principles of Group Solidarity'*, Berkeley: University of California Press.

Heckathorn, D. D. (2011) *Snowball versus Respondent-Driven Sampling'*, Sociological Methodology. Vol. 41, No. 1, pp. 355–366.

Heger, L. and Salehyan, S.I. (2007) Ruthless Rulers: Coalition Size and the Severity of Civil Conflict', *International Studies Quarterly*, Vol. 51, No. 2, pp. 385-403.

Hegre, H. *et al.* (2001) Towards a Democratic Civil Peace? Democracy, Political Change, and Civil War, 1816-1992', *American Political Science Review*, Vol. 95, No. 1, pp. 16-33.

Henderson, E. A. (1998) The Democratic Peace through the Lens of Culture, 1820- 1989', *International Studies Quarterly*, Vol. 42, No, 3, pp. 461-484.

Hendricks, K. B. and Singhal, V.R. (2005) *An empirical Analysis of the Effects of Supply Chain Disruption on Long-run Stock Price Performance and Equity Risk of the Firm'*, Production and Operations Management, Vol. 14, No. 1, pp. 22-53.

Herath, O. (2016) A *Critical Analysis of Positive and Negative Peace'*, pp. 104-107. http://www.repository.kln.ac.lk/bitstream/handle/.../journal1%20%281%29 [Accessed: 15/10/2017].

Herbst, J. (2000) *States and Power in Africa: Comparative Lessons in Authority and Control'*, Princeton: Princeton University Press.

Herring, E. and Rangwala, G. (2006) *Iraq in Fragments: The Occupation and Its Legacy'*, London: Hurst.

Herz, J. (1951) *Political Realism and Political Idealism: A Study in Theories and Realities'*, Chicago: University of Chicago Press.

Hesse-Biber, S. N. and Leavy, P. (2011) *The Practice of Qualification Research'*, 2nd (Eds.), Sage Publications, Inc. Oaks, California

Hindess, B. (1996) *Discourses of Power: From Hobbes to Foucault'*, Oxford:

Blackwell Publishers Ltd.

Hippler, J. (2004) *Nation-states for Export? - Nation-building between Military Intervention, Crisis Prevention and Development Policy'*, (pp. 173-190). In: Jochen Hippler (Ed.), Nation-Building – A Key Concept for Peaceful Conflict Transformation. London.

Hippler, J. (2005) *Nation-Building - A Key Concept of Peaceful Conflict Transformation'*, London Pluto Press, pp. 3-14.

Hirshleifer, J (2001) *The Dark Side of the Force: Economic Foundations of Conflict Theory'*, Cambridge: Cambridge University Press.

Hobbes, T. [1651] 1996. *Leviathan'*, (Ed.), Richard Tuck. Cambridge: Cambridge University.

Hobbs, D. (2006) *Fieldwork'*, In V. Jupp (Ed.), The Sage Dictionary of Social Research Methods', (pp. 120-122). London: Sage Publications Ltd.

Hoddie, M. and Hartzell. C. (2003) Civil War Settlements and the Implementation of Military Power-Sharing Arrangements', *Journal of Peace Research*, Vol. 40, No. 3, pp. 303-320.

Hoffman, J. and Graham, P. (2009) *Introduction to Political Theory'*, London: Pearson Longman.

Hoffmann, K. (2014) Ethnogovernmentality: The Making of Ethnic Territories and Subjects in Eastern Congo', PhD Thesis. University of Roskilde, Roskilde.

Hoffmann, K. and Vlassenroot, K. (2014) *Armed Groups and the Exercise of Public Authority, The Cases of the Mayi Mayi and Raya Mutomboki in Kalehe, South Kivu'*, Peacebuilding. Vol. 2, No. 2, pp. 202–20.

Höglund, K. and Oberg, M. (2011) *Understanding Peace Research: Methods and Challenges'*, New York: Taylor & Francis.

Høigilt, J., Falch, A. and Rolandsen, O. H. (2010) *The Sudan Referendum and Neighbouring Countries: Egypt and Uganda'*, Oslo: Peace Research Institute Oslo.

Holsti, K. (1996) *The State, War, and the State of War'*, Cambridge: Cambridge University Press.

Hooks, B. (1989) *Talking Back: Thinking Feminist, Thinking Black'*, Boston, MA: South End Press.

Horkheimer, M. (1982) *Critical Theory'*, New York: Seabury Press.

Horowitz, D. L. (1985) *Ethnic Groups in Conflict'*, Berkeley: University of California Press.

Horowitz, D. L. (1998) Structure and Strategy in Ethnic Conflict', *Paper Prepared for the Annual World Bank Conference on Development Economics*, Washington, DC.

Horwitz, T. (1991) *First Sounds of Defiance Emanating from Iraqis'*, Globe and Mail (Canada), Academic, Lexis-Nexis, University of Iowa Library, Iowa City, IA.

Howell, J. (1978) *Horn of Africa: Lessons from the Sudan Conflict'*, International Affairs. Vol. 54, No. 3, pp. 421-36.

HSBA (2011) *Women's Security and the Law in South Sudan Grow and Oxfam'*, Geneva: HSBA.

HSBA (2012) *Sudan Human Security Baseline Assessment, DDR in South Sudan'*, Geneva: HSBA.

Htun, M. (2004) *Is Gender like Ethnicity? The Political Representation of Identity Groups'*, Perspectives on Politics, Vol.2, No, 3, pp. 439-458.

Hughes, C., Öjendal, J. and Schierenbeck, I. (2015) *The Struggle versus* the Song—the local turn in Peacebuilding: An introduction', Third World Quarterly. Vol. 36, No. 5, pp. 817–824.

Humphreys, M and Weinstein, J. (2005) *Handling and Manhandling Civilians in Civil War'*, Unpublished Manuscript.

Humphreys, M. (2005) Natural Resources, Conflict, and Conflict Resolution: Uncovering the Mechanisms', *Journal of Conflict Resolution*, Vol. 49, No.4, pp. 508 – 537.

Humphreys, M. and Weinstein, J. (2004) *What the Fighters Say'*, Centre for Globalisation and Sustainable Development Working Paper, Columbia University.

Humphreys, M. and Weinstein, M. (2008) Who Fights? The Determinants of Participation in Civil War', Midwest Political Science Association, *American Journal of Political Science*, Vol. 52, No. 2, pp. 436-455.

Huntington, S. (1996) *The Clash of Civilisations and the Remaking of World Order'*, New York: Simon & Schuster.

Hurworth, R. (2003) *Overview of Qualitative Methods'*, Unpublished Manuscript, Melbourne.

Hutchinson S. (1996) *Nuer Dilemmas: Coping with Money, War, and the State'*, University of California Press, Berkeley.

Hutchinson, J. and Smith, A. (1996) *Ethnicity'*, Oxford University Press, Oxford and New York.

Hutchinson, S. (2000) *Nuer Ethnicity Militarised'*, Anthropol Today. Vol. 16, No. 3, pp. 6–13.

Hutchinson, S. (2001) A Curse from God? Religious and Political Dimensions of the post-1991 Rise of Ethnic Violence in South Sudan',

Journal of Modern African Studies, Vol. 39, No. 2, pp. 307–331.

Hutchinson, S. and Pendle. N.R (2015) *Violence, Legitimacy, and Prophecy: Nuer struggles with uncertainty in South Sudan'*, Am Ethnol. Vol 42, No. 3, pp. 415–430.

Hutton, L. (2014) *South Sudan: From Fragility at Independence to a Crisis of Sovereignty'*, Netherlands Institute of International Relations Clingendael', pp. 4-48. https://www.clingendael.org/sites/default/files/pdfs/South%20Sudan.pdf [Accessed: 15/10/2017].

Hyden, G. (1996) *Rethinking Theories of the State: An Africanist Perspective'*, Africa Insight, Vol. 26, No. 1, pp. 26 - 35.

Ibhawoh, B (2010) *Beyond Instrumentalism and Constructivism: Reconceptualising Ethnic Identities in Africa'*, Humanities Today, Vol. 1. No.1, pp. 221-9.

IDDRS, (2006) *Integrated DDR Standards',* United Nations, New York, http://pksoi.army.mil/doctrine_concepts/documents/UN Guidelines/IDDRS. Pdf [Accessed 20/03/2017].

Idris, A. H. (2001) *Sudan's Civil War: Slavery, Race, and Formational Identities'*, Lewiston, N.Y.: Edwin Mellen Press.

Idris, A. H. (2005) *Conflict and Politics of identity in Sudan'*, New York, Palgrave Macmillan.

Idris, A.H. (2010) *I Hate to Choose: Personal Reflections on the Referendum'*, http://www.sudantribune.com/I-hate-to-Choose-Personal,37003, [Accessed: 06/07/2018].

IGAD (2011) IGAD Support for the new Republic of South Sudan. Available at:

http://www.un.org/en/ecosoc/julyhls/pdf12/south_sudan_igad_br ochure.pdf, [Accessed: 11/09/2017].

Ignatieff, M. (1996) *There's No Place Like Home: The Politics of Belonging'*, In: S. Dunant and R. Porter (Eds), The Age of Anxiety. London: Virago.

Ignatieff, M. (2003) *Empire Lite: Nation-Building in Bosnia, Kosovo and Afghanistan'*, London: Vintage.

Ihonvbere, J. (1996a) *The Crisis of Democratic Consolidation in Zambia'*, Civilisations. Vol. 43, No. 2, pp. 83-109.

Ihonvbere, J. (1996b) *Economic Crisis, civil society and Democratisation: The Case of Zambia'*, Trenton, NJ: Africa World Press.

Ikenberry, D. and Ramnath, D. (2000) *Underreaction'*, Working Paper. Rice University.

Ingrid, V.B. and Rustad, S.A. (2018) *Conflict Trends in Africa, 1989–2017, Conflict Trends'*, Vol. 6. Oslo: PRIO.

International Crisis Group (2012) *Conflict Minerals in DRC'*, http://www.crisisgroup.org/en/publication-type/key-issues/country/conflict-minerals-in-drc.aspx [Accessed: 27/12/2017/].

International Crisis Group. (2003a) *Sudan: Towards an Incomplete Peace'*, Nairobi and Brussels: International Crisis Group.

International Crisis Group. (2003b) *Sudan's Other Wars'*, Nairobi and Brussels: International Crisis Group, Nairobi and Brussels: International Crisis Group.

International Crisis Group. (2005) *The Khartoum–SPLM Agreement: Sudan's Uncertain Peace'*, Nairobi and Brussels: International Crisis

Group.

International Crisis Group. (2011) *Divisions in Sudan's Ruling Party and the Threat to the Country's Future Stability'*, Nairobi and Brussels: International Crisis Group.

International Crisis Group. (2019) *Salvaging South Sudan's Fragile Peace Deal'*, Brussels.

Isajiw, W. (2000) Approaches to Ethnic Conflict Resolution: Paradigms and Principles', *International Journal of Intercultural Relations*, Vol. 24, No.1, pp.105-24.

Isike, C. and Okeke-Uzodike, U. (2010) *Moral Imagination, Ubuntu and African Women: Towards Feminising Politics and Peace-building in KwaZulu-Natal'*, Gandhi Marg. Vol. 31, No. 4, pp. 679-709.

Iyob, R and Khadiagala, G.M. (2006) *Sudan: The Elusive Quest for Peace'*, Colorado: Lynne Rienner Publishers.

Jabareen, Y. (2013) Conceptualising Post-Conflict Reconstruction and Ongoing Conflict Reconstruction of Failed States', *International Journal of Politics, Culture, and Society*, Vol. 26, No. 2, pp. 107-125.

Jabri, V. (2007) *War and the Transformation of Global Politics'*, Basingstoke & New York: Palgrave Macmillan.

Jackson, P. (2015) *Introduction: Security and Development'*, In: P. Jackson (Ed.), Handbook of International Security and Development (pp. 1-18). Cheltenham: Edward Elgar Publishing.

Jackson, R.H. (1990) *Quasi-States: Sovereignty, International Relations and the Third World'*, Cambridge: Cambridge University Press.

Jacoby, T. and Ozerdem, A. (2008) The Role of the State in the Turkish Earthquake of 1999', *Journal of International Development*, Vol. 20, No. 3, pp. 297–310.

James, C. and Oplatka, I. (2015) *An Exploration of the notion of the 'Good Enough School'*, Management in Education, Vol. 29, No. 2, pp. 77–82.

James, L. (2011) *From Slaves to Oil'*, In: J. Ryle, J. Willis, S. Baldo and J.M. Jok, (Eds). The Sudan Handbook. London: James Currey and the Rift Valley Institute.

Jarstad, A. K. (2009) *The Prevalence of Power-sharing: Exploring the Patterns of Post-election Peace'*, Africa Spectrum, Vol. 44, No. 3, pp. 41-62.

Jenkins, R. (1997) *Rethinking Ethnicity'*, London: Sage.

Jenne, E. (2006) *National Self-Determination: A Deadly Mobilising Device'*, In: Hannum and E. Babbitt (Ed.), Negotiating Self-Determination (pp. 7-36). Lanham: Lexington.

Jennings, K. M. (2009) The Political Economy of DDR in Liberia: A gendered Critique', *Conflict, Security and Development*, Vol. 9, No. 4, pp.475-494.

Jervis, R. (1976) *Perception and Misperception in International Relations'*, Princeton University Press.

Jervis, R. (1978) *Cooperation under the Security Dilemma'*, World Politics. Vol. 30, No. 2

Johnson, D. (1986) Judicial Regulation and Administrative Control: Customary Law and the Nuer, 1898–1954', *The Journal of African History'*, Vol. 27, No. 01, pp. 59–78.

Johnson, D. (2003) *The Root Causes of Sudan's Civil Wars'*, Indiana University Press.

Johnson, D. (2010) *When Boundaries Become Borders: The Impact of Boundary-making in Southern Sudan's Frontier Zones'*, London: Rift Valley

Institute.

Johnson, D. (2014) The Political Crisis in South Sudan', *African Study Review*, Vol.57, No. 3, pp. 167–174.

Johnson, H. (2011) *Waging Peace in Sudan: The Inside Story of the Negotiations that ended Africa's Longest Civil War'*, Brighton, UK: Sussex Academic Press.

Johnson, H. (2016) *South Sudan: The Untold Story from Independence to the Civil War'*, London: IB Tauris.

Johnson, K. and Hutchison, M. L. (2012) Hybridity, Political Order and Legitimacy: Examples from Nigeria', *Journal of Peacebuilding and Development*, Vol. 7, No. 2, pp. 37–52.

Johnson, M.J. (2002) *In-depth Interviewing'*, In J. F. Gubrium & J.A. Holstein (Eds.), Handbook of Interview Research: Context and methods (pp. 103-120). London: Sage.

Jok, A., Leitch, R. and Vandewint, C. (2004) *A study of Customary Law in Contemporary Southern Sudan'*, World Vision International and the South Sudan Secretariat of Legal and Constitutional Affairs. Juba; South Sudan.

Jok, M.J. (2005) *War, changing ethics and the position of youth in South Sudan'*, In: Jon Abbink and Ineke van Kessel (Eds), Vanguard or Vandals: Youth, Politics and Conflict in Africa (Brill, Leiden.

Jok, M.J. (2011) *Diversity, Unity, and Nation-Building in South Sudan'*, Special Report, Washington: United States Institute of Peace.

Jok, M.J. (2012) *Insecurity and Ethnic Violence in South Sudan: Existential Threats to the State'*, The Sudd Institute, Issue Paper No. 1.

Jok, M.J. (2012) *South Sudan: Building a Diverse Nation'*, In: Heinrich Böll

Foundation and Toni Weis (Eds.), Sudan after Separation: New Approaches to a New Region, Heinrich Böll Foundation, Berlin.

Jok, M.J. (2013) *Mapping Sources of Conflict and Insecurity in South Sudan'*, Special Report No. 1. The Sudd Institute. Juba; South Sudan.

Jok, M.J. (2014*) South Sudan and the Prospect of Peace amidst Violent Political Wrangling'*, Juba; The Sudd Institute. South Sudan

Jok, M.J. (2014) *South Sudan and the Prospects for Peace amidst Violent Political Wrangling'*, Policy Brief, No. 4, The Sudd Institute. Juba; South Sudan.

Jok, M.J. (2015) *Negotiating the end to the current Civil War in South Sudan: What Lessons can Sudan's Comprehensive Peace Agreement Offer?* Inclusive Political Settlements Papers, No. 19, Berghof Foundation, Berlin.

Jok, M.J. (2015) *The Paradox of Peace in Sudan and South Sudan; Why the Political Settlements Failed to Endure'*, Berghof Foundation Operations GmbH – CINEP/PPP, pp. 1-17.

Jok, M.J. (2017) *Introduction: The State, Security and Community Defence Groups in South Sudan'*, In: Jok, M.J., Schomerus M, Kuol LBD, Breidlid IM, Arensen M.J. (Eds.), Informal Armies: Community Defence Groups in South Sudan's Civil War. pp 1–6. Saferworld. London.

Jok, M.J. and Hutchinson, S.E. (1999) *Sudan's Prolonged Second Civil War and the Militarisation of Nuer and Dinka Ethnic Identities'*, African Studies Review. Vol. 42, No. 2, pp. 125–145.

Jones I.R. (2001) *Habermas or Foucault or Habermas and Foucault? The implications of a shifting debate for medical sociology'*, In: G. Scambler (Ed.), Habermas Critical Theory and Health London, (pp. 163–181). Routledge.

Jones, B. F and Olken, B.A. (2005) Do Leaders Matter? National Leadership and Growth Since World War II', *The Quarterly Journal of Economics*, Vol. 120, Issue 3, pp. 835–864.

Jones, M. (2011) *Somaliland and South Sudan—the Challenging Road Ahead'*, http://www.southsudannation.com/somalilandsschallengesahead%2078.htm [Accessed: 05/04/2018].

Jooma, M. (2007) *Dual realities: Peace and War in the Sudan – An update on the implementation of the CPA'*, Institute for Security Studies, Situation Report, www.issafrica.org/uploads/.

Jooma, M. (2005) *Feeding the Peace: Challenges Facing Human Security in Post-Garang South Sudan'*, Pretoria: Institute for Security Studies. http://www.reliefweb.int/library/documents/2005/iss-sdn-23aug.pdf.

Joseph, R. (1991) Africa: The Rebirth of Political Freedom', *Journal of Democracy*, Vol. 2, No. 4, pp. 11–24.

Joshi, M. and Mason, T. D. (2011) *Civil War Settlements, Size of Governing Coalition, and Durability of Peace in Post–Civil War States'*, International Interactions, Vol. 37, No. 4, pp. 388-413.

Josselson, R. (1996) *Ethics and Process in the Narrative Study of Lives'*, London: Sage.

Justice Africa, (2001) *Prospect for peace in Sudan: Briefing November 2001'*, http://www.sudanarchive.net. [Accessed 13/01/2018].

Justice Africa. (2002a) *Prospect for peace in Sudan: Briefing June–July 2002'*, http://www.sudanarchive.net [Accessed: 02/01/ 2018].

Justino, P. (2013) *Research and Policy Implications from a Micro-level*

Perspective on the Dynamics of Conflict, Violence and Development', In: P. Justino, T. Brück, and P. Verwimp (Eds.), A Micro-Level Perspective on the Dynamics of Conflict, Violence and Development', Oxford: Oxford University Press.

Justino, P. (2016) Supply and Demand Restrictions to Education in Conflict-affected Countries: New Research and Future Agendas', *International Journal of Educational Development,* Vol. 47, pp. 76–85.

Jütting, J. (2003) I*nstitutions and Development: A Critical Review'*, OECD Development Centre Working Papers, No. 210, OECD Publishing, Paris. https://doi.org/10.1787/341346131416.

Kabeer, N. (2000) *Social Exclusion, Poverty and Discrimination: Towards an Analytical Framework'*, IDS Bulletin, Vol. 31, No. 4, pp. 83-97

Kahmann, E. (2003*) Conceptualising Security Governance'*, Cooperation and Conflict, Vol. 38, No. 1, pp. 5–26.

Käihkö, I. (2014) *Once a Combatant, Always a Combatant?' Mats Utas blog,* (http://matsutas.wordpress.com/2014/01/07/once-a-combatant-always-a-combatant-by-ilmari-kaihko.

Kaldor, M. (1999) *New and Old Wars: Organised Violence in a Global Era'*, Stanford, CA: Stanford University Press.

Kaldor, M. (2001; 2006) *New and Old Wars, organised violence in a global era'*, Stanford: Stanford University Press.

Kaldor, M. (2009) *New Wars: Counter-Insurgency or Human Security'*, The Broker: http://www.thebrokeronline.eu/en/Dossiers/[Accessed 4 June 2017].

Kalyvas, S. (2001*) New and Old Civil Wars: A Valid Distinction?'* World Politics. Vol. 54, pp. 99-118.

Kalyvas, S. (2006) *The Logic of Violence in Civil War'*, Cambridge: Cambridge University Press.

Kalyvas, S. and Kocher, M. (2007) *How 'Free' Is Free Riding in Civil Wars? Violence, Insurgency and the Collective Action Problem'*, World Politics. Vol. 59, pp. 177–216.

Kameir, E.W. (2011) *The Political Economy of South Sudan: A Scoping Analytical Study'*, The African Development Bank. https://www.afdb.org/fileadmin/uploads/afdb/Documents/Project -and-Operations/2011%20Political_Economy_South_Sudan_- _24_October_20111.pdf.

Kandeh, J.D. (1992) *Politicisation of Ethnic Identities in Sierra Leone'*, African Studies Review. Vol. 35, pp. 81-99.

Kaplan, R. (1993) *Balkan conflicts: A Journey through History'*, New York: St. Martin's Press.

Karazsia, Z. (2015) Evaluating the Success of Disarmament, Demobilisation, and Reintegration Programs: The Case of Congo-Brazzaville', *Journal of Interdisciplinary Conflict Science*, Vol. 1, No. 2, pp.1-34.

Kareva, I. (2011) *Prisoner's Dilemma in Cancer Metabolism'*, PLoS One. Vol. 6, No. 12.

Karl, M. and Engels, F. [1968] (1848) *The Communist Manifesto'*, Middlesex: Penguin.

Karp, A. (2006) *Trickle and Torrent: State Stockpiles'*, Small Arms Survey 2006: Unfinished Business; Chapter 2 (Appendix I), p. 61. Oxford: Oxford University Press.

Kasfir, N. (1977*) Southern Sudanese Politics since the Addis Ababa

Agreement, African Affairs. Vol. 76, No. 303, pp. 143-66.

Kauffmann, C. (1996) *Possible and Impossible Solutions to Ethnic Civil Wars'*, International Security, Vol. 20, pp. 136-175.

Kaufman, S. (2006) *Symbolic Politics or Rational Choice? Testing Theories of Extreme Ethnic Violence'*, International Security, Vol.30, No. 4, pp.45-86.

Kaufmann, C. (2005) *Rational Choice and Progress in the Study of Ethnic Conflict: A Review Essay'*, Security Studies. Vol.14, No. 1, pp. 178-207.

Keating, V.C. and Wheeler, N.J. (2013) *Concepts and Practices of Cooperative Security: Building Trust in the International System'*, In: V. Mastny & Z. Liqun (Eds.), The Legacy of the Cold War: Perspectives on Security, Cooperation, and Conflict (pp. 57-78). Lanham, MD: Lexington Books.

Keen, D. (1998) *The Economic Functions of Violence in Civil Wars'*, Adelphi Paper 320. Oxford: Oxford University Press.

Keen, D. (2001) *War and Peace: What's the Difference?* In: Adebajo, A. and C.L. Sriram (Eds.). Managing Armed Conflict in the 21st Century (pp. 1-22). London: Frank Cass.

Keen, D. (2009) *A Tale of Two Wars: Great Expectations, Hard Times'*, Conflict, Security and Development, Vol.9, No, 4, pp. 515-534.

Keen, D. (2012) *Greed and Grievance in Civil War'*, International Affairs, Vol. 88, No. 4, pp.757-777.

Keili, F.L. (2008) *Small arms and light weapons transfer in West Africa: a stock-taking'*, Disarmament Forum 4.

Kellner, D. (1989) *Critical Theory, Marxism and Modernity'*, Cambridge: Polity Press. Keohane, R.O. and Nye, J.S. (Eds) 1971 Transnational

Relations and World Politics. Massachusetts: Harvard University Press.

Kellner, D. (1990) *Critical Theory and the Crisis of Social Theory'*, Sociological Perspectives, Vol. 33, No. 1, pp. 11–33.

Keohane, R.O. (2005) *After Hegemony: Cooperation and Discord in the World Political Economy'*, Princeton: Princeton University Press.

Keriga, L. and Bujra, A. (2009) *Social Policy, Development and Governance in Kenya: A Profile on Healthcare Provision in Kenya'*, Nairobi. Dpmf.

Kerr, P. (2013) *Human Security'*, In: Collins, A. 3rd (Ed.), Contemporary Security Studies (pp. 104-116) Oxford University Press.

Kettl, D.F. (1999) The Future of Public Administration', *Journal of Public Affairs Education*, Vol. 5, No. 2, pp. 127-133.

Kettl, D.F. (2015) *The Job of Government: Interweaving Public Functions and Private Hands'*, Public Administration Review, Vol. 75, No. 2, pp. 219-229.

Khalid, M. (1990) *The Government They Deserve: The Role of the Elite in Sudan's Political Evolution'*, London: Kegan Paul.

Khalid, M. (2003) *War and Peace in Sudan: A Tale of Two Countries'*, London: Keegan Paul Ltd.

Kidder, L. and Fine, M. (1987) *Qualitative and Quantitative Methods: When Stories Converge, Multiple Methods in Program Evaluation, New Directions for Program Evaluation'*, No. 35. San Francisco, CA: Jossey-Bass.

Kieh, G.K. (1996) The Taproots of the Liberian Civil War', *Twenty-First Century Afro-Review*, Vol. 2, No. 3, pp. 123-152.

Kieh, G.K. (2011) *Warlords, Politicians and the Post-First Civil War Election in Liberia'*, African and Asian Studies, Vol. 10, pp. 83-99.

Kilroy, W. (2008) *Disarmament, Demobilisation and Reintegration (DDR) as a participatory process: involving communities and beneficiaries in post-conflict disarmament programmes'*, In: European Consortium for Political Research (ECPR) Second Graduate Conference, 25-27 August 2008, Universitat Autonòma Barcelona.

Kilroy, W. (2010) *Disarmament, Demobilisation, and Reintegration: The co-evolution of concepts, practices, and understanding'*, Working Papers. N.Y.: Ralph Bunche Institute for International Studies.

Kilroy, W. (2014) *Does a more participatory approach to reintegrating Ex-Combatants lead to better outcomes? Evidence from Sierra Leone and Liberia'*, Conflict, Security and Development. Vol. 14, No. 3, pp. 275-308.

Kim, K. (2007) Clinical Competence among Senior Nursing Students after their Preceptorship experiences', Journal *of Professional Nursing,* Vol. 23, No. 6, pp. 369-375.

Kim, S. (2003) *Research Paradigms in Organisational Learning and Performance: Competing Modes of Inquiry'*, Information Technology, Learning, and Performance Journal, Vol. 21, No. 1, pp. 9-18.

Kimenyi, M. (2012) *Future engagement between South Sudan and the Republic of Sudan'*, In: South Sudan, one year after independence: Opportunities and Obstacles for Africa's Newest Country, The Brookings Africa Growth Initiative.

Kimenyi, M. and Mbaku, J. (2011) *South Sudan: Avoiding State Failure'*, the Brooking Institution.

King, G., Robert O. Keohane, R.O. and Sidney, V. (1994) *Designing social inquiry: In Scientific inference in Qualitative Research'*, Princeton: Princeton University Press.

King, J.A., Morris, L.L. and Fitz-Gibbon, C. T. (1987) *How to Assess*

Program Implementation', Beverly Hills, CA: Sage.

Kingma, K (2000) *Demobilisation in Sub- Saharan Africa: The Development and Security Impacts'*, London: Macmillan.

Kingma, K. (2001) *Demobilisation and Reintegration of Ex-Combatants in Post-War and Transition Countries: Trends and Challenges of External Support'*, Eschborn, Germany: GTZ.

Kisiangani, E. (2011) South Sudan and The Pitfalls of Power', *African Security Review*, Vol. 20, pp. 91-95.

Klabbers, J. (2008) *Treaty Conflict and the European Union'*, Cambridge: Cambridge University Press.

Klain, E. (2009) *Croatia: The Participant in Large-Group Conflict'*, In: Carter Judy, C, Irani George, I. and Vamik, V., (Ed.), Regional and Ethnic Conflicts: Perspectives from the Front Lines. New Jersey: Pearson.

Klaus, K. and Mitchell, M. I. (2015) Land grievances and the mobilisation of electoral violence: Evidence from Côte d'Ivoire and Kenya', *Journal of Peace Research*, Vol. 52, No, 5, pp. 622–635.

Klein, A. (2002) *The Horn of Turbulence: Political Regimes in Transition'*, In: Debiel, T and Klein, A., (Eds). Fragile Peace: State Failure, Violence and Development in Crisis Regions, (pp. 156 – 170). London: Zed Books in Association with the Development and Peace Foundation.

Klopp, J.M. (2002) *Can Moral Ethnicity Trump Political Tribalism? The Struggle for Land and Nation in Kenya'*, African Studies, Vol. 61, No. 2, pp. 269-94.

Knight, W.A. (2008) *Disarmament, Demobilisation, and Reintegration and Post-Conflict Peacebuilding in Africa: An Overview'*, African Security, Vol. 1, No. 1, pp. 24-52.

Knopf, K.A. (2016) *Ending South Sudan's Civil War. Council Special Report'*, Vol. No. 77. Council on Foreign Relations, New York.

Knotter, C. (2019) *The de facto Sovereignty of Unrecognised States: Towards a Classical Realist Perspective?* Ethno-politics, Vol.18, No. 2, pp. 119-138.

Knox, C. (2012) *The Secession of South Sudan: A Case Study in African Sovereignty and International Recognition'*, Political Science Student Work Paper   1.
https://digitalcommons.csbsju.edu/polsci_students/1[Accessed: 14/08/2018].

Koenig, T., Spano, R. and Thompson, J. (2019) *Human Behaviour Theory for Social Work Practice'*, Singapore: Sage Publications.

Kohnert, D. (2010) *Democratisation via Elections in an African 'Narco-State'?* The Case of Guinea-Bissau', GIGA Working Papers Series.

Körppen, D. (2011) *Space Beyond the Liberal Peacebuilding Consensus – A Systemic Perspective'*, In: Daniela Körppen, Norbert Ropers and Hans J. Giessmann (Eds.). The Non-Linearity of Peace Processes: Theory and Practice of Systemic Conflict Transformation (pp. 77-96) Opladen/Farmington Hill: Barbara Budrich Publications.

Krahmann, E. (2003) *Conceptualising Security Governance'*, Cooperation and Conflict. Vol. 38, No. 1, pp. 5-26.

Kraidy, M.M. (2002) *Hybridity in Cultural Globalisation'*, Communication Theory, Vol.12, No. 3, pp. 316-339.

Krain, M. and Myers, M. (1997) *Democracy and Civil War: A Note on the Democratic Peace Proposition'*, International Interactions, Vol. 23, No, 1, pp. 109-18.

Krasner, S.D., and Risse, T. (2014) *External Actors, State-Building, and*

Service Provision in Areas of Limited Statehood: Introduction', Governance, Vol. 27, No. 4, pp. 545-567.

Krause, J. (2018) *Resilient Communities: Non-violence and Civilian Agency in Communal War'*, Cambridge: Cambridge University Press.

Krebs, R.R. (2014) *Military Disintegration: Canary in the Coal Mine?* In: Licklider R (Ed.), New Armies from Old: Merging Competing Military Forces after Civil Wars (pp. 245–58). Washington, DC: Georgetown University Press.

Kriesberg, L. (2001) *Changing forms of Coexistence'*, In: Abu-Nimer, Mohammed (Ed) Reconciliation, Justice, and Coexistence (Chapter 3, pp. 47-64). Oxford, UK: Lexington Books.

Kron J. (2010) *Peace Hovers in Sudan, but most Soldiers Stay Armed'*, New York Times, Online: http://www.nytimes.com/2010/12/31/world/africa/31sudan.html[Accessed: 10/02/2017].

Kruger, D. (1988) *An introduction to Phenomenological Psychology'*, 2nd (Ed.). Cape Town, South Africa: Juta.

Kuhn, T. S. (1962*) The Structure of Scientific Revolutions'*, Chicago: The University of Chicago Press.

Kulusika, S.E. (1998) *Southern Sudan: Political and Economic Power Dilemmas and Options'*, London: Minerva Press.

Kumar, K. (1998) *Post-Conflict Elections, Democratisation and International Assistance*; London: Lynne Rienner.

Kumar, K. (1999) *Promoting Social Reconciliation in Post-Conflict Societies: Selected Lessons from USAID's Experience'*, USAID Program and Operations Assessment Report No. 24. Centre for Development

Information and Evaluation, U.S. Agency for International Development.

Kumar, R. (1996) *Research: A way of thinking. Research Methodology'*, A step-by-step guide for beginners, Melbourne, VIC, Longman, pp. 1-13.

Kumnar, K. (1998) *Post-conflict Elections and International Assistance'*, In: Krishna Kumnar (Ed.), Post-Conflict Elections, Democratisation, and International Assistance (pp. 5-14). Boulder, CO: Lynne Rienner Publishers.

Kuol, D.K. (2018) *Confronting the Challenges of South Sudan's Security Sector: A Practitioner's Perspective'*, African Centre for Strategic Studies, Special Report, No. 4, https://africacenter.org/spotlight/confronting-the-challenges-of-south-sudans-security-sector-a-practitioners-perspective/[Accessed: 28/07/2019].

Kupchan, C. (1998) *After Pax Americana: Benign Power, Regional Integration, and the Sources of a Stable Multi-polarity'*, International Security, Vol. 23, No. 2, pp. 40-79.

Kuperman, A.J. (2013) *A Model Humanitarian Intervention? Reassessing NATO's Libya Campaign'*, International Security. Vol. 38, No. 1, pp. 105-136.

Kustov, A. (2017) *How Ethnic Structure affects Civil Conflict: A model of Endogenous Grievance'*, Conflict Management and Peace Science. Vol. 34, No. 6, pp. 660–679.

Kvale, S. (1996) *Interviews: An Introduction to Qualitative Research Interviewing'*, London: Sage.

Kydd, A.H. (1997) *Sheep in Sheep's Clothing'*, Security Studies, Vol. 7, No.

1, pp. 114–154.

Kydd, A.H. (2005) *Trust and Mistrust in International Relations'*, Princeton, NJ: Princeton University Press.

Kymlicka, W. (1995) *Multicultural Citizenship: A Liberal Theory of Minority Rights'*, Oxford: Oxford University Press.

Kymlicka, W. (1995) *The Rights of Minority Cultures'*, Oxford: Oxford University Press.

Lacher, W. (2012) *South Sudan: International State-building and its Limits'*, SWP Research Paper. Berlin: German Institute for International and Security Affairs.

Lacina, B. (2006) Explaining the severity of civil wars', *Journal of Conflict Resolution*, Vol. 50, No. 2, pp. 276-289.

Lagrange, M. A. (2010) *Insurgencies in South Sudan: A Mandatory Path to Build a Nation?* Small Wars Journal (pp.1-7). https://smallwarsjournal.com/blog/journal/docs-temp/620-lagrange.pdf. [Accessed: 26/04/2017].

Lagu, J. and Alier, A. (1985) *Protest from the First-Generation Leadership of the South'*, Hom of Africa, Vol. 8. No.1, pp. 47-51.

Lake and Rothschild, D. (1998) *The International Spread of Ethnic Conflict: Fear, Diffusion, and Escalation'*, Princeton, NJ: Princeton University Press.

Lake, D. and Rothchild, D. (1996) *Containing Fear: The Origins and Management of Ethnic Conflict'*, International Security. Vol. 21, No. 2, pp. 41-75.

Lamb, G. and Stainer, T. (2018) The Conundrum of DDR Coordination: The Case of South Sudan. Stability', *International Journal of Security and Development*, Vol. 7, No. 1, pp. 1–16.

Lamoureaux, S. and Sureau, T. (2019) Knowledge and Legitimacy: The Fragility of Digital Mobilisation in Sudan', *Journal of Eastern African Studies*, Vol. 13, No, 1, pp. 35-53.

Lange, M. (2004) *British Colonial Legacies and Political Development*, World Development, Vol. 32, No. 6, pp. 905–22.

Lapin, L.L. (1987) *Statistics for Modern Business Decisions*, Harcourt Publishers Ltd. Wallingford, United Kingdom.

Laqueur, W. (1968) *Revolution, International Encyclopedia of the Social Sciences*, Vol. 13, pp. 501-507.

Larson, G., Biar, A. and Pritchett, L. (2013) *South Sudan's Capability Trap: Building a State with Disruptive Innovation*, Harvard University Center for International Development Working Paper No. 268. Cambridge, MA: MIT Press.

Laudati, A. (2011) Victims of discourse: Mobilising narratives of fear and insecurity in post-conflict South Sudan —The case of Jonglei State', *African Geographical Review*, No. 30, Vol. 1, pp. 15–32.

Lax, D.A. and Sebenius, J.K. (1991) Negotiating Through an Agent', Journal of Conflict Resolution. Vol. 35, No. 3, pp. 474-493.

Le Billon, P. (2008) Diamond wars? Conflict diamonds and geographies of resource wars', *Annals of the Association of American Geographers*, Vol. 98, No. 2, pp. 345–372.

Le Billon, P. and Cervantes, A. (2009) Oil Prices, Scarcity and Geographies of War', *Annals of the Association of American Geographers*, Vol. 99, No. 5, pp. 836-844.

LeBrun, E. and Jonah, L. (2014) *Weapons Tracing in Sudan and South*

Sudan – Introduction', Small Arms Survey 2014: Women and Guns; (pp. 213-214). Cambridge University Press.

Lederach, J.P. (2001a) *Building Peace. Sustainable Reconciliation in Divided Societies'*, Washington DC, U.S.: United States Institute of Peace Press.

Lederach, J.P. (2001b) *Civil Society and Reconciliation, Turbulent Peace: The Challenges of Managing International Conflict'*, (Ed.), Chester A. Crocker, Fen Osler Hampson, and Pamela Aall. Washington: United States Institute of Peace Press.

Lederach, J.P. (2003) *The Little Book of Conflict Transformation'*, Intercourse, PA: Good Books.

Leibfried, S. and Zürn, M. (2005) *Transformations of the State*? UK: Cambridge University Press.

Lema, A. (2000) *Causes of Civil War in Rwanda: The Weight of History and Socio-Cultural Structures'*, In: 'Ethnicity Kills? The Politics of War, Peace and Ethnicity in Sub-Saharan Africa, McMillan Press Ltd.

Lemay-Herbert, N. (2009) State-building without Nation-building? Legitimacy, State Failure and the Limits of the Institutional Approach', *Journal of Intervention and Statebuilding*, Vol. 3, No.1, p. 21-45.

Leonardi, C. (2007) *Liberation or Capture: Youth in-between 'Hakuma', and 'Home' during Civil War and its Aftermath in Southern Sudan'*, African Affairs. Vol. 106, No, 424, pp. 391-412.

Leonardi, C. (2011) Paying Buckets of Blood for the Land: Moral Debates over Economy, War and State in Southern Sudan', *The Journal of Modern African Studies*, Vol. 49, No, 2, pp. 215-240.

Leonardi, C., Moro, L.N., Santschi, M., and Deborah, H.I. (2010) *Local Justice in Southern Sudan'*, United States Institute for Peace, Washington

DC.

LeRiche, M. (2014) *Sudan 1972-1983'*, In: New Armies from Old, Merging Competing Military Forces after Civil War, Roy Licklider, (Eds.), Washington, DC: Georgetown University Press.

LeRiche, M. and Arnold, M. (2012) *South Sudan: From Revolution to Independence'*, New York: Columbia University Press.

Lesch, A.M. (1998) *The Sudan: Contested National Identities'*, Bloomington: Indiana University Press.

Leuprecht, C. (2010) International Security Strategy and Global Population Aging', *Journal of Strategic Security*, Vol. 3, No. 4, pp. 27-48.

Levin, D.M. (1988) *The opening of vision: Nihilism and the Postmodern Situation'*, London: Routledge.

Lewis, I. (1983) *Nationalism and Self-Determination in the Horn of Africa'*, London: Ithaca Press.

Leysens, A.J. (2006) Social Forces in Southern Africa: Transformation from Below? *Journal of Modern African Studies*, Vol. 44, No. 1, pp. 31-58.

Licklider, R. (1995) The Consequences of Negotiated Settlements in Civil Wars, 1945-1993', *American Political Science Review*, Vol. 89, pp. 681-690.

Lincoln, Y.S. and Guba, E.A. (1985) *Naturalistic Inquiry'*, Beverly Hills, CA: Sage.

Lindley C.A. (2005) *Story and Narrative Structures in Computer Games'*, In: Developing Interactive Narrative Content: Sagas/Sagasnet Reader, Bushoff, B. (Ed.), Munich: High Text.

Linklater, A. and Suganami, H. (2006) *The English School of International Relations: A Contemporary Reassessment'*, Cambridge: Cambridge

University Press.

Lonsdale, J. (1994) *Moral Ethnicity and Political Tribalism'*, In: P. Kaarsholm and J. Hultin (Eds.), Inventions and Boundaries: Historical and Anthropological Approaches to the Study of Ethnicity and Nationalism, Roskilde University.

Lotze, W., Yvonne, K., and de Carvalho, G. (2008) *Peacebuilding Coordination in African Countries: Transitioning from Conflict: Case Studies of the Democratic Republic of the Congo, Liberia and South Sudan'*, Occasional Paper Series: Vol. 3, No. 1, Durban: Accord.

Luborsky, M. (1994) *The Identification and Analysis of Themes and Patterns'*, In: Gubrium, J. and Sankar, A. (Eds.), Qualitative Methods in Aging Research. Sage; Thousand Oaks, CA.

Luckham, R. and Kirk, T. (2013*) Understanding Security in the Vernacular in hybrid political contexts: a Critical Survey'*, Conflict, Security and Development. Vol. 13, No. 3, pp.339-359.

Lujala, P. (2010) The Spoils of Nature: Armed Civil Conflict and Rebel Access to Natural Resources', *Journal of Peace Research*, Vol. 47, No. 1, pp. 15–28.

Lunde, L. (2002) *Economic Driving Forces of Conflict (Econ Report 27/01)'*, Oslo: Econ Institute.

Lunde, L., Taylor, T., and Huser, A. (2003) *Commerce or Crime? Regulating Economies of Conflict'*, Fafo Report 424. Oslo: Fafo Institute.

Lyman, P. and Knopf, K. A. (2016) *To save South Sudan, Put it on Life Support'*, Financial Times (July 20). http://blogs.ft.com/beyond-brics/2016/07/20/to-save-south-sudan-put-it-on-life-support/ [Accessed: 06/09/2018].

Lynch, G. (2011) *I Say to You: Ethnic Politics and the Kalenjin in Kenya'*, Chicago: Chicago University Press.

Lynch, M. (2013) *Civilian-on-civilian Violence: An Ethnography of Choices during Civil War'*, ProQuest, UMI Dissertations Publishing.

Lyons, T. (2002) *Post-conflict Elections: War Termination, Democratisation, and Demilitarising Politics'*, Working Paper No. 20. Arlington, VA: Institute of Conflict Analysis and Resolution, George Mason University.

Lyons, T. (2002) *The Role of Post-Settlement Elections'*, Ending Civil Wars: The Implementation of Peace Agreements', (Ed.) by Elizabeth M. Cousens, Donald Rothchild, and Stephen John Stedman. Boulder, CO: Lynne Rienner.

Maanen, J. V. (1996) Commentary: On the Matter of Voice', *Journal of Management Inquiry*, Vol. 5, No. 4, pp. 375–381.

Mac Ginty, R. (2006) *No War, No Peace: The Rejuvenation of Stalled Peace Processes and Peace Accords'*, New York: Palgrave Macmillan.

Mac Ginty, R. (2010) *Hybrid Peace: The Interaction between Top-Down and Bottom-Up Peace'*, Security Dialogue, Vol. 41, No.4, pp. 391–412.

Mac Ginty, R. (2011) *International Peacebuilding and Local Resistance: Hybrid Forms of Peace'*, Palgrave Macmillan.

Mac Ginty, R. (2012) Against Stabilisation', Stability, *International Journal of Security and Development*, Vol. 1, No. 1, pp. 20-30.

Mac Ginty, R. (2014) *Everyday Peace: Bottom-up and Local Agency in Conflict-affected Societies'*, Security Dialogue, Vol 45, No. 6, pp. 548–564.

Mac Ginty, R. and Richmond, O. (2007) *Myth or Reality: Opposing Views on the Liberal Peace and Post-war Reconstruction'*, Global Society, Vol. 21,

No.4, pp. 491-497.

Mac Ginty, R. and Sanghera, G. (2012) Hybridity in Peacebuilding and Development: An Introduction', *Journal of Peacebuilding and Development*, Vol.7, No. 2, pp. 3–8.

Mack, A. (2005) *Human Security Report 2005: War and Peace in the 21st Century'*, New York and Oxford: Oxford University Press.

Mack, A. (2007) *Global Patterns of Political Violence'*, Working Paper, New York: International Peace Academy.

Madut-Arop, A. (2006) *Sudan's Painful Road to Peace; A Full Story of the Founding and Development of the SPLM/SPLA'*, North Charleston, SC: Book Surge.

Mailer, M. and Poole, L. (2010) *Rescuing the Peace in Southern Sudan'*, Joint NGO Briefing Paper.

Major, C. H. and Savin-Baden, M. (2011) *Integration of Qualitative Evidence: Towards Construction of Academic Knowledge in Social Science and Professional Fields'*, Qualitative Research, Vol. 11, No. 6, pp. 645–663.

Makombe, G. (2017) *An Expose of the Relationship between Paradigm, Method and Design in Research'*, The Qualitative Report, Vol. 22, No. 12, pp. 3363-3382.

Malejacq, R. (2016) *Warlords, Intervention, and State Consolidation: A Typology of Political Orders in Weak and Failed States'*, Security Studies, Vol. 25, No. 1, pp. 85-110.

Malesevic, S. (2004) *The Sociology of Ethnicity'*, London, GB: Sage Publications Ltd, 2004.

Malesevic, S. (2006) *Identity as Ideology: Understanding Ethnicity and Nationalism'*, New York: Palgrave Macmillan.

Malwal, B. (1985) *The Sudan: A Second Challenge to Nationhood'*, New York: Thornton Books.

Malwal, B. (2014) *Sudan and South Sudan: From One to Two'*, Palgrave MacMillan.

Mamdani M. (2017) *Can the African Union save South Sudan from Genocide?* New York Times 8 Jan. https://www.nytimes.com/2017/01/08/opinion/canafrican-union-save-south-sudan-fromgenocide.html [Accessed: 14/09/2018].

Mamdani, M. (1996) *Subject and Citizen'*, Princeton: Princeton University Press.

Mampilly, Z. (2011) *Rebel Rulers: Insurgent Governance and Civilian Life during War'*, Ithaca: Cornell University Press.

Manning, C. (2003) *Local-level Challenges to Post-conflict Peacebuilding, International Peacekeeping'*, No.10, Vol 3, pp. 25–43.

Mansfield, E.D. and Snyder, J. (2002) *Democratic Transitions, Institutional Strength, and War'*, International Organisation, Vol. 56, No. 2, pp. 297-337.

Mansfield, E.D. and Snyder, J. (2005) *Electing to fight: Why emerging Democracies go to War'*, Cambridge: MIT Press.

Marijan, B. (2015) *Neither War nor Peace: Everyday Politics, Peacebuilding and the Liminal Condition of Bosnia-Herzegovina and Northern Ireland'*, Theses and Dissertations (Comprehensive). Paper 1770.

Markakis, J. (1999) *Nationalism and Ethnicity in the Horn of Africa'*, In: Paris Yeros (Ed.), Ethnicity and Nationalism in Africa: Constructivist Reflections and Contemporary Politics, (pp. 65-80). Basingstoke: Macmillan.

Markula, P. and Silk, M. (2011) *Paradigmatic Approaches to Physical Culture*, In: P. Markula and M. Silk (Eds.), Qualitative Research for Physical Culture (pp. 24-56). New York: Palgrave.

Marshall, M. and Cole, B. (2008) *Global Report on Conflict, Governance and State Fragility*', Foreign Policy Bulletin, Vol. 18, No. 1, pp. 3-21.

Marshall, M. G. and Gurr, T. R (2005) *Peace and Conflict 2005: A Global Survey of Armed Conflicts, Self-Determination Movements, and Democracy*', College Park: Centre for International Development and Conflict Management, University of Maryland.

Marwick, A., Blackwell, L. and Lo, K. (2016) *Best Practices for Conducting Risky Research and Protecting Yourself from Online Harassment*', (Data & Society Guide). New York: Data & Society Research Institute.

Mason, J. (2002) *Qualitative Researching*', London: Sage, 2nd (Ed.), — (2006) Six Strategies for Mixing Methods and Linking Data in Social Science Research, Real Life Methods NCRM Node Working Paper.

Mastropaolo, A. (2012) *Is democracy a Lost Cause? Paradoxes of an Imperfect Invention*', Translated by Clare Tame, Publications from the ECPR Press.

Mathew, S, Boyd, R. (2011) *Punishment Sustains Large-scale Cooperation in Pre-state Warfare*', Proc Natl Acad Sci, Vol. 108, No, 28, pp. 11375–11380.

Mathews, J. (1997) *Power Shift*', Foreign Affairs, Vol. 76, No. 1, pp.50–66.

Mattes, M. and Savun, B. (2009) Fostering Peace after Civil War: Commitment Problems and Agreement Design', *International Studies Quarterly*, Vol. 53, No. 3, pp. 737-759.

Matthew, R. (2005) William James on Emotion and intentionality', *International Journal of Philosophical Studies,* Vol. 13, No. 2, pp. 179-202.

Maynard, D. (1989) *On the Ethnography and Analysis of Discourse in Institutional Settings'*, In: J. Holstein and G. Miller. (Ed.), In: Perspectives on Social Problems, Vol. 1, pp. 127–46.

Mayring, P. (2000) *Qualitative Inhaltsanalyse, Grundlagen und Techniken'*, 7th (Eds.), Weinheim: Deutscher Studien Verlag.

Mayring, P. König, J., Birk, N. and Hurst, A. (2000) *Opfer der Einheit, Eine Studie zur Lehrerarbeitslosigkeit in den neuen Bundesländern'*, Opladen; Leske & Budrich.

Mazurana, D.E., McKay, S.A., Carlson, K.C., and Kasper, J.C. (2002) *Girls in fighting forces and groups: Their recruitment, participation, Demobilisation, and Reintegration'*, Peace and Conflict: Journal of Peace Psychology, Vol 8, No. 2, pp. 97-123.

Mbaku, J.M and Smith, J.E. (2012) *South Sudan-One Year after Independence: Opportunities and Obstacles for Africa's Newest Country'*, Brookings Africa Growth Initiative.

Mc Fate, S. (2010) *The Link Between DDR and SSR in Conflict-Affected Countries'*, Special Report, No. 238, USIP. Washington.

McEvoy, C. and LeBrun, E. (2010) *Uncertain future: armed violence in Southern Sudan'*, Geneva: HSBA.

McMullin, J.R. (2013) Integration or Separation? The stigmatisation of Ex-Combatants after war', *Review of International Studies*, Vol. 39, pp. 385-414.

Mcneish, H. and Nicholls, P. (2014) *Hunger amid tragedy for South Sudan Refugees'*, As Fears Grow of New Violence in the World's Newest

Nation, Refugees in Ethiopia Relive the Terror of the Conflict. https://www.aljazeera.com/indepth/features/2014/11/[Accessed: 02/07/2017].

Mearsheimer, J. (1994) *The False Promise of International Institutions'*, International Security, Vol. 19, No 3, pp. 5-49.

Mearsheimer, J. (2001) *The Tragedy of Great Power Politics'*, New York: W.W. Norton & Company.

Mecca, J.T., Gibson, C., Giorgini, V., Medeiros, K. E., Mumford, M. D., and Connelly, S. (2015) *Researcher Perspectives on Conflicts of Interest: A Qualitative Analysis of Views from Academia'*, Science and Engineering Ethics, Vol. 21, No. 4, pp. 843–855.

Meek, S. and Malan, M. (2004) Identifying Lessons from DDR Experiences in Africa', Institute for Security Studies, Monograph No. 106. Pretoria, South Africa: Institute for Security Studies.

Mehler, A. (2004) *Oligopolies of Violence in Africa South of the Sahara'*, In: Nord-Süd-Aktuell, Vol. 18, No. 3, p. 539-548.

Mehler, A. (2009) *Hybrid Regimes and Oligopolies of Violence in Africa: Expectations on Security Provision from Below'*, In: Martina Fischer and Beatrix Schmelzle (Eds.), Building Peace in the Absence of States: Challenging the Discourse on State Failure, Berghof Handbook Dialogue Series, No. 8.

Mehreteab, A. (2007) *Border Conflict' –1998-2000 and its Psychological Impact on the Youth'*, Conference paper in Healy, Op.cit. pp. 23-77.

Melber, H. (2009a) Southern African Liberation Movements as Governments and the Limits to Liberation', *Review of African Political Economy*, Vol. 121, pp. 453-461.

Melber, H. (2009b) *Namibian Politics: The Pathology of Power and Paranoia'*, the Namibian, Windhoek, A Weekly Electronic Forum for Social Justice in Africa.

Merriam S. B. (2009) *Qualitative Research: A Guide to Design and Implementation'*, 3rd (Ed.), San Francisco, CA: Jossey-Bass.

Messner, J.J., Haken, N., Taft, P., Blyth, H., Lawrence, K., Graham, S.P. (2017) *Fragile States Index*. (T.F. Peace, Ed.). [PDF file]. http://fundforpeace.org/fsi/2017/05/14/fragile-states-index-2017-annual-report/951171705-fragile-states-index-annual-report-2017.

Meyer C. B. (2001) *A Case in Case Study Methodology'*, Field Methods, Vol. 13, No. 4, pp. 329–352.

Meyer, J.W., & Scott, W.R. (1983b) *Centralisation and the Legitimacy Problems of Local Government'*, In J.W. Meyer & W.R. Scott (Eds.), Organisational environments: Ritual and rationality, (pp. 199-215). Beverly Hills, CA: Sage.

Miall, H. (2004) *Conflict Transformation: A Multi-Dimensional Task'*, Berghof Handbook for Conflict Transformation, Berghof Research Centre for Constructive Conflict Management, Berlin.

Migdal, J. (1988) *Strong Societies and Weak States: State-Society Relations and State Capabilities in the Third World'*, Princeton: Princeton University Press.

Miles, M. B. and Huberman, A. (1984) *Qualitative Data Analysis'*, London: Sage.

Miles, M.B. and Huberman, A.M. (1994) *Qualitative Data Analysis'*, 2nd (Ed.), Newbury Park, CA: Sage.

Milgram, S. and Jodelet, D. (1976) *Psychological Maps of Paris'*, In:

Proshansky, Ittelson, Rivlin (Eds.) Environmental psychology: People and their physical settings, pp. 104-124). New York, Holt Rinehart and Winston.

Miller, C. (2005) A *Glossary of Terms and Concepts in Peace and Conflict Studies*, 2nd (Ed.), University of Peace, Africa Programme, from http://www.africa.upeace.org/documents/GlossaryV2.pdf.

Mitchell, C. (2012) *Introduction: Linking National-Level Peacemaking with Grassroots Peacebuilding*, In: Mitchell, C.R & Hancock, L.E. (Eds.), Local Peacebuilding and National Peace: Interaction between Grassroots and Elite Processes (pp. 1-18). London: Continuum International Publishing Group.

Mittelman, J.H. and Chin, C.N. (2005) *Conceptualising Resistance to Globalisation'*, In L. Amoore (ed.), the Global Resistance Reader', London: Routledge.

Mkutu, K.A. (2008) Uganda: Pastoral Conflict and Gender Relations', *Review of African Political Economy*, Vol. 35, No. 116, pp. 237-254.

Molloy, D.J. (2013) *An Unlikely Convergence: The Evolution of Disarmament Demobilisation and Reintegration (DDR) Theory and Counter-insurgency (COIN) Doctrine'*, PhD Dissertation Tokyo University of Foreign Studies.

Montalvo, *et al.* (2002) *The Effect of Ethnic and Religious Conflict on Growth'*, Available at: <http://www.econ.upf.edu/~montalvo/sec1034/jde.pdf[Accessed: 26/12/2018].

Moore, B. Jr. (1966) *Social Origins of Democracy and Dictatorship'*, Boston: Beacon Press.

Morgan, J. and Olsen, W. (2008) Defining Objectivity in Realist Terms', *Journal of Critical Realism*, Vol. 7, No. 1, pp.107-132.

Morrisey, E.L. (2010) *Lessons from the Past: Power Transitions and the Future of U.S. –China Relations'*, Washington DC: Georgetown University.

Morrison, J. (2004) *Sudan at the Crossroads'*, Whitehall Papers, Vol. 62, No. 1, pp.23-30.

Morrow, R.A. and Brown, D.D. (1994) *Critical Theory and Methodology'*, London: Sage.

Morrow, S. (2005) Quality and trustworthiness in qualitative research in counselling psychology', *Journal of Counselling Psychology*, Vol. 52, No. 2, pp. 250-260.

Moustakas, C. (1994) *Phenomenological Research Methods'*, Thousand Oaks, CA: Sage.

Mouton, J. (2010) *Research Designs in the Social Sciences'*, Class Notes. African Doctoral Academy Summer School, Stellenbosch: University of Stellenbosch.

Mueller, J. (2000) *The Banality of Ethnic War'*, International Security, Vol. 25, No.1, pp. 42-70.

Muggah, R and O'Donnell, C. (2015) Next-generation Disarmament, Demobilisation and Reintegration', Stability: *International Journal of Security and Development*, Vol. 4, No. 1. pp. 1–12.

Muggah, R and Rieger, M. (2012) *Negotiating Disarmament and Demobilisation in Peace Processes: what is the State of the Evidence?* Noref Report, pp.1-11. https://www.files.ethz.ch/isn/155994/84c0656455ff43ac35123eaf64 9015f9.pdf [Accessed: 12/05/2017].

Muggah, R, Nat Colletta, N. and de Tessières, S. (2009) *Alternatives to Conventional Security Promotion: Rethinking the Case of Southern Sudan,'* In HSBA. http://smallarmssurveysudan.org/pdfs/HSBA-Sudan-conference-papers.pdf.

Muggah, R. (2005) *Securing Haiti's Transition: Reviewing Human Insecurity and the Prospects for Disarmament, Demobilisation, and Reintegration',* Occasional Paper 14, Geneva: Small Arms Survey.

Muggah, R. (2005a) *No Magic Bullet: A Critical Perspective on Disarmament, Demobilisation and Reintegration (DDR) and Weapons Reduction in Post-conflict Contexts',* the Round Table, Vol.94, No, 379, pp. 239–252.

Muggah, R. (2005b) *Listening for a Change! Participatory Evaluations of DDR and Arms Reduction in Mali, Cambodia and Albania',* UNIDIR/2005/23. Geneva: United Nations Institute for Disarmament Research.

Muggah, R. (2005c) *Securing Haiti's Transition: Reviewing Human Insecurity and the Prospects for Disarmament, Demobilisation, and Reintegration',* Occasional Paper 14, Geneva: Small Arms Survey.

Muggah, R., Molloy, D. and Halty, M. (2009) *Disintegrating DDR in Sudan and Haiti? Practitioners views to overcome integration inertia',* In: Muggah, R. (Ed.), Security and Post-conflict Reconstruction: Dealing with Fighters in the Aftermath of War, (pp. 206–225). New York, N.Y.: Routledge.

Muller, E. N. (1972) A Test of a Partial Theory of Potential for Political Violence', *American Political Science Review,* Vol 66, No, 3, pp. 928–959.

Muller, E.N. (1985) Income Inequality, Regime Repressiveness, and Political Violence', *American Sociological Review,* Vol. 50, pp. 47-61.

Muller, E.N. and Weede E. (1990) Cross-National Variations in Political Violence: A Rational Action Approach', *Journal of Conflict Resolution*, Vol. 34, No, 4, pp. 624–51.

Multi-Country Demobilisation and Reintegration Program (2010) *MDRP Final Report: Overview of Program Achievements'*, Washington, DC: World Bank.

Munive, J. (2013a) *Context Matters: The conventional DDR template is Challenged in South Sudan'*, International Peacekeeping, Vol. 20, No. 5, pp. 585–599.

Munive, J. (2013b) *Disarmament, demobilisation and reintegration in South Sudan: The limits of conventional peace and security templates'*, Copenhagen: Danish Institute for International Studies', http://pure.diis.dk/ws/files/58204/RP2013_07_Jairo_Disarmament_SouthSudan_web.jpg.pdf [Accessed; 20/03/2018].

Munive, J. (2014) Invisible Labour: The Political Economy of Reintegration in South Sudan', *Journal of Intervention and Statebuilding*, Vol. 8, No. 4, pp. 334-356.

Munive, J. and Stine, J. (2012) *Revisiting DDR in Liberia: Exploring the power, agency and interests of local and international actors in the 'making' and 'unmaking' of combatants'*, Conflict, Security and Development, Vol, 12, No, 4, pp. 359-385.

Münkler, H. (2005) *The New Wars'*, Cambridge: Polity Press.

Murdoch, J.C. and Sandler, T. (2002) Economic growth, civil wars, and Spatial Spillover', *Journal of Conflict Resolution*, Vol 46, pp. 91-110.

Murshed, S. (2002) Conflict, Civil War and Underdevelopment: An Introduction', *Journal of Peace Research*, Vol. 39, Vol 4, pp. 387–393.

Murshed, S. and Tadjoeddin, M. (2009) Revisiting the Greed and Grievance Explanations for Violent Internal Conflict', *Journal of International Development*, Vol.21, No 1, pp.87-111.

Musso, G. (2011) *From one Sudan to two Sudan: from war to Peace?* ISPI - Working Paper, Africa Program.

Mutengesa, S. (2013) *Facile Acronyms and Tangled Processes: A Re-Examination of the 1990s 'DDR' in Uganda'*, International Peacekeeping, Vol. 20, No. 3, pp. 338-356.

Myrdal, G. (1972) How Scientific Are the Social Sciences?' *Journal of Social Issues*, Vol. 28, pp. 151-70.

Narayan, D., Raj Patel, R., Schafft, K., Rademacher, A. and Koch-Schulte, S. (1999) *Can Anyone Hear Us?* Washington D. C.: World Bank.

Natsios, A. S. (2012) *Sudan, South Sudan and Darfur: What Everyone Needs to Know'*, New York: Oxford University Press.

Nelson, C. (2004) *Learning from Clients, Assessment Tool for Microfinance Practitioners'*, the Small Enterprise Education and Promotion Network (SEEP), Washington D. C.

Newman, E. (2001) Human Security and Constructivism', *International Studies Perspectives*, Vol 2, No, 3, pp. 239–251.

Newman, E. (2009) *Conflict Research and the Decline of Civil War'*, Civil Wars. Vol. 11, No. 3, pp. 255-278.

Newman, E. (2013) *The International Architecture of Peacebuilding'*, In: R. Mac Ginty (Ed.), Routledge handbook of peacebuilding (pp. 266–276). London: Routledge.

Newman, E., Paris, R. and Richmond, O.P. (2009) *New perspectives on liberal peacebuilding'*, New York: United Nations University Press.

Nezam, T. and Alexandre, M. (2009) *Disarmament, Demobilisation and Reintegration*', Social Development Department Working Paper; no. 119. Conflict, Crime, and Violence, Washington, DC: World Bank.

Nichols, R. (2011) *DDR in South Sudan*', HSBA, Small Arms Survey, Geneva, Switzerland, http://www.smallarmssurveysudan.org/fileadmin/docs/archive/DDR/DDR-South-Sudan-Sept-2011.pdf.[Accessed: 04/07/2017].

Nitzschke, H. (2003) *Transforming War Economies: Challenges for Peacemaking and Peacebuilding*', IPA Conference Report, New York: International Peace Academy.

Nnoli, O. (1995) *Ethnicity and Development in Nigeria*', Aldershot: Avebury.

Noblit, G.W., and Hare, R.D. (1988) *Meta-ethnography: synthesising Qualitative Studies*', Newbury Park: Sage.

Nordlinger, E. A. (1972) *Conflict Regulation in Divided Societies: Occasional Papers in International Affairs No. 29*', Cambridge, Mass.: Harvard University. Centre for International Affairs, American Behavioural Scientist, Vol. 15, No. 6, pp. 952–952.

Nordstrom, C. (2004) *Shadows of War: Violence, Power, and International Profiteering in the Twenty-First Century*', Berkley/Los Angeles: University of California Press.

North, D. Wallis, J. and Weingast, B. (2009) *Violence and Social Orders: A conceptual framework for Interpreting Recorded Human History*', Cambridge, Cambridge University Press.

Nyaba, P.A. (2014) *South Sudan: The Crisis of Infancy*', Cape Town: The Centre for Advanced Studies of African Society.

Nyaba, P.A. (2000) *Politics of Liberation in South Sudan: An Insider's View'*, Kampala, Uganda: Foundation Publishers.

Nyaba, P.A. (2019) *South Sudan: Elites, Ethnicity, Endless Wars and the Stunted State'*, Dares-Salaam: Mkuki na Nyota.

Nyadera, I.N. (2018) *South Sudan Conflict from 2013 to 2018 Rethinking the causes, Situation and Solutions'*, Accord, https://www.accord.org.za/ajcr-issues/south-sudan-conflict-from-2013-to-2018.[Accessed: 28/04/2019].

O'Brien, A. (2009) *Shots in the Dark: The 2008 South Sudan Civilian Disarmament Campaign'*, HSBA Working Paper No. 16. Geneva: Small Arms Survey. http://smallarmssurveysudan.org/pdfs/HSBA-SWP-16-South-Sudan-Civilian-Disarmament-Campaign.pdf.

OECD (2007) *Handbook on Security Sector Reform (SSR): Supporting Security and Justice'*, Paris.

OECD (2012) *Peacebuilding and State-Building Priorities and Challenges: A Synthesis of Findings from Seven Multi-Stakeholder Consultations'*, International Dialogue on Peacebuilding and State-building, Dili, Timor-Leste.

Olson, M. (1965) *The Logic of Collective Action'*, Cambridge, MA: Harvard University Press.

Omondi, P. (2011) *Climate Change and Inter-community Conflict over Natural Resources in Jonglei State, South Sudan'*, Boma Development Initiative Report, London: Minority Rights Group International.

Omosulu, R. (2013) The Main Features and Constraints of Social Science's Research Methods', *International Journal of Development and Sustainability*, Vol. 2 No. 3, pp. 1907-1918.

Opongo, E. (2017) *An Assessment of Illicit Small Arms and Light Weapons Proliferation and Fragility Situations: Burundi'*, Nairobi: Regional Centre on Small Arms and Light Weapons.

Organski, A.F. (1958) *World Politics'*, New York: Knopf.

Osaghae, E. (1995) *Structural Adjustment and Ethnicity in Nigeria'*, Research Report No. 98. Uppsala: Nordic Africa Institute.

Osaghae, E. (1999) *The Post-Colonial African State and its Problems'*, In: P. McGowan and P. Nel (Eds.), Power, Wealth and Global Order, Cape Town: University of Cape Town Press.

Osaghae, E. (2005) The state of Africa's Second Liberation', Interventions: *International Journal of Post-colonial Studies*, Vol. 7, No. 1, pp. 1-20.

Osuala, E. C. (2001) *Introduction to Research Methodology*, 3rd (Ed.), Africana-First Publishers Limited, Onitsha.

Ottaway, M. (2002) *Rebuilding State Institutions in Collapsed States'*, Development and Change, Vol. 33, No. 5, pp. 1001–23.

Otterbein, K.F. (2004) *How War Began'*, College Station: Texas A&M Press.

Owegi, J., Ruth, T. and Kwambai, J. (2014) *Militarisation of Ethnic Conflict, Paradigms of Military Ethnicity, Intervention and Prevention'*, A presentation at the University of Nairobi for the Institute for Diplomacy and International Studies, pp.1-15.

Owen, J.M. (1994) *How Liberalism Produces Democratic Peace'*, International Security, Vol. 19, No. 2, pp. 87-125.

Oyugi, W. (2003) *The Politics of Transition in Kenya, 1999-2003: Democratic Consolidation or Deconsolidation'*, In: W.O. Oyugi *et al.* Eds. The Politics of Transition in Kenya: From KANU to NARC, Nairobi: Heinrich Böll Foundation.

Özerdem, A. (2012) *A Re-conceptualisation of Ex-combatant Reintegration: Social Reintegration Approach*', Conflict, Security and Development, Vol. 12, No. 1, pp. 51-73.

Ozkirimli, U. (2000) *Theories on Nationalism: A Critical Introduction*', St. Martin's Press, New York.

Paffenholz, T. and Spurk, C. (2006) *Civil Society, Civic Engagement, and Peacebuilding*', Social Development Papers: Conflict Prevention and Reconstruction, Paper No. 36.

Paffenholz, T., Abu-Nimer, M. and McCandless, E. (2005) Peacebuilding and development: Integrated approaches to evaluation', *Journal of Peacebuilding and Development*, Vol. 2, No. 2, pp. 1-5.

Pareto, V. (1935) *The Mind and Society*', London: Jonathan Cape Limited.

Paris, R. (2004) *At War's End: Building Peace after Civil Conflict*', Cambridge: Cambridge University Press.

Paris, R., and Sisk, T. D. (2009) *The Dilemmas of State Building: Confronting the Contradictions of Post-war Peace Operations*', New York: Routledge.

Parkinson, S.E. (2013) Organising rebellion: Rethinking high-risk mobilisation and social networks in war', *American Political Science Review*, Vol.10, No.3, p. 418.

Patton, M.Q. (1987) *How to Use Qualitative Methods in Evaluation*', California: Sage Publications, Inc.

Patton, M.Q. (1990) *Qualitative Evaluation and Research Methods*', Sage Publications, Newbury Park London New Delhi.

Patton, M.Q. (2002) *Qualitative Research and Evaluation Methods'*, 3rd (Ed.), Thousand Oaks, CA: Sage.

Paudel, D. (2016) *Ethnic Identity Politics in Nepal: Liberation from, or Restoration of Elite Interest?* Asian Ethnicity, pp. 1-18.

Pavkovic, A. and Radan, P. (2007) *Creating New States: Theory and Practice of Secession'*, Aldershot: Ashgate Publishing Limited.

Pavković, A. and Radan, P. (2011) *The Ashgate Research Companion to Secession'*, Farnham, UK; Burlington, VT: Ashgate Publishing.

Pelto, P., and Pelto, G. (2007) *Studying Knowledge, Culture and Behaviour in applied Medical Anthropology'*, Med Anthropol Q, Vol. 11, No. 2, pp. 147-63.

Pelto, P.J., and Pelto, G.H. (1997) *Ethnography: The Fieldwork Enterprise'*, In: J. Honigmann (Ed.), Handbook of Social and Cultural Anthropology, (pp. 241-288). New Delhi: Rawat Publications, India.

Pendle, N. (2015) They are Now Community Police: Negotiating the Boundaries and Nature of the Government in South Sudan through the identity of militarised cattle keepers', *International Journal of Minority Group Rights*, Vol. 22, No 3, pp. 410–434.

Persson, T., Roland, G. and Tabellini, G. (1997) Separation of Powers and Political Accountability', *Quarterly Journal of Economics*, Vol. 112, pp.1163-1202.

Petersen, R.D. (2001) *Resistance and Rebellion: Lessons from Eastern Europe'*, New York: Cambridge University Press.

Plummer, K. (1995) *Telling Sexual Stories: Power, Change, and Social Worlds'*, London: Routledge

Polese, A. and Santini, R.H. (2018) *Limited Statehood and its Security*

Implications on the Fragmentation Political Order in the Middle East and North Africa', Small Wars and Insurgencies, Vol. 29, No. 3, pp.379-390.

Polit, D.F. and Beck, C. T. (2004) *Nursing Research: Appraising Evidence for Nursing Practice'*, 7th (Ed.), Philadelphia, PA: Wolters Klower/Lippincott Williams & Wilkins.

Ponce, O. and Pagán-Maldonado, N. (2015) A mixed methods Research in Education: Capturing the complexity of the profession', *International Journal of Educational Excellence*, Vol. I, No. 1, pp. 111-135.

Porto, J.G. and Parsons, I. (2003) *Sustaining the Peace in Angola: an Overview of Current Demobilisation, Disarmament and Reintegration'*, Bonn, Bonn International Centre for Conversion, ISS Paper 27.

Posner, D. (2005) *Institutions and Ethnic Politics in Africa'*, Cambridge, Cambridge University Press.

Powell, G.B (1982) *Contemporary Democracies: Participation, Stability, and Violence'*, Cambridge: Harvard University Press.

Powell, R.   (2004) The Inefficient Use of Power: Costly   Conflict with   Complete Information', *American Political Science Review*, Vol. 98, No. 2, pp. 231-242.

Powell, R. (1999) *In the Shadow of Power'*, Princeton: Princeton University Press.

Powell, R. (2006) *War as a Commitment Problem'*, International Organisation, Vol. 60, pp. 169–203.

Powney, J. and Watts, M. (1987) *Interviewing in Educational Research'*, London: Routledge & Kegan, Paul.

Prendergast, J. (1991) *The Political Economy of Famine in Sudan and the Horn of Africa'*, Issue: A Journal of Opinion, Vol. 19, No. 2, pp. 49-55.

Pritchett, L., Woolcock, M., and Andrews, M. (2012) *Looking Like a State: Techniques of Persistent Failure in State Capability for Implementation'*, UNU-WIDER Working Paper, No. 63.

Prunier, G. (1995) *The Rwanda Crisis: History of a Genocide'*, New York: Columbia University Press.

Pugel, J. (2009) *Measuring Reintegration in Liberia: Assessing the Gap between Outputs and Outcomes'*, In: Muggah, R. (Ed.), Security and Post-Conflict Reconstruction: Dealing with Fighters in the Aftermath of War. New York: Routledge.

Pugh, A.J. (2011) *Distinction, boundaries or bridges? Children, Inequality and the uses of Culture'*, Poetics, Vol. 39, No. 1, pp. 1-18.

Pugh, M.C. and Sidhu, P.S. (2003) *The United Nations and Regional Security: Europe and Beyond'*, Boulder, Colorado: Lynne Rienner Publishers.

Putnam, R. (1993) *Making Democracy Work: Civic Traditions in Modern Italy'*, Princeton, N.J.: Princeton University Press.

Qu, S. Q. and Dumay, J. (2011) The qualitative Research Interview', *Qualitative Research in Accounting and Management*, Vol. 8, No. 3, pp. 238-264.

Quinn, J., Mason, D. Gurses, M. (2007) *Sustaining the Peace: Determinants of Civil War Recurrence'*, International Interactions, Vol. 33, No. 2, pp.167-193.

Rabianski, J.S. (2006) *Primary and Secondary Data: concepts, Errors and Issues'*, Appraisal Journal, Vol. 71, No. 1, pp. 43-55.

Radon, J. and Logan. S. (2014) South Sudan: Governance Arrangements, War, and Peace', *Journal of International Affairs*, Vol. 68,

No. 1 pp. 147–167.

Ramanathan, R. (2008) *The Role of Organisational Change Management in Offshore Outsourcing of Information Technology Services'*, Universal Publisher.

Ramose, M. (1999) *African Philosophy through Ubuntu'*, Harare: Mond Books.

Ramsbotham, O.W, T and Miall, H. (2009) *Contemporary Conflict Resolution'*, 2nd (Ed.), Cambridge: Polity Press.

Rands, R.B. and LeRiche, M. (2012) *Security Responses in Jonglei State in the Aftermath of Inter-ethnic Violence'*, London: Saferworld, Available at: http://www.burtonrands.com/documents

Ranger, T. (1991) *Missionaries Migrants and the Mayinka: The Invention of Ethnicity in Zimbabwe'*, In: Leroy Vail (Ed.), Creation of Tribalism in Southern Africa, Berkeley: University of California Press.

Rasmussen, J. (2018) *Parasitic Politics: Violence, Deception, and Change in Kenya's Electoral Politics'*, In: M. S. Kovacs, & J. Bjarnesen (Eds.), Violence in African Elections. Between Democracy and Big Man Politics, (pp.176-196). Zed Books, Africa Now.

Reed, S.K. (2016) The structure of ill-structured (and well-structured) problems re-visited', *Educational Psychology Review*, Vol. 28, No. 4, pp. 691–716.

Reeves E. (2013) The Coup Attempt in South Sudan: What we know. Sudan Tribune, http://www.sudantribune.com/spip.php?article49226 [Accessed 06/04/2017].

Reilly, B. (2002) *Elections in Post-Conflict Scenarios: Constraints and Dangers'*, International Peacekeeping, Vol.9. No. 2, pp. 118–139.

Reilly, B. (2006) *Political Engineering and Party Politics in Conflict-Prone*

Societies', Democratisation Vol.13, No. 5 pp. 811–27.

Reno, W. (1999) *Warlord Politics and African States'*, Boulder, CO: Lynne Rienner Publishers

Reno, W., (2000) *Shadow States and the Political Economy of Civil Wars'*, In Berdal, M. & Malone, D.M. (Eds.), Greed and Grievance: Economic Agendas in Civil Wars, London: Lynne Rienner Publishers.

Reychler, L. (2001) *From Conflict to Sustainable Peacebuilding: Concepts and Analytical Tools'*, In: Reychler, L & Paffenholz, J. (Eds.), Peacebuilding: A Field Guide, (pp. 3-20). London: Lynne Rienner Publishers.

Richards, L. and Richards, T. (1994) *From Filing Cabinet to Computer'*, In A. Bryman & R. G. Burgess (Eds.), Analysing qualitative data (pp. 146-172). London: Routledge.

Richards, P. (2002) Militia conscription in Sierra Leone', *Comparative Social Research*, No. 20, pp. 255-276.

Richards, P. (2005) *To fight or to farm? Agrarian dimensions of the Mano River conflict (Liberia and Sierra Leone'*, African Affairs, Vol. 104, No. 417, pp. 571-590.

Richmond O.P. (2012) *Beyond Local Ownership and Participation in the Architecture of International Peacebuilding'*, Ethno-politics, Vol. 1, No. 4, pp. 354-357.

Richmond, O.P. (2002) *Maintaining Order, Making Peace'*, London: Palgrave.

Richmond, O.P. (2013) *Failed Statebuilding versus Peace Formation'*, Cooperation and Conflict, Vol. 48, No. 3, pp. 378-400.

Richmond, O.P. (2005) *The Transformation of Peace'*, London: Palgrave.

Richmond, O.P. (2008) *Peace in IR'*, London: Routledge.

Richmond, O.P. (2009) *The Romanticisation of the Local: Welfare, Culture and Peacebuilding*, The International Spectator, Vol. 44, No. 1, pp. 149-169.

Richmond, O.P. (2013) *Failed Statebuilding versus Peace Formation*, Cooperation and Conflict, Vol. 48, No. 3, pp. 378–400.

Richmond, O.P. (201la) *Critical Agency, Resistance, and a Post-colonial civil society*, Cooperation and Conflict, Vol. 46, No. 4, pp. 419-440.

Richmond, O.P. (201lb) *A Post-Liberal Peace*, London: Routledge.

Richmond, O.P. and Franks, J. (2009) *Liberal Peace Transitions: Between Statebuilding and Peacebuilding*, Edinburgh: Edinburgh University Press.

Riehl, V. (2001) *Who is Ruling in South Sudan? The Role of NGOs in Rebuilding Socio-Political Order*, Studies on Emergencies and Disaster Relief, Uppsala: The Nordic Africa Institute.

Risse, T. (2010) *Governance without a State? Policies and Politics in Areas of Limited Statehood*, Columbia University Press, New York, N.Y.

Rodaway, P. (1995) *Exploring the Subject in Hyper-Reality*, In: Steve, Pile & Nigel, Thrift. Eds. Mapping the Subject: Geographies of Cultural Transformation', London; New York: Routledge.

Rodney, W. (1972) *How Europe Underdeveloped Africa*, Washington, DC: Howard University Press.

Rogier, E. (2005) *No More Hills Ahead? The Sudan's tortuous Ascent to Heights of Peace*, The Hague: Netherlands Institute of International Relations.

Rolandsen, O.H. (2005) *Guerrilla government: Political changes in the Southern Sudan during the 1990s*, Oslo: Nordiska Afrikainstitutet.

Rolandsen, O.H. (2011) A Quick Fix? A Retrospective Analysis of the

Sudan Comprehensive Peace Agreement', *Review of African Political Economy*, Vol. 38, No 130, pp. 551-564.

Rolandsen, O.H. (2015) Another Civil War in South Sudan: the failure of Guerrilla Government? *Journal of Eastern African Studies*, Vol.9, No. 1, pp. 163-174.

Rolandsen, O.H. and Breidlid, I.M. (2012) *A Critical Analysis of Cultural Explanations for the Violence in Jonglei State, South Sudan*', Conflict Trends, Vol.1, pp. 49–56.

Rolandsen, O.H. and Breidlid, I.M. (2013) *What is Youth Violence in Jonglei*', The Peace Research Institute Oslo (PRIO) Paper', https://www.prio.org/utility/DownloadFile.ashx?id=367&type=publicationfile [Accessed: 10/03/2020].

Rosen, D.M. (2005) *Armies of the Young: Child Soldiers in War and Terrorism*', New Jersey: The Rutgers Series in Childhood Studies).

Ross, M.H. (2004) What do we know about Natural Resources and Civil War? *Journal of Peace Research*, Vol. 41, pp.337–56.

Ross, M.H. (2007) *Cultural Contestation in Ethnic Conflict*', Cambridge Studies in Comparative Politics, Cambridge: Cambridge University Press.

Rotberg, R. (2004) *The Failure and Collapse of Nation-States: Breakdown, Prevention and Repair*', In: R. Rotberg (Ed.), When States Fail: Causes and Consequences, Princeton University Press, Routledge.

Rotberg, R. (2007) The Challenge of Weak, Failing, and Collapsed States', Leashing the Dogs of War, pp. 83-94.

Rothchild, D. and Roeder, G. (2005) *Power-sharing as an Impediment to Peace and Democracy,*' In: P. G Roeder and D. Rothchild (eds.),

Sustainable Peace: Power and Democracy after Civil Wars (pp. 29-50). Ithaca, N.Y.: Cornell University Press.

Rottenburg, R. and Komey, G. (2011) *The Genesis of Recurring wars in Sudan: Rethinking the violent conflicts in the Nuba Mountains / South Kordofan'*, Work Paper, Affiliation: Lost Research Group, University of Halle.

Rozema, Z. *et al.* (2008) *Governance for Sustainable Development: A Framework'*, Sustainable Development, John Wiley & Sons, Ltd., vol. Vol. 16, No. 6, pp. 410-421.

Rubin, H.J. Rubin, I.S. (2004) *Qualitative interviewing: The Art of Hearing Data'*, 2nd (Ed.), Thousand Oaks, CA. Sage Publications.

Rubinstein, R. (1990) The Environmental Representation of Personal Themes by Older People', *Journal of Aging Studies*, Vol. 4, No. 2, pp. 131–8.

Ruggeri, A., Dorussen, H., and Gizelis, T. (2017) *Winning the peace locally: U.N. peacekeeping and local conflict'*, International Organisation, Vol. 71, No, 1, pp. 163–185.

Russett, B.M., O'neal, J.R. and Cox, M. (2000) *Clash of Civilizations, or Realism and Liberalism Déjà Vu?* Some Evidence.

Ruzicka, J. and Wheeler, N.J. (2010) *The Puzzle of Trusting Relationships in the Nuclear Non-Proliferation Treaty'*, International Affairs, Vol. 86, No. 1, pp. 69-85.

Ryan, G. and Bernard, R. (2000) *Data Management and Analysis Methods'*, In: N. Denzin & Y. Lincoln (Eds.), Handbook of Qualitative Research (pp. 769–802). Thousand Oaks, CA: Sage.

Saferworld (2008) *Developing Integrated Approaches to Post-Conflict Security and Recovery: A Case Study of Integrated DDR in Sudan'*, London and

Nairobi: Saferworld.

Saferworld, (2012) *Civilian disarmament in South Sudan: A Legacy of Struggle*, http://www.saferworld. org.uk/downloads/pubdocs/South Sudan civilian disarmament.pdf.

Salant, P. and Dillman, D. A. (1994) *How to Conduct your own Survey'*, John Wiley & Sons, Inc.

Samatar, A. and Samatar, A.I. (1987) The Material Roots of the Suspended African State: Arguments from Somalia', *The Journal of Modern African Studies*, Vol. 25, No. 4, pp. 669-690.

Sambanis, N. (2000) *Partition as a Solution to Ethnic War: An Empirical Critique of the Theoretical Literature'*, World Politics, Vol. 52, pp. 437-483.

Sambanis, N. (2001) Do Ethnic and Non-ethnic Civil Wars have the same causes? A theoretical and Empirical Inquiry', *Journal of Conflict Resolution*, Vol. 45, No. 3, pp.259-282.

Sambanis, N. (2004) What is Civil War? Conceptual and Empirical Complexities of an Operational Definition', *Journal of Conflict Resolution*, Vol. 48, pp. 814-585.

Sandelowski, M. (1995) *Focus on Qualitative Methods: Sample Size in Qualitative Research'*, Research in Nursing and Health, Vol.18, pp.179-183.

Sanford, V. (2006) *The Moral Imagination of Survival: Displacement and Child Soldiers in Guatemala and Colombia'*, In: S. McEvoy-Levy (Ed.) Troublemakers or Peacemakers? Youth and Post Accord Peacebuilding, (pp. 49–80). Notre Dame, University of Notre Dame.

Sawant, A.B. (1998) *Ethnic Conflict in Sudan in Historical Perspective'*, International Studies, Vol. 35, No. 3. New Delhi: Sage Publications, pp. 343-363.

Schedler, A. (2001) *Measuring Democratic Consolidation'*, St Comp Int Dev, Vol.36, pp.66–92.

Schelling, T.C. (1960) *The Strategy of Conflict'*, Cambridge, MA: Harvard University Press. Schelling, T.C. (1966) Arms and Influence', New Haven, CT: Yale University Press.

Schermerhorn, R. A. (1970) *Comparative Ethnic Relations: A Framework for Theory'*, New York, Random House.

Scheurich, J.J and Delamont, K. B. (2005) *Foucault's Methodologies: Archaeology and Genealogy'*, In: N.K. Denzin & Y. S. Lincoln (Eds.), The Sage Handbook of Qualitative Research (3rd ed., pp. 841-868). Thousand Oaks: Sage Publications.

Scheurich, J.J. (1995) A Postmodernist Critique of Research Interviewing', *Qualitative Studies in Education*, Vol. 8, No.3, pp. 239–252.

Scheye, and Peake, G. (2005) To Arrest Insecurity: Time for a Revised SSR Agenda', *Conflict, Security and Development*, Vol. 5, No. 3, pp. 295-327.

Scheye, E. and McLean, A. (2006) *Enhancing the Delivery of Justice and Security in Fragile States'*, Organisation for Economic Cooperation and Development - Development Assistance Committee (OECD/DAC) Network on Conflict, Peace and Development Co-operation, Paris (CPDC).

Schilling, J. (2012) *Raiding Pastoral Livelihoods: Motives and Effects of Violent Conflict in North-Western Kenya'*, Pastoralism Res Policy Pract, Vol. 2, No. 25, pp.1-16.

Schirch, L. (2008) Strategic Peacebuilding- State of the Field', Peace

Prints: *South Asian Journal of Peacebuilding'*, Vol. 1, No. 1, pp. 1-17.

Schlee, Y. and Watson, E. (2009) *Changing Identifications and Alliances in Northeast Africa'*, New York: Berghahn.

Schmeidl, S. (2009) *Prêt-a-Porter States: How the McDonaldization of State-Building Misses the Mark in Afghanistan'*, http://www.berghofhandbook. [Accessed: 23/11/2017].

Schomerus, M. (2008a) *Perilous border: Sudanese communities affected by conflict on the Sudan/Uganda border'*, London: Conciliation Resources.

Schomerus, M. (2008b) *Violent Legacies: Insecurity in Sudan's Central and Eastern Equatoria'*, Working Paper 13. Human Security Baseline Assessment. Geneva: The Small Arms Survey.

Schomerus, M. and Allen, T. (2010) *Southern Sudan at Odds with itself: Dynamics of Conflict and Predicaments of Peace'*, Development Studies Institute, LSE. London.

Schroeder, M., and Lamb, G. (2018) The Illicit Arms Trade in Africa: A Global Enterprise', *Small arms proliferation and control in Southern Africa.* https://www.researchgate.net/publication/326462123_The_Illicit_Arms_Trade_in_Africa_A_Global_Enterprise [Accessed: 08/05/2019].

Schultz, A. l. (1967) *The Phenomenology of the Social World'*, Evanston, IL: North-Western University Press.

Scott, G. (2002) Recruitment and Allegiance: The Micro-foundations of Rebellion', *Journal of Conflict Resolution*, Vol 26, pp. 111-30.

Scott, J. (1990) *A Matter of Record: Documentary Sources in Social Research'*, Cambridge: Polity Press.

Scroggins, D. (2002) *Emma's War'*, New York: Pantheon Security Responses in Jonglei State, (Final).pdf.

Sedra, M. (2006) *SSR in Afghanistan: The Slide towards Expediency'*, International Peacekeeping, Vol. 13, No. 1, pp. 94–110.

Sedra, M. (2013) *The Hollowing-out of the Liberal Peace Project in Afghanistan: The Case of SSR'*, Central Asian Survey, Vol. 32, No. 3, pp. 371–387.

Sedra, M. (2018) Adapting SSR to Ground-Level Realities: The Transition to a Second-Generation Model', *Journal of Intervention and Statebuilding*, Vol. 12, No. 1, pp. 48-63.

Segovia, A. (2009) *Transitional Justice and DDR: The Case of El Salvador'*, New York: ICTJ.

Sekaran, U. (1992) *Research Methods for Business: A Skills-Building Approach'*, New York: Wiley and Sons.

Selby, J. (2007) *The Political Economy of the Israeli-Palestinian and Indo-Pak Peace Processes: Full Research Report'*, ESRC End of Award Report, RES-228-25-0010. Swindon: ESRC.

Senehi, J. (2009) *The Role of Constructive, Transcultural Storytelling in Ethno-political Conflict Transformation in Northern Ireland'*, In Carter Judy, I. George, V. Vamik. (Ed)., Regional and Ethnic Conflicts: Perspectives from the Front Lines. New Jersey: Pearson.

Senehi, J., Flaherty, M., Sanjana, C., Kirupakaran, L.K., Matenge, M. and Skarlato, O.

Senghaas, D. (2002) *The Clash within Civilisations: Coming to terms with Cultural Conflicts'*, 1st English (Ed.), Routledge, New York.

Sesay, A., Ukeje, C. and Gbla, O. (2009) *Post-War Regimes and State Reconstruction in Liberia and Sierra Leone'*, Dakar, Council for the Development of Social Science Research in Africa.

Shapcott, R. (2004) IR as Practical Philosophy: Defining a 'Classical

Approach', *The British Journal of Politics and International Relations*, Vol. 6, No. 3, pp. 271–291.

Sharkey, H. (2008) *Arab Identity and Ideology in Sudan: The Politics of Language, Ethnicity, and Race'*, African Affairs, Vol. 107, pp. 21-43.

Shaw, T.M. and Mbabazi, P. (2007) *Two Uganda's and a Liberal Peace? Lessons from Uganda about Conflict and Development at the Start of a New Century'*, Global Society, Vol. 24, No. 4, pp.567-78.

Shinn D.H. (2004) *Addis Ababa Agreement: Was it destined to Fail and are there Lessons for the Current Sudan Peace Process?* Annales d'Ethiopie, Vol. 20, pp. 239-259.

Siebert, H. (2014) *National dialogue and legitimate change', Legitimacy and Peace Processes: from Coercion to Consent'*, Accord//ISSUE 25//www.c-r.org Conciliation Resources Burghley Yard, London.

Simangan, D. (2017) *The Limits of Liberal Peacebuilding and Pitfalls of Local Involvement Cambodia, Kosovo, and Timor-Leste in retrospect'*, PhD Thesis. The Australian National University, Canberra, Australia.

Simmons, M. and Dixon, P., eds. (2006) *Peace by piece: Addressing Sudan's Conflicts'*, London: Conciliation Resources.

Singh, G. (2000) *Ethnic Conflict in India'*, New York: St Martin's Press.

Sisk, T.D. (1996) *Power-Sharing and International Mediation in Ethnic Conflict'*, Perspective Series, United States Institute of Peace, Washington DC.

Sisk, T.D. (2002) *Spiritual Intelligence: The Tenth Intelligence that Integrates all other Intelligence'*, Gifted Education International, Vol. 16, No. 3, pp. 208–213.

Skocpol, T. (1979) *States and Social Revolutions'*, Cambridge, MA:

Cambridge University Press.

Small Arms Survey (2006–2007) *Anatomy of civilian disarmament in Jonglei state: Recent experiences and implications*', Sudan Issue Brief Number 3 (2nd Ed.) Human Security Baseline Assessment. http://www.smallarmssurveysudan.org/fileadmin/docs/issue-briefs/HSBA-IB-03-Jonglei.pdf. [Accessed 20/08/2017].

Small Arms Survey (2011) *Failures and Opportunities, Rethinking DDR in South Sudan*', HSBA Issue Brief No 17, Small Arms Survey, Geneva.

Small Arms Survey (2012a) *Reaching for the Gun: Arms Flows and Holdings in South Sudan'*, HSBA Issue Brief No 19. Small Arms Survey, Geneva.

Small Arms Survey, (2012b) *My neighbour, my enemy', Inter-tribal violence in Jonglei*', HSBA Issue Brief No 21. Small Arms Survey, Geneva.

Smith, A.D. (1988) *Ethnic Origins of Nations*', London, UK: Blackwell.

Smith, A.D. (1983) *Theories of Nationalism*', London.

Smith, A.D. (1998) *Nationalism and Modernism*', London: Routledge

Smith, A.D. (2004) *Towards a Strategic Framework for Peacebuilding: Getting their Act Together*', the Royal Norwegian Ministry of Foreign Affairs.

Smith, M.G. (1986) *Pluralism, Race and Ethnicity in Selected African Countries*', In J. Rex and D. Mason (Eds.), Theories of Race and Ethnic Relations Cambridge: Cambridge University Press.

Smith, T.L. (1999) *Decolonizing Methodologies: Research and Indigenous Peoples*', London, New York, Dunedin: Zed Books and University of Otago Press

Snow, D.M. (1996) *Uncivil Wars: International Security and the New Internal Conflicts*', London: Lynne Rienner Publishers, Inc.

Snowden, J. (2012) *Work in Progress: Security Force Development in South*

Sudan through February 2012', HSBA Working Paper, No. 27. Small Arms Survey, Geneva.

Solomon, C., Ginifer, J. (2008) *Disarmament, Demobilisation and Reintegration in Sierra Leone –Case Study*', Centre for International Cooperation and Security, University of Bradford.

Sørbø, G.M. (2010) Local Violence and International Intervention in Sudan', *Review of African Political Economy*, Vol. 37, No. 124, pp. 173–186.

South, A. (2018) Hybrid Governance and the Politics of Legitimacy in the Myanmar Peace Process', *Journal of Contemporary Asia*, Vol. 48, No. 1, pp. 50-66.

Spear, J. (1996) *Arms Limitations, Confidence-Building Measures, and Internal Conflict*', In: M.E. Brown (Ed.), The International Dimensions of Internal Conflict, CSIA Studies in International Security Cambridge, Mass.: The MIT Press.

Spear, J. (2002) *Disarmament and Demobilisation*', In: S.J Stedman *et al.* (Ed.), Ending Civil Wars: The implementation of peace agreements (pp. 141-82). Boulder, CO: Lynne Rienner.

Spikes, D. (1993) *Angola and the Politics of Intervention: From Local Bush War to Chronic Crisis in Southern Africa*', McFarland & Co. Publishers, Jefferson, N.C. and London.

SPLM/A News Agency, (2002) *Government Forces Evacuate Torit*', http://www.Sudan Net/news/press/postedr/176.Shtml [Accessed 21/12/2016].

SSDDRC and UNDP (2006) *Jonglei Community Security and Arms Control (CSAC)*', Program Initial Emergency Phase.

Stahl, I. (1972) *Bargaining Theory: Computer Programs*', The Economic Research Institute, Stockholm. Sweden.

Stake, R. (1978) *The Case study Method in Social Inquiry*', Educational Researcher, Vol. 7, No. 2, pp. 5-8.

Stake, R. (1995) *The Art of Case Study Research*', Thousand Oaks, CA: Sage.

Stake, R. (1998) *Case studies*', In: Denzin N. K, Lincoln Y. S. Strategies of Qualitative Inquiry, (pp. 86–109). Thousand Oaks, CA: Sage.

Stedman, S. (1991) *Peacemaking in Civil War: International Mediation in Zimbabwe*', 1974-1980. Boulder: Lynne Rienner.

Stedman, S. (1997) *Spoiler Problems in Peace Processes*', International Security, Vol 22, No. 2, pp. 5-53.

Stedman, S. (2001) *Implementing Peace Agreements in Civil Wars: Lessons and Recommendations for Policymakers*', International Peace Academy (IPA) Policy Paper Series on Peace Implementation, New York: Centre for International Security and Cooperation.

Stedman, S. (2001) *International Implementation of Peace Agreements in Civil Wars*', In Turbulent Peace, Washington DC U.S.: U.S. Institute of Peace.

Steenkamp, C. (2011) In the Shadows of War and Peace: Making Sense of Violence after Peace Accords', *Conflict, Security and Development*, Vol. 11, No. 3, pp. 357–383.

Stewart, F. Brown, G. and Mancini, L. (2005) *Why Horizontal Inequalities Matter: Some Implications for Measurement*', Crise Working Paper No. 19, Oxford: Centre for Research on Inequality, Human Security and Ethnicity.

Stewart, F. (2000) *Crisis Prevention: Tackling Horizontal Inequalities'*, Oxford Development Studies, Vol 28, No 3, pp.245-262.

Stewart, F. (2003) Conflict and the Millennium Development Goals', *Journal of Human Development*, Vol 4, No 3, pp. 325-352.

Stewart, F. (2004) *Social Exclusion and Conflict: Analysis and Policy Implications'*, Report prepared for the UK Department for International Development, London

Stewart, F. (2004) *The relationship between Horizontal Inequalities, Vertical Inequality and Social Exclusion'*, Crise Newsletter, Winter.

Stewart, F. (2008) *Horizontal Inequalities and Conflict: Explaining Group Violence in Multiethnic Societies'*, Basingstoke: Palgrave Macmillan.

Stewart, F. (2011) *Horizontal Inequalities as a Cause of Conflict'*, World Development Report Background Paper, a Review of Crise Findings.

Stockholm Initiative on (SIDDR) (2006) *Final Report'*, Ministry for Foreign Affairs, Sweden.

Stone, L. (2011) *Rethinking DDR in Post-Independence Sudan'*, the SAS report, Global Policy Forum, https://www.globalpolicy.org/security-council/index-of-countries-on-the-security-council-agenda/sudan/50424-rethinking-ddr-in-post-independence-sudan.html [Accessed: 24/05/2017].

Strauss, A. and Corbin, J.M. (1990) *Basics of qualitative research: Grounded Theory Procedures and Techniques'*, Sage Publications, Inc.

Stringer, E.T. (1999) Action research', 2nd (Ed.), Thousand Oaks, CA: Sage.

Stringham, N. and Forney, J. (2017) It Takes a Village to Raise a Militia: Local Politics, the Nuer White Army, and South Sudan's Civil Wars',

The Journal of Modern African Studies, Vol 55, No. 2, pp. 177-199.

Stubbs, J.M. (1934) *Notes on Beliefs and Customs of the Malwal Dinka of Bahr el Ghazal Province*', Sudan Notes Rec, Vol. 17, pp. 243-54.

Stubbs, J.M. Morison, C.G. (1938) *The Western Dinkas, their Land and their Agriculture*', Sudan Notes Rec, Vol. 21, pp. 251-65.

Suchman, M. (1995). Managing Legitimacy: Strategic and Institutional Approaches', The *Academy of Management Review*, Vol. 20, No. 3, pp. 571-610.

Sudan Human Security Baseline Assessment (HSBA) (2012) *Small Arms Survey*', No. 47 Avenue Blanc, Geneva, Switzerland http://www.smallarmssurveysudan.org.

Sudman, S. (1985) *Efficient Screening Methods for the Sampling of Geographically Clustered Special Populations*', Marketing Res. Vol. 22, pp. 20-29.

Suleiman, M. A. (2011) *Britain Looking into Debt Relief for Sudan: Envoy*', Sudan Tribune: Plural news and Views on Sudan, http://www.sudantribune.com/Britain-looking-into-debt-relief,37988. [Accessed 19/02/2016].

Suri, H. (2011) *Purposeful Sampling in Qualitative Research Syntheses*', Qualitative Research Journal, Vol.1. No.2, pp. 63-75.

Swarbrick, P. (2007) *Avoiding Disarmament Failure: The Critical Link in DDR; An Operational Manual for Donors, Managers, and Practitioners*', Geneva: Small Arms Survey, http://www.smallarmssurvey.org.[Accessed: 27/08/2018].

Swift, J.J. (1996) *Desertification: Narratives, Winners and Losers*', In: Leach M. and Mearns, R. (Eds.), the lie of the Land, Oxford: James Currey publishers.

Sylvester, A. (1977) *Sudan Under Nimeiri'*, London: Bodley Head.

Tadjbakhsh, S. (2011) *Rethinking the Liberal Peace: External Models and local alternatives'*, Routledge Cass Series on Peacekeeping, Routledge, Milton Park, UK.

Tarimo, A. (2010) Politicisation of Ethnic Identities: The Case of Contemporary Africa', *Journal of Asian and African Studies*, Vol. 45, No. 3, pp. 297–308.

Tasić, S. and Feruh, M (2012) Errors and Issues in Secondary Data Used in Market Research Data, socioeconomic', *The Scientific Journal for Theory and Practice of Socioeconomic Development*, Vol. 1, No. 2, pp. 326-335.

Tatiana, C. and Pangburn, A. (2018) *What Works in Security Interventions: Rethinking DDR in Today's Violent Conflicts'*, Peace and Security, https://blogs.lse.ac.uk/crp/2018/10/03/what-works-in-security-interventions-rethinking-ddr-in-todays-violent-conflicts/[Accessed: 08/04/2020].

Taylor, I. (2007) *What fit the liberal peace in Africa?* Global Society, Vol. 21, No. 4, pp. 553-566.

Tellis, W. (1997) *Introduction to Case Study'*, The Qualitative Report, Vol. 3, No. 2. pp. 1-14.

Temitope, O. (2014) Ethnic   Conflict and   African   Women's Capacity for   Preventive   Diplomacy', *International Research Journal*, Global Journals Inc. pp. Vol. 1, 4   Issue, 2. pp. 61-66.

Terpstra, N. and Frerks, G.   (2017) *Rebel Governance and Legitimacy: Understanding the Impact of Rebel Legitimation on Civilian Compliance with the LTTE Rule'*, Civil Wars, Vol. 19, No. 3, pp. 279-307.

Thakur, S. and Venugopal, R. (2018) *Parallel Governance and Political order in Contested Territory: Evidence from the Indo-Naga Ceasefire*, Asian Security, Vol. 15, No. 3, 285-303.

The Comprehensive Peace Agreement between the Government of the Republic of Sudan and the Sudan People's Liberation Movement/Sudan People's Liberation Army', January 2005. Available at: http://www.sd.undp.org/doc/CPA.pdf.[Accessed: 02/10 2016].

The CPA Monitor-Monthly Report on the Implementation of the CPA', UNMIS, https://unmis.unmissions.org/sites/default/files/CPA%20Monitor%20December%202009.pdf[Accessed on 20/12/2017].

The CPA Monitor-Monthly report on the Implementation of the CPA', UNMIS, December 2010. https://unmis.unmissions.org/sites/default/files/CPA%20Monitor%20December%202009.pdf[Accessed on 20/12/2017].

The Department for International Development (DFID) (2004) Non-State Justice and security system. London.

The Government of the Republic of South Sudan (2011b) South Sudan', Available at: http://geography.about.com/gi/o.htm?zi=1/XJ&zTi=1&sdn=geography&cdn=education&tm=184&gps=326_6_1366_618&f=00&su=p284.13.342.ip_&tt=2&bt=0&bts=0&zu=http%3A//www.goss.org/[Accessed: /10/16/2016].

The United Nations (2000) *Report of the Panel of Experts on Violations of the Security Council Sanctions against UNITA*', U.N. Document S/2000/203.

The United Nations (2000) *The Role of United Nations Peacekeeping in Disarmament, Demobilisation, and Reintegration*', Report of the Secretary-General.

The World Bank (2017) World Bank Annual Report', Washington, DC: World Bank Group. http://documents.worldbank.org/curated/en/143021506909711004 /pdf/119779-BR-REPLACE-ON-FRINDAY-OUO-9-SecM2017- 0254-1-World-Bank-Annual-Report-2017-Rev-09292017.pdf. [Accessed: 17/09/2019].

The World Bank. (1993) *Demobilisation and Reintegration of Military Personnel in Africa: The Evidence from Seven Country Case Studies*', Discussion Paper: Africa Regional Series. Washington, DC: The World Bank.

Themnér, A. and Ohlson, T. (2014) *Legitimate Peace in Post-civil War States: Towards Attaining the Unattainable, Conflict, Security AND Development*', Vol.14, No. 1, pp. 61-87.

Thomas, E. (2015) *South Sudan: A Slow Liberation*', London: Zed Books.

Thompson, J.B. (2012) *Rethinking the Clinical vs. Social Reform Debate: A Dialectical Approach to Defining Social Work in the 21st Century*', PhD Dissertation, University of Kansas, Lawrence, KS, USA.

Thorne, S. (2000) *Data Analysis in Qualitative Research Evidence-Based Nurse*', Vol. 3, Issue, 3, pp. 68-70.

Tilly, C. (1969) *Collective Violence in European Perspective*', In: Violence in America, H. O. Graham and T. R. Gurr (Eds.), (pp. 4-45). New York: Bantam.

Tilly, C. (1975) *The Formation of National States in Western Europe*',

Princeton University Press, Princeton, NJ.

Tilly, C. (1990) *Coercion, Capital, and European States, A.D. 990–1992'*, Cambridge, MA: Wiley-Blackwell.

Tilly, C. (1990) *Coercion, Capital, and European States, AD 990-1990'*, Studies in Social Discontinuity, Basil Blackwell, Inc. 3 Cambridge Centre, Cambridge, Massachusetts, USA.

Timonen, V., Foley, G. and Conlon, C. (2018) *Challenges When Using Grounded Theory: A Pragmatic Introduction to Doing GT Research'*, International Journal of Qualitative Methods.

Titeca, K. and De Herdt, T. (2011) *Real Governance Beyond the Failed State: Negotiating Education in the Democratic Republic of the Congo'*, African Affairs, Vol. 10, No. 439, pp. 213–31.

Toft, M. (2003) *The Geography of Ethnic Violence: Identity, Interests, and the Indivisibility of Territory'*, Princeton University Press.

Toft, M. (2007) *Getting Religion? The Puzzling Case of Islam and Civil War'*, International Security, Vol.31, No 4, pp.97-131.

Toft, M. (2010) *Securing the Peace: The Durable Settlement of Civil Wars'*, Princeton NJ: Princeton University Press.

Toki, M. (2004) *Peace-building and the Process of Disarmament, Demobilisation, and Reintegration: the Experiences of Mozambique and Sierra Leone'*, Institute for International Cooperation. Japan: Japan International Cooperation Agency, IIC/JR 03-64.

Torjesen, S. (2006) *The Political Economy of Disarmament, Demobilisation and Reintegration (DDR): Selective Literature Review and Preliminary Agenda for Research'*, Paper No. 709. Oslo: Norwegian Institute of International Affairs.

Torjesen, S. (2013) Towards a Theory of Ex-Combatant Reintegration', *International Journal of Security and Development*, Vol. 2, No. 3, pp. 1-13.

Torjesen, S. and MacFarlane, S. Neil. (2007) *R before D: The Case of Post-Conflict Reintegration in Tajikistan*', Conflict, Security and Development, Vol 7, No 2, pp. 311–332.

Touray, O. (2005) *The Common African Defence and Security Policy*', African Affairs, Vol. 104, No. 417, pp. 635-656.

Tschirgi, N. (2004) *Political Economy of Armed Conflicts and Peacebuilding*', Conflict, Security and Development, Vol. 4, No. 3, pp. 377-382.

Tsebelis, G. (2000) Veto Players and Institutional Analysis', Governance: *An International Journal of Policy and Administration*, Vol. 13, No. 4, pp. 441-474.

Tsebelis, G. (2002) *Veto Players: How Political Institutions Work*', Princeton, NJ: Princeton University Press.

Turse, N. (2016) New Nation, Long War: In South Sudan, It's Hard to Tell the Soldiers from the Criminals',https://theintercept.com/2016/06/16/in-south-sudan-its-hard-to-tell-the-soldiers-from-the-criminals/[Accessed: on 13/03/2017].

Turyamureeba, R. (2014) *The CPA-DDR Program in South Sudan: What went wrong?* ALC Research Report, No. 7, pp. 1-29.

United Nations Department of Peacekeeping Operations (UNDPO) (2010) *DDR in Action: the Democratic Republic of the Congo*', DDR in peace operations – a retrospective, United States: United Nations.

UNMIS (2006) *United Nations Mission in Sudan, CPA Monitor: Monthly*

Report on the implementation of the CPA', December 2006, http://www.unmis.org.

UNSG, (2012a) *Report of the Secretary-General on South Sudan'*, UN Doc. S/2012/486, 26 June.

UNSG, (2012b) *Report of the Secretary-General on South Sudan'*, UN Doc. S/2012/820, 8 November.

UNSG, (2013) *Report of the Secretary-General on South Sudan'*, UN Doc. S/2013/140, 12 March.

Vale, R. J. (2011) *Is the Sudan Conflict best Understood in terms of Race, Religion, or Regionalism? Katholieke Universiteit Leuven'*, https://www.e-ir.info/pdf/8854 [Accessed: 25/1/2017].

Vallings, C, Moreno-Torres, M. (2005) *Drivers of Fragility: What Makes States Fragile?* PRDE Working Paper 7. London: Department for International Development, pp. 1–31.

Van Evera, S. (1994) *Hypotheses on Nationalism and War'*, International Security, Vol. 18, No. 4, pp.5-39.

Van Evera, S. (2001) *Primordialism Lives!; APSA-CP: Newsletter of the Organised Section in Comparative Politics of the American Political Science Association'*, Vol. 12, No. 1, pp. 20-22.

Vangen, S and Huxham, C. (2003) Nurturing Collaborative Relations: Building trust in inter-organisational collaboration', *The Journal of Applied Behavioural Science*, Vol. 39, No. 1, pp. 5–31.

Varese, F. (2010) *General Introduction', what is Organised Crime?* In: Varese F (Ed.) Organised Crime, Vol. 1. London and New York: Routledge.

Vinck, P., Pham, P.N and Kreutzer, T. (2011) *Talking Peace: A population-based Survey on Attitudes about Security, Dispute Resolution, and Post-conflict Reconstruction in Liberia'*, Berkeley, CA: Human Rights Centre, University of California, Berkeley.

Vlassenroot, K. (2016) *The Challenges of Multi-Layered Security Governance in Ituri'*, JSRP Policy Brief 3: http://www.lse.ac.uk/internationalDevelopment/research/JSRP/downloads/JSRP-Brief-3.pdf.

Wa Thiong'o, N. (1986) *Decolonising the Mind Delhi'*, Worldview Publication.

Waever, Ole. (1998) *Securitisation and Desecuritisation'*, On Security, (Ed.), Ronnie D. Lipschutz. New York: Columbia University Press.

Wagner, R.H. (1993) *The Causes of Peace. In: Roy Licklider, Stopping the Killing: How Civil Wars End'*, (Eds.), (pp. 235-268). New York: New York University Press.

Wai, O.M. (1981) *The African-Arab Conflict in the Sudan'*, New York: Africana Publishing Company.

Waihenya, W. (2006) *The Mediator: Gen. Lazaro Sumbeiywo and the Southern Sudan peace Processes'*, Nairobi: Kenway Publications.

Wakoson, E.N. (1984) *The Origin and Development of the Anya-Nya movement, 1955–1972'*, In: Beshir, M.O. (Ed.), Southern Sudan: Regionalism and Nationalism, Khartoum.

Wakoson, E.N. (1993) *The Politics of Southern Self-Government 1972-83'*, in M. W. Daly & Ahman Alawad Sikainga, (Eds), Civil War in the Sudan', London: British Academic Press, pp. 27-50.

Wallenstein, I. (1980) *The Modern World-System II: Mercantilism and the Consolidation of the European World-Economy, 1600-1750'*, San Diego, CA:

Academic Press.

Wallis, J. (2017) *Is Good Enough Peacebuilding Good Enough? The potential and pitfalls of the Local Turn in Peacebuilding in Timor-Leste'*, The Pacific Review, Vol. 30, No. 2, pp. 251-269.

Walsham, G. (1993) *Interpreting Information Systems in Organisations'*, John Wiley & Sons, Inc. New York, United States.

Walsham, G. (1995) Interpretive Case Studies in is Research: Nature and Method', *European Journal of Information Systems*, Vol. 4, No. 2, pp. 74–81.

Walter, B. (1995) *Designing Transitions from Civil War: Demobilisation, Democratisation, and Commitments to Peace'*, International Security, Vol 24, No. 1, pp. 127.

Walter, B. (1997) *The Critical Barrier to Civil War Settlement'*, International Organisation, Vol 51, No. 3, pp. 335-364.

Walter, B. (2002) *Committing to Peace: The Successful Settlement of Civil Wars'*, Princeton, NJ: Princeton University Press.

Warner, L.A. (2016) The Disintegration of the Military Integration Process in South Sudan (2006–2013) Stability', *International Journal of Security & Development*, Vol. 5, No. 1, pp. 1–20.

Wassara, S. (2002) Conflict and State Security in the Horn of Africa: Militarisation of Civilian Groups', *African Journal of Political Science*, Vol 7 No. 2. pp. 39-60.

Wassara, S. (2007) *Traditional Mechanisms of Conflict Resolution in Southern Sudan'*, Berghof Foundation for Peace Support, Berlin-Germany.

Wassara, S. (2015) South Sudan: State Sovereignty Challenged at Infancy', *Journal of Eastern African Studies*, Vol. 9, No. 4, pp. 634-649.

Wassara, S. and Kurimoto, E. (2017) Negotiating statehood: Handling crisis of South Sudan. In: Gebre, Yntiso, Itaru Ohta and Motoji Matsuda, (Eds.), *African Virtues in the Pursuit of Conviviality: Exploring Local Solutions in Light of Global Prescriptions'*, Bamenda, Langaa.

Webb, K. (1995) *An Introduction to Problems in the Philosophy of Social Sciences'*, New York, A Cassell Imprint, New York.

Weber, M. (1946) *Politics as a Vocation'*, In: From Max Weber: Essays in Sociology, translated by H. H. Gerth and C. Wright Mills, Oxford University Press.

Weber, M. (1978) *Ethnic Groups'*, In: G. Roth, & C. Wittich, (Ed.), Economy and Society, Vol. 1, (pp. 389-95). Berkeley: University of California Press.

Weber, M. (1979) *Economy and Society: An Outline of Interpretive Sociology'*, (Eds.), Wittich, C. and Roth, G. Berkeley: University of California Press.

Webster, M. (1985) *Webster's Ninth new Collegiate Dictionary.* Meriam - Webster Inc.

Weinstein, J.M. (2005) Resources and the Information Problem in Rebel Recruitment', *Journal of Conflict Resolution*, Vol. 49, pp. 598–624.

Wendt, A. (1992) *Anarchy is What States Makes of It'*, International Organisation, Vol. 46, No. 2, pp. 391–425.

Wendt, A. (1994) Collective Identity Formation and the International State', *American Political Science Review*, Vol. 88, No. 2, pp. 384-396.

Wennmann, A. (2009) *Getting Armed Groups to the Table: Peace Processes, the Political Economy of Conflict and the Mediated State'*, Third World Quarterly, Vol. 30, No. 6, pp. 1123–38.

Wesley, M. (2008) *The State of the Art on the Art of State Building'*, Global Governance, No.14: pp. 369-385.

Wheeler, N.J. (2012) Trust-Building in International Relations', Peace Prints, *South Asian Journal of Peacebuilding*, Vol. 4, No. 2, pp. 1-13.

Wickham, M. and Woods, M. (2005) *Reflecting on the strategic use of CAQDAS to manage and report on the qualitative research process'*, The Qualitative Report, Vol. 10, No. 4, pp.687-702.

Wight, P. (2017) South Sudan and the Four Dimensions of Power-Sharing: Political, Territorial, Military, and Economic', *African Conflict and Peacebuilding Review*, Vol. 7, No. 2, 1-35.

Wild, H., Jok, J.M. and Patel, R. (2018) The militarisation of Cattle Raiding in South Sudan: How a Traditional Practice became a tool for political violence', *International Journal Humanitarian Action*, Vol 3, No. 2, pp.1-11.

Wilkof, M.V., Brown, D.W., and Selsky, J.W. (1995) When the Stories are Different: The Influence of Corporate Culture Mismatches on Inter-organisational Relations', *The Journal of Applied Behavioural Science*, Vol. 31, No. 3, pp. 373–388.

Willems, R. Kleingeld, J., and van Leeuwen, M. (2010) *Connecting Community Security and DDR: Experiences from Burundi'*, The Hague: Working Group on Community Security and Community-based DDR in Fragile States, Peace, Security and Development network.

Willems, R., Kleingeld, J., and Rouw, H. (2009) *Security Promotion in Fragile States: Can Local Meet National'*, The Hague: Working Group on Community Security and Community-based DDR in Fragile States, Peace, Security and Development Network.

Williams, G. (1984) *The Genesis of Chronic Illness: Narrative Reconstruction'*, Sociology of Health and Illness, Vol. 6, No. 2, pp. 175–200.

Williams, P. (2004) *Peace Operations and the International Financial Institutions: Insights from Rwanda and Sierra Leone,'* International Peacekeeping, Vol. 11, No. 1, pp.103-23.

Williamson, O.J. (2000) The new institutional economics: Taking stock, looking ahead', *Journal of Economic Literature*, Vol. 38, pp.595-613.

Williamson, O.J. (2006) *The disarmament, demobilisation and reintegration of child soldiers: Social and Psychological Transformation in Sierra Leone'*, Intervention, Vol. 4, No. 3, pp. 185–205.

Willis, J., Battahani, A., and Woodward, P. (2009) *Elections in Sudan: Learning from Experience'*, Rift Valley Institute, Commissioned by the UK Department for International Development (DFID)https://riftvalley.net/sites/default/files/publicationdocuments/RVI%20Elections%20in%20Sudan_0.pdf.[Accessed: 25/08/2018].

Wilson, J.Q. (1989) *Bureaucracy: What Government Agencies do and why they do it'*, New York, N.Y.: Basic Books.

Wolff, S. (2004) *The Institutional Structure of Regional Consociations in Brussels, Northern Ireland, and South Tyrol'*, Nationalism and Ethnic Politics, Vol.10, No.3, pp. 387-414.

Wolff, S. (2006) *Ethnic Conflict: A Global Perspective'*, Oxford University Press.

Wolff, S. (2007) Conflict resolution between power-sharing and power dividing, or beyond?' Political Studies Review, Vol. 5, No. 3, pp. 363-79.

Wolfsfeld, G. (2004) *Media and the Path to Peace'*, New York: Cambridge University Press.

Wondu, S. and Lesch, A. (1999) *Battle for peace in Sudan: an analysis of the Abuja conferences 1992–1993'*, Lanham, MD: University Press of America.

Wood, E.J. (2008) The Social Processes of Civil War: The Wartime Transformation of Social Networks', *Annual Review of Political Science*, Vol.11, No.1, pp. 539-561.

Woodward, P. (1990) *Sudan 1898-/989: The Unstable State'*, Boulder: Lynne Rienner Publishers.

Woodward, P. (1995) *Balkan Tragedy: Chaos and Dissolution after the Cold War'*, Washington, DC: Brookings Institution.

Woolcock, M. (1998) *Social Capital and Economic Development: Towards a Theoretical Synthesis and Policy Framework'*, Theory and Society, Vol. 27, No. 2, pp. 151-208.

World Bank, (2006) *World Development Indicators'*, World Bank, Washington DC.

Yamokoski, A. and Dubrow, J. (2008) *How Do Elites Define Influence? Personality and Respect as Sources of Social Power'*, Sociological Focus, Vol. 41. pp. 319-336.

Yang, P. (2000) *Ethnic Studies: Issues and Approaches'*, New York: State University of New York Press.

Yeros, P. (1999) *Ethnicity and Nationalism in Africa: Constructivist Reflections and Contemporary Politics'*, Basingstoke: Macmillan Press.

Yiftachel, O. (1992) *The State, Ethnic Relations and Democratic Stability: Lebanon, Cyprus and Israel'*, Geo Journal, Vol. 28, pp. 319–332.

Yin, R. (1984) *Case Study Research: Design and Methods'*, Newbury Park, CA: Sage.

Yin, R. (1994) *Case Study Research: Design and Methods*, London: Sage.

Yin, R. (2003) *Case study Research: Design and Methods'*, 3rd (Ed.), Thousand Oaks, CA: Sage.

Ylonen, A. (2012) *Limit of Peace through Statebuilding' in Southern Sudan: Challenges to State Legitimacy, Governance and Economic Development during the CPA Implementation, 2005-2011'*, Journal of Conflictology, Vol. 3, No. 2, pp. 28–40.

Ylonen, A. (2005) *Grievances and the Roots of Insurgencies: Southern Sudan and Darfur', Peace, Conflict and Development: An Interdisciplinary Journal*, Vol.7 http://www.peacestudiesjournal.org [Accessed: 11/07/2018].

Yokwe, E. M. (1997) *Conflict Resolution in the Sudan: A Case Study of Intolerance in Contemporary African Societies'*, Africa Media Review, Vol. 11, No.3, pp. 80-103.

Young, C. (1976) *The Politics of Cultural Pluralism'*, Madison: University of Wisconsin Press.

Young, C. (1986) *Nationalism, Ethnicity, and Class in Africa'*, A retrospective, Cahiers d'Études Africaines, pp. 421–495.

Young, C. and Turner, T. (1985) *The Rise and Decline of the Zairian State'*, Madison: The University of Wisconsin Press.

Young, J. (2003) *Sudan Liberation Movements, Regional Armies, Ethnic Militias and Peace'*, Review of African Political Economy, No. 97, 423–434.

Young, J. (2005) John Garang's Legacy to the Peace Process, the

SPLM/A & the South', *Review of African Political Economy*, No.106: pp. 535-548.

Young, J. (2006) The SSDF in the Wake of the Juba Declaration', HSBA Working Paper, No. 1, Small Arms Survey, Geneva.

Young, J. (2007) *Sudan IGAD Peace Process: an Evaluation*', [online]. Sudan   Tribune, http://www.sudantribune.com/IMG/pdf/Igad_in_Sudan_Peace_Pr ocess.pdf[Accessed: 9/02/2018].

Young, J. (2007) *Sudan People's Liberation Army: Disarmament in Jonglei and its Implications*', Institute for Security Studies, Occasional Paper 137

Young, J. (2012) *The Fate of Sudan: The Origins and Consequences of a Flawed Peace Process*', Zed Books, London.

Yuar, A. (2014) *The polarised political dimensions in South Sudan's Conflict*', Sudan Tribune, online: www.sudantribune.com/spip.php?rubrique12 [Accessed 08/07/2016].

Yuval, D. (2003) *Belonging: from the Indigene to the Diasporic,*' In: U. Ozkirinli (ed.), Nationalism and Its Futures. Basingstoke: Palgrave Macmillan.

Zachariah, A.B and Mampilly, C. (2005) Winning the War, but Losing the Peace? The Dilemma of SPLM/A Civil Administration and the Tasks Ahead', *The Journal of Modern African Studies*, Vol. 43, No. 1, pp. 1-20.

Zambakari, C. (2013) South Sudan and the Nation-building Project: Lessons and Challenges', *International Journal of African Renaissance Studies*' Vol. 8, No. 1, pp.5-29.

Zambakari, C. (2015) *Sudan and South Sudan: Identity, Citizenship, and*

Democracy in Plural Societies, Citizenship Studies', Vol. 19, No. 1, pp. 69-82.

Zambakari, C. (2016) The misguided and mismanaged intervention in Libya: Consequences for peace', *African Security Review*, Vol. 25, No. 1, pp.44-62.

Žarkov, D. (2008) *Gender, Violent Conflict and Development*, New Delhi: Zubaan (Imprint of Kali for Women).

Zartman, I.W. (1993) *The Unfinished Agenda: Negotiating Internal Conflicts'*, in Stopping the Killing: How Civil Wars End, pp. 20–35.

Zartman, I.W. (1995) *Collapsed States: The Disintegration and Restoration of Legitimate Authority'*, Boulder, CO: Lynne Rienner Publishers.

Zartman, I.W. (2003) *The Timing of Peace Initiatives: Hurting Stalemates and Ripe Moments. In Contemporary Peacemaking'*, Springer pp. 19–29.

Zartman, J. (2008) *Negotiation, exclusion and durable peace: dialogue and peacebuilding in Tajikistan'*, International Negotiation, Vol. 13, No. 1, pp. 55-72.

Zartman, W. and Touval, S. (1996) *International Mediation in the Post-Cold War Era'*, In: Chester Crocker, Fen Hampson and Pamela Aall, (Ed.), Managing Global Chaos, (pp. 445-461). Washington, DC: United States Institute of Peace Press.

Zaum, D. (2012) *Review essay: Beyond the 'liberal peace' Global Governance'*, Vol. 18, No. 1, pp. 121–32.

Zena, P. N. (2013) *The Lessons and Limits of DDR in Africa', Africa Security Brief: A Publication of the Africa Centre for Strategic Studies'*, No. 24: pp.1-8.

Zürcher, C. (2007) *The Post-Soviet Wars: Rebellion, Ethnic Conflict, and Nationhood in the Caucasus'*, New York: New York University Press.

ABOUT THE AUTHOR

Doctor Marial Mach Aduot is an extraordinary young talented political scientist, security policy strategies and international laws expert based in Melbourne Australia. He is an academic researcher at Deakin University in Melbourne, Victoria.

www.ingramcontent.com/pod-product-compliance
Lightning Source LLC
Chambersburg PA
CBHW070759280326
41934CB00012B/2977